Transition Farms

by

Bev Buckley

Farming across Australia is changing as farmers question the sustainability of practices that have been accepted without question for the past 60 years and look to new and better ways to produce healthy food. "Transition Farms" tells the story of 18 farmers who are making the transition. It provides a detailed account of how and why these farmers are making the changes and outlines the benefits of doing so.

Transition Farms

Published by Castelen Press
3 Golfcourse Road
Mt Tamborine,
Queensland 4272
Australia

Website: www.growinghealthyorganicfood.com

Published 2010

ISBN: 978-0-9808395-0-0

Foreword

Agriculture in Australia is transforming. It has been for the last 40 years or so! Over the last 10 years this transformation has gathered pace and most of our 'agri' institutions have been left behind: scientific, government, multinational corporations, think tanks, industry and research institutions, wholesalers and retailers are all fighting to stay in the game. The problem is that the game is up. What they've failed to realise is that agriculture is now on a trajectory of working with nature, not against it. *Real* farmers live and work with the land and there is a movement occurring that is exciting, challenging and morally just. It's a movement that is, at long last, finally putting 'culture back into agriculture'.

The farmers in this book epitomise the ingenuity and courage of the pioneering ecological farmers who have gone before them. They are seeking solutions so that they can farm in harmony with nature, grow high quality, nutritionally-dense food, and more importantly leave the landscape in better shape than it was when they started.

If the farmers in this book were to be measured in the same way as our sporting men and women, these farmers would be our Olympians. Most of them would have a medal around their necks. Of course, these farmers are so humble about their achievements, that they would be embarrassed or even annoyed by me saying that. This is all the more reason why this book should be read.

Bev Buckley is like these farmers. She is one of a growing number of landholders with amazing ability to grow great food ecologically and is connected to the land in a way that drives her to endlessly research better ways.

Robert Pekin
Chief Executive
Food Connect Foundation.

Bonus Offer

You are now the owner of "Transition Farms" and I believe you will be as excited by the information it contains as I became during the year I spent getting to know 18 very special farmers.

Interviewing the farmers whose stories are told in this book has provided confirmation for me that the strategies I have developed and teach in my on-line training programme "Healthy Growing" are ones that really work in both large and small enterprises. I have been on a journey similar to the one described by these farmers and have come to the same conclusions. My "farm" is small. It is, in fact, more like a large garden than a conventional farm. Like the farmers in the book I started out believing that to grow successfully, it was necessary to use agricultural poisons and artificial fertilizers. I know now that there is a much better way. I use my garden to demonstrate a way to produce highly nutritious, organically grown fruit and vegetables using a system that maximises productivity. I have taken the concepts and applied them in a community garden to prove that they are easily learnt and applied. Additionally, I have developed a marketing strategy to maximise my financial returns as many of these farmers have done.

The "Healthy Growing" on-line training programme shows you how you can do this too. It provides an easyto-understand explanation of the science that underpins the methodology and takes you, step by step through the process to take the guesswork out of successful growing.

Check it out at _www.growinghealthyorganicfood.com_ and register to receive a copy of my **FREE** "Secrets of Organic Gardening".

Ben Buckley.

Contents

Chapter 1
Motivation for Change

In increasing numbers, farmers throughout Australia are making a transition away from "conventional" ways of farming. Conventional farming methods normally involve the production of a small range of products grown or raised on large areas of land in ways that involve high capital investment, low inputs of labour, use of large inputs of chemical fertilizers, insecticides, pesticides and fungicides and high levels of mechanisation. Frequently a large percentage of production is grown for export.

A number of farmers were interviewed for this book. Most of them are smallholders with farms less than 50 acres in size. A couple have much larger farms but are making the transition to organic, bio-dynamic or nutrition farming strategies on only a portion of their total land. The reasons they give for moving away from conventional methods of farming are usually related to concerns over falling standards of living because of decreasing financial returns, compromised health arising from the use of agricultural chemicals, the perceived production of food that is less than optimally nutritious, diminishing resources such as fertile soil, water and oil, and the increase in prices of needed inputs: energy, chemical fertilizers and agricultural sprays. They have been aware of problems arising from practices which they have used which no longer seem to be working and are causing serious concerns with regard to climate change, soil infertility, soil erosion, water depletion, insect and disease pressures and reduced yields.

Unbelievably, food prices have not increased in 20 years but everything else has. Small farmers are squeezed between giant agribusinesses at the input end and by giant supermarkets at the farm gates. Over the past two generations they have seen their returns dwindle to a fraction of what they were two generations ago as costs of production, insurance and general living increase.

Many of the farmers I spoke to believe that their farms would have become unsustainable if they had continued as they were doing. They were actively searching for alternatives and open to ideas that were presented to them. Others, who had observed conventional farming practices when they were working on family farms or were employed by others, went into organic, biodynamic or nutrition farming strategies as soon as they had the opportunity to do so. A few have done it with the support of their families. All wanted to find better ways of doing things because they sensed that what they were doing and what they were observing was not viable for long-term ecological sustainability or for economic return. Available evidence, some of which is provided in Chapter 2, indicates that their fears are well founded.

Additionally, some of the farmers interviewed see control of what they do by big business, organic accreditation bodies, multinational corporations and government as a major disincentive to smallholders. Unlike agribusinesses they are extremely innovative in finding ways to make a living without government assistance. They are involved in farmers' markets, direct selling, export, packing and marketing co-operatives and community supported agricultural systems, trying wherever possible to eliminate middlemen and thus maximise their share of the sale price. Some sell through agents, but the majority seek to develop loyal customers who appreciate the quality of the food they produce. Many of the farmers we interviewed are quite prepared to get in a truck and take their produce to where it is needed.

An exciting thing I discovered about the farmers who agreed to be interviewed for this book is that they are totally dedicated to what they are doing, intent on doing better what they already do, and excited by the long term prospects. They are resilient, often highly educated and always highly motivated. Their education is ongoing and self-directed and is motivated by the desire to find solutions to problems they are experiencing.

In Australia we are witnessing a groundswell of support for small farmers whose innovative approaches are totally unsupported by most government agencies and industry groups. This support is provided by network of highly qualified experts. Farmers no longer have to "go it alone" as many have had to do in the past. The experts who are changing the face of Australian horticulture are generally individuals who have travelled down the path of sustainable agriculture and want to share their experiences with other growers. They generally do not represent government agencies or educational institutions such as the CSIRO or the Department of Agriculture. The demonstrated success of some of the strategies they are using is arousing interest at the ground level but not as yet by industry bodies or government agencies.

The book only contains interviews of Australian farmers and they provide a glimpse of just part of the picture. Worldwide there is a movement that is occurring at a number of different levels and is gaining momentum. There is evidence of it in the huge upsurge of interest in backyard food growing, in community gardens and in a trickle of people moving away from cities to country areas where they can own a small area of land and grow their own food. We see it in the number of TV programmes relating to food, cooking, gardening and small-scale farming.

We see evidence of the trend in growing opposition to World Trade Agreements and in the development of groups such as the Campesina Movement of Santiago del Estoro, which comprises the families of traditional farmers and indigenous tribes people, who actively oppose the takeover of their land by large-scale, international companies for farming.

Each year, April 17th has been designated as International Day of Small Farmers' Struggle. The date marks the day in 1996 when nineteen Brazilian peasants who were defending their right to produce food on their own land were massacred by the military police at El Dorado dos Carajas. La Via Campesina, an international movement of peasants, small and medium-sized producers, the landless, rural women, indigenous peoples and agricultural workers, initiated this day to highlight the plight of small farmers worldwide. They promote a model of peasant or family-farm agriculture based on sustainable production with local resources and in harmony with local culture and tradition. Representatives of La Via Campesina from Japan, Indonesia, South Korea and East Timor visited Australia in June, 2010 and shared experiences with Australian small farmers.

We see the same trend towards sustainable agriculture in the increasing preparedness by the media to tell the story of damage caused by use of poisonous sprays, which are still "approved" for use by government agencies. A hard-hitting "60 Minutes" TV interview shown in March 2010 blamed agricultural poisons for clusters of horrendous birth defects and health problems in Australia and India. Official approval is still given for use of these poisons in spite of massive evidence, from both in Australia and overseas, that proves conclusively that these sprays cause catastrophic birth defects, distortion of reproductive systems and major health problems. We should be asking the question: "Whose interests are being looked after here?"

We are increasingly seeing in newspapers, magazines, books, on the Internet and television, information that refutes the claims put out by companies such as Monsanto that genetic modification is safe and will lead to increased production of food. Research organizations are undertaking studies to test safety.

Early in 2010 an English newspaper[1] reported that Austrian researchers had confirmed a direct link between a decrease in fertility and a diet containing GM food. The study was commissioned by the Austrian Agency for Health and Food Safety and carried out by the Veterinary University Vienna. They found significant litter size and pup weight deceases in the third and fourth litters in GM-fed mice. The GM produce in question was corn genetically modified with genes that produce a pesticide toxin as well as genes that allow the corn to survive applications of the herbicide Roundup.

Sixty-five serious health risks from genetically modified products of all kinds were documented in the book "Seeds of Deception"[2]. Health risks include:

• offspring of rats fed GM soy showed a five-fold increase in mortality, lower birth rates and inability to reproduce

•male mice fed GM soy had damaged young sperm cells

• embryonic offspring of GM soy-fed mice had altered DNA functioning

• sterility or fertility problems among pigs and cows fed on GM corn varieties

• fertility problems, abortions, premature births and other serious health issues, including deaths, among buffaloes in India fed GM cottonseed products.

Whilst no one knows for sure the long term effect of eating genetically modified food, the immediate consequences are known: between 1991 and 2001, the period during which GMO food flooded the market, food related illnesses doubled because GMO foods can be allogenic, toxic, carcinogenic and anti-nutritional.

For decades we have been told, over and over again, that the only way to feed the world's population is by being big, mechanised and "scientific". Most large-scale farmers believe this to be true. Evidence from the yield and productivity figures available over several decades proves conclusively that it isn't. Farm productivity per hectare decreases with increase in size. It is only farm output per person that increases with increased size.

The most efficient and productive farms are small family owned and run farms. This book demonstrates conclusively that big does not necessarily mean "clever". It is obvious from the interviews that Australian small farmers are prepared to sift through massive amounts of information and develop appropriate strategies for their requirements. They are forward thinking and highly intelligent problem solvers who are determined to be successful in what they do.

From the evidence available, some of which is provided in this book, it does seem that many small farmers in Australia are in the forefront of thinking and practice in terms of small-scale horticultural production. Changes are happening and they're happening fast. Whilst a massive switch in direction is required if we are to avoid the future we can expect if we continue "business as usual," the farmers interviewed for "Transition Farms" show that it is possible to create an entirely different, sustainable future.

Chapter 2
The future we can expect
if we continue "business as usual"

The world is experiencing a huge range of problems, any of which is capable of causing catastrophic disruption of the status quo.

Production based on the agribusiness model has been responsible for displacement of millions of people, an upsurge in health problems, depletion of non-renewable resources by profligate use of energy, massive areas of "dead" seas and rivers which can no longer sustain life, depletion of river and underground water storage and, if the evidence is to be believed, the killing of billions of bees on which horticulture depends.

Amazingly, these problems and more would lessen to an enormous degree if we were to change how we grow our food and start to eat food that is locally produced in ways that restore, rather than destroy, natural resources.

What follows is intended to put you in the picture with regard to the problems that humans have created by unsustainable food growing practices. These are examples of the sorts of things our farmers have been worried about and have sought to remedy in their own farming practice.

Probably the most serious problems on a world scene relate to peak oil and climate change. One without the other would be serious enough. Together they represent a huge challenge.

Peak Oil

The world's oil and gas are finite resources. Production in at least 60 of the world's 98 oil-producing nations is in decline. Even mighty oil-producing countries like Saudi Arabia are not increasing production even in a situation of increasing demand and escalating prices.

Peak oil is the point where further expansion of oil production becomes impossible because new production flows are fully offset by production declines. It is the point where oil demand exceeds supply because we have used up more oil than we have in reserve.

Once we pass the peak (and the evidence strongly suggests that we are already there), supply levels become the significant factor. This means that the prices will start to rise suddenly and steeply and the people with control of remaining oil reserves really get to dictate price and supply levels.

If you need to be persuaded that peak oil is a reality, there is one set of statistics that is totally convincing. In the 1960s the world consumed 4 billion barrels of oil per year and the average rate of discovery annually was around 30 billion barrels. Now, we consume 30 billion barrels of oil per year and the discovery rate is approaching 4 billion barrels of crude per year.[1]

Analysis of the rise and decline of oil exploration and extraction for individual countries shows that there is a forty-year gap between the peak in oil discovery and the peak in oil extraction. That is, it takes forty years for 50% of identified reserves to be extracted. Oil discoveries were highest in the 1960's and 1970's. The number of oilfields located since then has declined dramatically. This has not been for want of trying. If the same trend holds true for the whole world, as it does for individual countries, then there is certainly convincing evidence that oil production has peaked and is now in decline.

Discoveries have fallen since their peak in 1965. Oil is still being found but the average size of the fields is declining and the cost of extraction is increasing dramatically. The events in 2010 in the Gulf of Mexico, are indicative also, of the danger and risks involved in deep sea oil extraction.

If you need further convincing, the fact that oil companies are contracting staff and buying back their own shares rather than investing in oil exploration indicates that those who are "in the know" are taking action to safeguard their investments and ensure they benefit from price rises that are inevitable as oil supplies run down. Exxon is spending US$30 billion each year buying back its own shares, which is a clear indicator that oil companies are starting to plan for their own contraction.

Since January 2005, world oil production has levelled out between 84 and 87 million barrels of oil per day, in spite of very high prices.

Even though many countries are very secretive about oil reserves, evidence points to the fact that the figures for likely future reserves have been grossly inflated.

One of the really troubling things about the peak oil debate is that few people seem to be very interested. The fact that politicians in Australia have totally failed to start planning for a world without supplies of cheap or even relatively cheap oil is absolutely astounding, considering the magnitude of the problems that must result. Action that is being taken is happening at grass roots level. [2] China seems to be one of the few countries that is making serious efforts to produce sustainable energy supplies.

Modern mechanised farming methods are extremely demanding in terms of oil inputs. Not only is oil used for diesel to run machinery, it is also used for transport, water pumping, packaging, inputs such as chemical fertilizers (in particular nitrogenous fertilizers), insecticides, fungicides, herbicides, heating and cooling and refrigeration.

Oil is also the major component of a multitude of pieces of equipment used on a regular basis by farmers: poly pipe, drainage pipes, drums, hoses, and tanks of all shapes and sizes.

Sustainable agricultural practices substitute manpower for oil-driven machines to a large degree. This makes them far less vulnerable to increasing oil prices. Smallholdings generally, are far less mechanised than large-scale enterprises. They have replaced chemical fertilizers insecticides and herbicides, which are derived from oil, with products, which are not oil based.

Some farmers are developing strategies for building soil balance and fertility, which eliminate the need for any poisonous agricultural sprays. Since small-scale farms cannot afford to be far from their markets, the use of oil for transport is generally far less than it is for farms that transport food from one end of the country to the other.

As a consequence of rising prices caused by diminishing supplies of oil and increasing costs of production as all the "easy" oil is used up, transport costs are rising, which means the prices of everything brought into an area from outside that area must increase. We are already seeing this. Food prices are rising rapidly and will rise even more steeply in the near future.

Climate Change

Chemical fertilizers are badly named. They're not "fertilizers" in actual fact, but salts. Their role is to speed up the decomposition of humus in soil, release nutrients held in the humus and make them available for plant growth. Over time, chemical fertilizers strip the soil of its humus content. Chemical fertilizers such as super phosphate are the reason that Australian soils have declined from an average of 5% humus content to just on 1% in less than 50 years.

What people generally don't realise is that humus is made up of 58% carbon. The process just described where chemical fertilizers accelerate the breakdown of organic matter, releases carbon into the atmosphere as CO_2. Release of carbon into the atmosphere as a result of some farming practices, including ploughing, is a major cause of the increase in CO_2 levels in the atmosphere, which is widely accepted as the reason for global warming. What is not widely known is that Australian farming practices are, to a large degree, responsible for Australia having the highest per capita rate of greenhouse gas emissions in the world.

Sustainable agriculture is a cost effective system that could effectively mop up most of the excess carbon being emitted into the atmosphere if it were practiced everywhere. Every tonne of carbon lost from the soil adds 3.67 tonnes of CO_2 to the atmosphere. Organic farming practices such as incorporating vegetable waste in to the soil, composting and growing green manure crops helps sequester carbon. When cropping and grazing lands are nurtured in ways that improve both the level of humus and biological activity in the form of increased micro-organisms, not only will our food be healthier for us but we will be sequestering carbon as a bonus.

Theoretically, the benefits associated with improving levels of soil carbon should provide sufficient impetus for change. Carbon is, after all, the basis of life and the key measure of soil fertility. Changes are happening, but on too small a scale. People in positions of power are looking in the wrong direction for solutions to two of Australia's major problems: climate change and the health crisis.

Funds directed towards encouraging farmers to earn carbon credits by increasing the humus levels in their soil could provide an impetus for change.

Soil humus is rich in carbon. If carbon were to be stored in soil as a deliberate policy, rather than in the atmosphere, carbon levels in the atmosphere could be reduced dramatically. A 1% increase in organic carbon in the top 20 centimetres of soil represents a 24 tonne per hectare increase in organic carbon, which is equivalent to 88 tonnes of CO_2 per hectare. It is possible to increase carbon levels in soils by 1% in a year. Many of the farmers interviewed for the book, are doing this.

The more carbon in soils, the greater the number of soil micro-organisms. This leads to better soil structure, more nutrients available for plant growth and increased water and oxygen content in the soil. These are all important benefits that come from improving carbon levels in soil.

Greenhouse gas emissions from agricultural soils currently represent huge losses of valuable farm resources. A carbon credits trading scheme for soil carbon would create the economic incentive for rapid development of market-based innovative technologies to reverse this trend. [3]

Stories of farmers being forced into debt or off their land by catastrophic natural events such as floods, fire, drought, hail and hurricanes are becoming more and more common. This is caused by severe climate events, which as we know are a concomitant of global warming. Whilst returns on crops are high, the costs associated with preparation and planting in order to produce a crop are also extremely high. Farmers in many locations across Australia are seeing not one failed harvest, but failures year after year because of these disastrous natural events.

The idea that we are likely to experience more and more extreme climatic events as CO_2 levels rise and affect the Earth's climate is generally accepted. We are already experiencing these types of climate extremes and farmers are bearing the brunt of seasonal abnormalities and extreme climatic events.

Consequences of the Peak Oil and Climate Change combination

Unless governments do something incredibly foolish, like going to war to take control of the scarce resources that are left, expensive oil will inevitably cause economic contraction. It has certainly caused some of the farmers I have interviewed to reconsider how they have been operating and make the switch to different strategies, which demand lower energy inputs. One benefit is that this sort of thinking may slow down the impact of climate change if it is widely adopted.

Some doomsday thinkers believe that the peak oil and climate change challenges indicate the "end of the world" but perhaps, if we change our perspective, we see that it is not "the end", but rather the start of a whole new, and better, world: one we have the opportunity of creating for ourselves.

Perhaps these challenges represent a blessing in disguise. Without cheap energy, wars on the scale we have seen in recent decades, cannot be fought. Mindless manufacture of goods we don't need will be curtailed. Pollution levels will drop. Lower production levels will reduce the strain on Earth's resources. At the community level, we may benefit from greater self-sufficiency, cohesiveness and diversity. When energy costs increase we will need to provide products for our communities in ways that are not necessarily the most economical in terms of production costs, but are the most energy efficient.

There is no doubt that, as the effect of climate change and peak oil start to impact, farming methods will be forced to change. Some farmers, including the ones interviewed in this book, have "jumped the gun". They have seen that the methods they have been using are unsustainable for the planet as well as for themselves and are seeking different strategies. The sooner everyone starts planning for changes that will be inevitable, the easier the transition will be.

Water Depletion

Depletion of surface and underground water supplies is a major problem. Underground water supplies, worldwide, are being depleted.[4] Some of the farmers, interviewed for this book, are vulnerable because of possible water shortages. Without water nothing will grow. Without some sort of guarantee of water availability, investment in future plantings is risky, particularly in marginal regions where irrigation is a vital part of the horticultural scene.

India is facing severe food shortage because 175 million Indians are fed with grain produced using underground water supplies. Twenty-one million wells have been drilled and half of these have already dried up.

In Chennai, in southern India, there is a thriving tanker industry, which supplies water to the city's residents. Thirteen thousand tankers haul water to Chennai from surrounding rural areas every day. Farmers are happy because they get more money for water than they do from their crops. Predictably, water tables are falling and already many wells have gone dry. Eventually, with this level of water usage, the farmers, who have sold their water, will no longer be able to farm their land. Chennai is not an isolated case.

The vast Ogallala aquifer under the U.S. Great Plain will soon be depleted. Farmers will have no option but to return to lower-yield dry-land farming.

Falling water tables are already adversely affecting harvests in China, which rivals the US as the world's largest grain producer. The level of the deep aquifer under the North China Plain is dropping 3 metres per year. When the aquifer is depleted, grain harvests will drop by 40 millions tons and China will lose the food supply for 130 million of its people.

Pakistan faces a similar situation to India. Observation wells near Islamabad and Rawalpindi show a fall in the water table averaging between 1 and 2 metres per year. Iran is over-pumping its aquifers by an average of 5 billion tons of water per year. In Mexico, in the agricultural state of Guanajuato, the water table is falling by 2 metres or more a year. At the national level, 51% of all water extraction is from aquifers that are being over-pumped.

In Australia, the Murray-Darling river basin covers 14% of Australia's landmass. It is Australia's most important agricultural region, accounting for 40% of the national gross value of agricultural production. It supports one-quarter of Australia's cattle, half the sheep and half the cropland. From this river basin comes one-third of Australia's wheat, all of its cotton and rice, half of its fruit and a substantial share of the country's vegetables.

The Murray-Darling river system is drying up. In the season of 2007-2008 there was no water available for irrigation. There is not sufficient water to flush out the Coorong, the wetland area at the mouth of the Murray River. One of the reasons for the shortage of water in the river is over-allocation of water resources to farmers for irrigation. Water is stored in reservoirs along the river and evaporation rates are high. Moreover, towns along the Murray River and Darling River compete with farmers for water resources. The Murray River is the major source of water for Adelaide, the largest city in South Australia.

Whilst evaporation, drought and over-usage go a long way towards explaining the lack of water flow along the Murray, these account for only a relatively small percentage of the water lost. Only 10 - 15% of the loss is through evaporation. A much more serious problem is that half of the water loss is through the soil.

Based on observations from the GRACE satellite mission, it has been found that from 2002 - 2009 the Murray-Darling basin lost 200 cubic kilometres of water, which is equivalent to 400 times the volume of water in Sydney Harbour. The satellite data shows that while there is water loss from the surface streams and flows, the greatest losses, equivalent to half of the total, have occurred beneath the surface.

It is likely that the Murray-Darling system river system is the source of Australia's underground water storage system as a whole. Water from the Murray-Darling basin is the probable source of the Great Artesian Basin's enormous storage of underground water: water on which the farms and towns distant from rivers depend on for watering livestock. [5] If this is what is happening it is not going to be possible for the water that has been used up in the Artesian Basin to be replaced and continue to maintain large-scale, horticultural activity along the Murray River.

With accelerating depletion of aquifers worldwide comes the potential for massive levels of unrest, migration and famine caused by severe food and water shortages.

Soil erosion

The quality of the food we grow depends on the fertility of the soil in which that food is grown. Throughout the world depleted soils are a problem caused by "robber" farming techniques and by processes such as soil erosion and soil salting.

If we look at soil erosion in Western Australia as typical of the problem throughout Australia, we see it is a serious matter indeed. Thick dust storms originating in central and Western Australia have covered vast areas of Australia and taken topsoil as far away as New Zealand. Storms such as these demonstrate conclusively that soil erosion is a very serious problem for the country.[6]

Studies carried out on 70 sites throughout Western Australia showed that 10% of the sites had soil losses in excess of 20 tonnes per hectare per year, or approximately 15 - 20 millimetres per decade. Since it is estimated that soil formation is likely to be in the order of one metre every million years in some of the areas tested, soil loss of the magnitude recorded is clearly unsustainable.

Soil Salinity

Soil salinity was identified as a problem in Australia back in 1924 but it has only been since the 70s that attempts have been made to understand the problem and find solutions. Lost agricultural production due to salinity has been estimated to be $130 million a year and increasing. Soil salt renders soil useless for growing crops. Land available for cultivation is shrinking because of this problem at the same time that the population is increasing.

Salinity is a problem not only for farming. Urban centres are being seriously affected as roads, footpaths, sewage pipes and buildings are being corroded by saline seepage.

The problem has been caused by the clearing of many billions of trees to make way for large scale farming which is not sustainable.

Native Australian vegetation evolved to be salt-tolerant. Many woodland species have deep roots and a high demand for water. While the system was in balance the salt stayed put. One solution to the problem is to replant the trees that have been removed, allowing agro-forestry to be established in the wetter areas and full-scale forestry elsewhere.

Insects and disease

Many of the farmers I have interviewed speak of having formerly used insecticides and pesticides that have been banned in recent years. What appear to be miraculous solutions to serious problems are in fact the creators of even more serious problems. What follows is a sample of the effects of some of the agricultural poisons that have been used by the farmers I have interviewed:

(a) Parathion is an organic phosphorous compound used as an insecticide. It is extremely toxic to humans. The compound works in humans and insects as a cholinesterase inhibitor, disrupting the normal functioning of the nervous system and causing respiratory failure.

(b) DDT is an organo-chlorine contact insecticide, which has been shown to bio-accumulate with the potential to disrupt endocrine systems in humans and wildlife.

(c) Lead Arsenate poisons were used extensively to control agricultural pests. The pesticide residues bind tightly to the soil surface layer where they remain for decades and may pose a human health risk. Arsenic can lead to several types of cancer.

(d) Gramoxone has been used worldwide since the 1960s. The active ingredient is paraquat, which is highly toxic. It is a known carcinogen, a cholinesterase inhibitor, and a known reproductive and developmental toxicant. It was banned in 1992 in the USA and in 2003 in Europe.

(e) The jury is still out on *RoundUp* but the evidence against it is stacking up. France's highest court ruled in 2009 that Monsanto had not told the truth about the safety of its best-selling weed-killer, Roundup. The court confirmed an earlier judgment that Monsanto had falsely advertised its herbicide as "biodegradable".

Glyphosate, the active ingredient in RoundUp, is the most commonly reported cause of pesticide illness in California. According to Dr. Joseph Mercola, it is suspected of causing genetic damage, is acutely toxic to fish, birds, beneficial insects and soil organisms that maintain ecological health. Studies are showing that RoundUp residues cause cell damage and death even at very low levels. The ingredients added to glyphosate to create the product called RoundUp, make the product even more damaging than glyphosate on its own.

There is no need to worry about poisons and insects when the soil is healthy and nutritionally balanced, with a pH of 6·4. Healthy soil produces healthy plants. Healthy plants are full of minerals and sugars, which give insects alcohol poisoning. This makes sense when you realise that insects and diseases are nature's garbage disposal agents. They get rid of the rubbish! There's no prize for guessing who eats the rubbish when we eliminate most of the insects and diseases with poisons.

Plants have defence systems to fight against insect attack and disease. This may take the form of thick skin on fruit or spines or hairs on the plants. It may involve feedback systems of bio-chemical pathways, which operate in a similar way to our immune system. An external cue, such as an insect sting, prompts a cascade of responses that trigger the production of bio-chemicals. These deter or kill invading pests. This response takes only minutes in a healthy plant, but unhealthy plants do not have adequate energy resources to activate their defences.

From the above it is clear that the solutions that have been provided for the pest and disease problems are probably far more dangerous to our health than we have been led to believe. When we look at some of the major health problems in our society and link them with the practices used in conventional farming, it seems that there is cause for alarm.

Health

Farmers have at their disposal a huge range of agricultural poisons to control the pests and diseases that are attacking their plants. At last count there were something like 74,000 registered man-made poisons, the vast majority of which were designed to fight pests and diseases in agriculture.

The downside of this approach is that a recent study of thousands of American schoolchildren showed that all of them had traces of one or more agricultural poisons in their bodies.

We are told that these chemicals are safe, but the toxic smorgasbord of chemicals used by many commercial farmers has unintended and undesirable side effects, including poisoning the soil, water and soil micro-organisms.

Governments have an interesting method for determining the "safe" level of toxins in food. When actual levels become higher than the "recommended safe level," they increase the recommended level. The European Union has raised the legal daily limit of glyphosate (the active ingredient in most herbicides and weedicides) residue to 20mg per kilogram of food. This is sixty times higher than the limits recommended by the World Health Organization. The Environmental Protection Agency in the United States has raised the legally acceptable level to 100 mg per kilogram of food. This is 10 times the level at which birth and reproductive anomalies have been observed in animals.

A troubling side effect that comes from using a chemical to control a pest is that the rich suite of biological compounds that plants naturally synthesise in order to protect themselves is not produced. This reduces the flavour, nutritional value and even medicinal properties that plants offer because beneficial bio-chemicals have been replaced by toxic, man-made chemicals.

Australian authorities ignore the overwhelming evidence about adverse effects of using a huge number of poisonous pesticides, fungicides and herbicides in Australian gardens and farms. More than 7,200 registered biocide products are used in Australia. There is virtually no testing to detect the residues of poison in our food and little research has been done to determine safe intake levels, if indeed any level is "safe".

Regulatory authorities assure us our food is safe. However, the facts demonstrate clearly that it is a myth that agricultural chemicals leave few residues and do not persist in our food: residues from 37 poisons were found in Australian foods in 2003. Most agricultural poisons leave residues of breakdown chemicals when they degrade and in some cases they become even more toxic as they break down. Many of the chemicals currently in use are as residual as the now banned organo-chlorines such as Dieldrin and Heptachlor. Residues from chemicals currently in use cause as many health and reproductive problems as Dieldrin and Heptachlor.

Whilst contamination statistics are not available in Australia, the story from the USA provides a very grim picture. In a study carried out in 2007 with 97,000 tests, the findings were as follows: 97% of nectarines, 96.7% peaches and 94.1% of apples tested positive for pesticide. Even more worrying was the fact that 87% of peaches, 85.3% of nectarines and 82.3% of apples contained 2 or more pesticide residues.

The figures for vegetables were almost as bad with 94.1% of celery, 81.5% of capsicum and 82.3% of carrots containing pesticide residues and 79.8% of celery and 62.2% of capsicum containing two or more different poisons.

If this isn't scary enough, the following statistics are even worse. Peaches and apples contained a total of 9 different poisons. Capsicum won the award for having the most number of different poisons. They contained 11. These tests show that farmers use a wide variety of pesticides. The combined 2007 tests showed that 53 different chemicals were used for peaches. An even greater variety of pesticides were used for vegetables.

Pesticides do not just pollute our food. They also poison our water and air. In 1999 Swiss research demonstrated that rain falling in Europe contained higher levels of pesticides than were allowed for drinking water. A Greek study in

1999 showed rain contained one or more pesticides in 90% of the 200+ samples tested.

One and a half billion kilograms of pesticides are used in the world annually. The emerging body of science indicates that many chemical cocktails work synergistically but even one chemical alone can do great damage. For example, in 2006 Atrazine was banned in Europe because it was shown to cause tumours of mammary glands, uterus and ovaries in test animals and was believed to be a cause of cancer in humans. Australian authorities have ignored the overwhelming evidence about the adverse effects caused by this chemical.

Swedish studies have also linked non-Hodgkins lymphoma to pesticide. Before 1940, this was one of the world's rare forms of cancer. It is now the most common one. Moreover, glyphosate, the active ingredient in Roundup, causes gene mutations and chromosomal aberrations. Denmark banned glyphosate in 2003 because it was so persistent that it polluted most of the groundwater.[8]

Unable to eliminate unrecognisable toxic chemical substances, the body deals with them in the only way it knows: it stores them. It accumulates them in our fat cells, our livers and kidneys. It stores them in our brain. It stores them in our glands, particularly the thyroid and adrenal glands. It stores them throughout our central nervous system. Pesticides, herbicides and fungicides accumulate in fatty tissues and tend to settle in the bones.

Virtually all of us are now in a state of toxic overload because of exposure to toxic chemicals. Cumulatively, the toxic residues in our daily diet have been demonstrated to exceed 500% of the recommended daily maximum. Several studies have shown that the average person, no matter where that person lives, has 40 to 75 man-made chemical residues stored in fat tissue.

Accumulation of toxic chemicals and metals means our bodies can't assimilate and utilize essential minerals such as iron, calcium and magnesium. Enzyme dysfunction, nutritional deficiencies, hormonal imbalances, neurological disorders, damage to brain chemistry may result. Accumulated toxins can lead to auto-immune disorders, cancer and other debilitating chronic conditions.

Tests have shown that organically grown foods have substantially lower levels of pesticides and insecticides than conventionally grown food. They cost more than conventionally produced food, because they are more expensive to produce, but scientific findings world-wide, suggest they are worth it.

Food Quality

Scientific studies are demonstrating that what many of the farmers I interviewed believe to be true about the quality of the food they are producing, actually is true.

A study was carried out in England recently to show that food grown using organic farming methods has significantly higher mineral content than food grown by conventional farming methods. Two farm plots, adjacent to one another, used different growing techniques for the same vegetables, and analysis of the crops proved that what consumers have known for ages is true. The conclusions from this study were published in *The Australian* newspaper. Whilst consumers haven't needed to be convinced, the scientific community needs to hear this.

Food produced by large-scale, conventional, commercial farming practices generally contains 3 major nutrients (nitrogen, potassium and phosphorous) and 4 minor nutrients (boron, copper, manganese and molybdenum).

The bad news is that living things need 72 biological elements for normal metabolic function, reproduction and maintenance of the immune system. Many of the farmers I have interviewed for this book mention that their soils are deficient in calcium. Since calcium is required in every cell in our body, it is vitally important for health and, of course, to the production of healthy crops.

Soils containing all 72 elements in the correct balance are healthy. Because the soil is healthy, plants grown in this soil are healthy. Insects and diseases do not attack healthy plants. Disease is also nature's way of eliminating those things that are not healthy, whether they are plants, animals or humans. The purpose for this plan is to ensure survival of the species. If unhealthy plants are allowed to produce seeds, then the next generation of plants will be weaker. By eliminating all but the healthy, nature ensures that the next generation of plants will also be strong.

The food we eat is severely deficient in over 60 vitally important elements. Many practitioners of alternative medicine and a growing number of doctors believe that this is the cause of large numbers of physiological and mental diseases such as cancer, auto–immune disease, late onset diabetes, degenerative and chronic diseases, allergies and birth defects. The reason that trace elements are so important is because they are:
•   essential in the assimilation and utilisation
        of vitamins
•   an aid in digestion
•   a catalyst for hormones and enzymes
•   an aid in replacing electrolytes lost through
        perspiration
•   a protection against toxic reactions.

Reinstatement of trace elements in our soils eliminates all plant diseases, pest and insect attack. If there are no pests and diseases attacking our plants, we have no need to use toxic agricultural chemicals. The fact that farmers need to use these substances with such frightening frequency is a clear indication that the food that they are producing is not healthy.

Much more research needs to be done to highlight the importance of every one of the minerals and trace elements that occur on Earth and probably have a role to play in all living things.[9] Nevertheless, we have enough evidence already to persuade us to protect the trace elements in our food.

Business and government disincentives

It seems that our economic environment is actively working against sustainable agriculture and the small farmer. Not only are there no incentives to grow more nutritious food in a way that supports the environment, big business and government actually create disincentives for small farming, in the belief that corporate farming is more profitable. This is in spite of the fact that there is a huge amount of information that supports the idea that productivity decreases with size and the most efficient and productive farm unit is small and family owned and run.

Worldwide, industrial mono-cultural farming has displaced traditional food production and farmers, wreaking havoc on food prices and local food availability. This is particularly true in less developed countries where peasants and small farmers have been pushed off the land to make way for large agribusiness.

In Argentina, for example, the 2008 agricultural census showed that more than 60,000 farms shut down between 2002 and 2008, while the average size of farms increased from 421 to 538 hectares. Problems of land access and disputes over land titles has become one of the central issues for traditional farmers, who primarily grow a range of food for their own use and a little for sale. Once displaced from their land, farmers are then replaced by machinery.

Canada lost almost three-quarters of its farm population between 1941 and 1996. The six founding countries of Europe's Common Agricultural Policy had 22 million farmers in 1957 and now have fewer than 7 million. In the USA there were almost 7 million farms in 1935. Now there are fewer than 2 million.

Argentina has been described as South America's breadbasket because it once produced grain and beef for much of the region. Production has now shifted to soybeans, displacing traditional food production by farmers who occupied what were formerly forest areas. A growing number of the large landholders are financial investors from other countries. Members of indigenous communities evicted from their lands have been arrested, injured and occasionally killed as a result of violence erupting because of protests.

This problem is not Argentina's alone. According to a statement by Vanana Shiva, in the *Nation* magazine, "a billion people are without sufficient food because industrial monocultures rob them of their livelihoods in agriculture". Corporatization of food has been a boon for multinational businesses, which market everything industrial farmers need: equipment, fuels, seeds, antibiotics, pesticides, and more. When farmers produce a small but diverse range of crops, their entire harvest can be marketed within their own local economy, but when swallowed into the global food system, farmers need to market single crops in amounts far larger than the local economy can absorb. These farmers can no longer market their own production and have come to depend on agribusinesses to do it for them.

Corporate agribusinesses have thus taken control of the entire food system. They not only supply almost all the needs of industrial farmers (in some cases owning the farms themselves), but they also act as middlemen, processors, distributors and retailers - buying, packaging and selling food on markets that have grown to encompass the entire planet. Many agribusinesses have become huge, vertically integrated enterprises, with subsidiaries profiting from every aspect of a farm's operation.[10]

The concerns discussed above are the sorts of things that have caused most of the transition farmers profiled in this book to take the organic[11], biodynamic[12] or biological[13] approach to farming. They are probably more aware than the general population of the links between farming practices and good health, soil erosion and the problems caused by rising oil prices. They have chosen to take action by changing their farming practices to ones that rely less on oil, sequester carbon, reduce water usage, reduce soil erosion and create healthier food by cutting down or eliminating chemical poisons.

In the following chapters you will discover how they have done this.

Chapter 3

Nut Cases

Three nut farmers have chosen to share the story of their transition from chemical farming to something more sustainable.

They are:

Geoff Bugden from Lismore in Northern NSW

Martin Brook from Byron Bay in northern NSW

Jim Velehris from Renmark in South Australia

Geoff Bugden
Pecan Nut grower in Lismore, NSW

Geoff Bugden is a boilermaker by trade. He claims to be uneducated, having left school at an early age. He worked in the building trade in Sydney and taught himself carpentry, concreting and roof plumbing. He also played 13 years of professional Rugby League in Sydney with teams that won premierships. When he retired from Rugby League he joined the police force in Sydney before moving to Lismore and working for 12 years as a detective.

How did you get into farming, Geoff?

Whilst still working for the police I bought a small farm. I've always loved gardening and farming and I wanted something for when I retired. I researched what would suit that farm because it was in an area that has heavy frosts. Pecans seemed to be a good crop to grow. They were, I thought, particularly good because they are deciduous and go to sleep for three months, which would give my wife and myself a period each year when we could hook up the caravan and go away.

I joined the Pecan Association, did a lot of research on pecans and eventually planted 600 pecan trees. It was just the best experience. When I started I knew nothing about farming. I knew nothing about fertilizer. I knew nothing about how to grow anything. It was my hobby.

We were on that farm for about 8 years when one of my friends, who was a pecan nut grower, told me he was selling his farm and asked me if I wanted to buy it. He owned 150 acres with 100 of them on the flood plain. He had a 25-acre pecan orchard of mature trees that were bringing in a small return.

I went home and told the wife that I was thinking of selling our farm and buying a bigger one. She cried. She loved our little farm. I took her to see the new farm and we decided it would be a good move.

What sort of farming methods did you use when you first bought the new farm?

It's a beautiful river flat farm. It used to be a dairy farm and it had been flogged for generations prior to the previous farmer owning it. When I moved onto the farm the first thing I asked the old fella I'd bought it from was: "What sort of fertilizer regime do you use?"

He told me he used NPK and asked: "Do you know what that is?" Well I didn't but I looked it up and found it was a nitrogen, phosphorus and potassium mix. He also put on nitrogen in the form of urea, using a fertigation system. He needed the fertigation system because, to be commercially viable, pecans have to be irrigated and they are heavy feeders. To grow and produce they also need a certain time under 7^0C. He told me the amount of urea he was putting on was calculated by looking at the diameter of the tree trunk. In winter he put out extra phosphorous in the form of single super or triple super phosphate, whichever was cheapest. His application rate depended on how much the fertilizer people told him was appropriate. For extra potassium he used muriate of potash.

I got the low down from the old fella and proceeded to do exactly the same as he had done but I did do some research. When I looked up all these things I found out that urea is a petroleum chemical salt-based fertilizer. When I put it into my fertigation tank it burnt my hands. One day my son asked me: "Do you know that when the Romans used to sack towns they put salt on the land so that it would be infertile?" I told him I was doing it because that was what the old fella used to do.

This area is full of iron. When the CSIRO did tests here, they found out that within 30 minutes, the phosphorus in the super phosphate combined with the iron and turned into iron phosphate and became like cement. From then on it is unavailable to the trees. The old farmer put it on every year religiously, as if he was putting money into the bank.

Lastly I found out about muriate of potash. It's a chlorine-based product that is actually just the waste from chlorine factories. You put chlorine into your swimming pool to kill the bugs and they use muriate of potash on roads up north during the wet season to make the surface hard.

When I found all this out I thought: "This can't be doing the soil any good!" It might make the trees grow but it's not sustainable.

When I bought the farm I also bought all the old fella's implements. With pecans you have to grab hold of the tree and shake it. The nuts fall onto the ground, which is where they get picked up. What he used was a macadamia harvester that had been modified to pick up pecans without breaking them. It was a type of harvester that doesn't pick up pecans in grass very well. As a result he had to herbicide the grass leaving just bare dirt under the trees. We used herbicide 3 or 4 times a year to keep the grass from growing.

Using these strategies I felt I was waging a form of "warfare" farming and I wondered why we were having trouble keeping the trees healthy. The ground here was bare like a landing strip because I was using all these sulphate chemicals and herbicides. The "enemy" was well and truly dead!

One day I was in the local farm shop getting more super and more urea and I saw a leaflet about someone called Graeme Sait who was giving a 1-day seminar in Lismore. It was a workshop about sustainable agriculture and saving money on fertilizer.

I went. I walked out of that workshop saying: "You beauty!" I immediately signed up for Graeme's 4-day workshop and when I completed that my head was buzzing. It was unbelievable. My eyes were opened and my thinking had changed. Farming wasn't just a matter of using three elements. There's a whole range of other things you need. Once I realized that I didn't look back.

Now when I started farming, I wouldn't use pesticides and fungicides. That was probably my only good decision. I thought they were far too dangerous. Poisons were one of the reasons I decided to grow pecans rather than macadamias. One day I was at a macadamia farm talking to a bloke and I just leaned up against the 5,000-litre spray tank he used for his foliar spraying. He jumped up and said: "Don't lean on that! Quick, come here and wash your hands!" I asked: "What's in it?" but he wouldn't tell me. That incident made me decide not to grow macadamias.

What did you do once you realized that there was a different way to farm?

I needed more knowledge. I subscribed to *Acres* magazine and I enrolled in an 18-week TAFE course on biological farming. That was a fantastic course. I joined the "Soil Care" group at Wollongbar.

The first thing I did was to get rid of my harvester. Originally, macadamia growers used to use pecan harvesters brought out from America. I found an old farm with two old pecan harvesters that had been parked in the shed for 20 years. I bought them and replaced all the bearings, chains and belts. They can pick up pecans in 6 inches of grass.

I started encouraging the grass to grow. I even re-seeded it and I'm planning to put pinto peanuts under the trees. Now I've got a beautiful lawn under my trees and the microbes that live on the roots of the grass feed the trees. I've got the old American pecan harvester that picks up nuts for me beautifully, so I don't have to worry about the grass any more.

Then I started thinking: "Trees need nitrogen. Everything needs nitrogen. In Graeme's Sait's course I learned that there's heaps of nitrogen everywhere.

The trees just have to be able to get it, and for that to happen you need to have the soil in balance and lots of microorganisms. "

Having sorted the harvesting problem, my next job was to get the soil into balance. The trees are planted on the flood plain, which is fine because pecans come from the Mississippi wetlands and are used to floods. I've had small trees with floodwater 10ft over the top of them. I might lose one or two because of water speed, but generally floods do more good than harm. We just have to manage the flood plains.

The soil on the flood plain was so out of whack that to fix the imbalances it was going to cost me something like $20,000 for a prescription blend[2]. I couldn't afford that so I decided to put on just half of what I needed. I had to be careful with timing when I put out the prescription blend because I could lose it all if the river were to flood after I put it out.

In that first year I was expecting to harvest 8 tonnes. I actually harvested 20 tonnes.

We originally had 500 mature trees and another 4,000 were just starting to produce and a further 2,000 were still to be planted. That will give us between 300 and 500 tonnes of pecans a year, which is a big increase over the 8 tonnes we started with. I've already tripled my crop and the fertilizer costs have remained the same.

Now that we've built up the soil biology the fertilizer gets taken into the soil really quickly. I know this is happening because when I walk the farm, I see the nuts that have fallen off the tree start to decompose in about 14 days. Previously the nuts just used to sit on the ground for weeks and weeks. And another thing tells me we're on track. Back in the beginning I couldn't even find any earthworms. Now they're coming back. We've still got a long way to go but we're getting there.

It hasn't all been trouble free. Back in 2005, when I was so excited at seeing the production level increase, I was having a problem with the lower leaves on the trees going black and the nuts also turning black and falling off.

The leaf of the tree is the solar panel and these black spots were covering a large percentage of the solar panels on the tree. While this was happening the photosynthesis process wasn't working as well as it should do and the sugars weren't available to the trees. They were losing half their growth energy.

I sent some samples to the Sydney Botanical Garden's pathology laboratory and they told me I was in big trouble because I had anthracnose. I said: "What's that?" Apparently it's a disease caused by a particular type of fungus and it had the potential to inflict major damage. It infects the nut through the pollen causing the nut to rot from the inside out.

Their recommendation was to rake up all the nuts, leaves and sticks and burn them as soon as the trees lost their leaves and then to sanitise the area with a fungicide poison. Now I won't put fungicides on our farm so I had to find another way and the idea of picking up 30 tonnes of sticks and leaves didn't impress me.

Graeme Sait told me that pathogens come from the ground up and since the problem was worst closer to the ground so I thought he was probably right. I followed his recommendation to use a predator fungus called trichoderma that eats the anthracnose.

I had this old 1,000-litre mist tank that I'd bought at a clearance sale. The spray could only go 20 ft into the air but that's what I had and I wasn't going to invest in fancy equipment. I'd learnt how to make compost tea so I bought the anthracnose inoculant[3], brewed it up and sprayed it on.

I sent away a second sample a year later and got a report back that the anthracnose wasn't as well developed but that anthracnose had been joined by another fungus living in the diseased nuts.

In the third year, the Botanic Gardens pathology laboratory people phoned me because they wanted to do a trial with anthracnose and thought our place would be ideal. As it turned out, there was a problem with this plan: when they tested our trees that year, there was no evidence of anthracnose.

Now I don't believe we've eradicated the anthracnose, and if I stop doing what I've been doing it will come back. I'm fine with that. What's great is that a lot of farmers in the area are now using trichoderma fungus and they're happy with the changes that are being made.

What is your general fertilization routine and soil improvement strategy now?

I now plant a root-friendly zone between the tree rows. Pecan nut trees have a taproot and lateral roots that go out as far as the tree is high. I put in soybeans, sorghum, lucerne, 3 different types of clover, cowpeas and lablab. All these go in at the one time and it's all worm food. I mow it and in three weeks, the cut stuff is all gone.

Where I used to have hard ground that I could drive up and down, now I get bogged because the ground is so soft and springy.

I put on a foliar spray using a product called Bio-N. That's a bacterium that goes to the roots and sucks the nitrogen out of the air so that the tree has all the nitrogen it need because of the bacteria around the root zone. I know this works because of the leaf tests. I sprayed Bio-N on and the next time I did a leaf test, there was a 12% increase in nitrogen in the leaf. I spray on Bio-N twice a year, at the start and the end of the season. The urea I bought the day I saw the leaflet advertising Graeme Sait's workshop is still sitting in the shed.

I know now that to sustain a horticultural crop you need 33 ppm of phosphorus in your soil. I've got over 3,000 ppm locked up in my soil, thanks to the previous owners. I can access that using legumes, microbes and soft rock phosphate. I no longer put any phosphorus on the soil but if I see that my trace elements are a bit deficient, I just put a bit of guano or phosphorus on the tree as a foliar spray. In addition I use potassium sulphate to keep up the potassium levels.

Urea used to cost me $5,000 per year. Now nitrogen inputs cost me $500. My potassium sulphate is twice the price of muriate of potash but it is good for my soil, unlike muriate of potash, which does a lot of harm. For all my trace elements I use chelated products when I need them. I need different ones at different times of the year.

I'm planning a 3-year soil enhancement rotation. I'll put on 200 cubic metres of chicken manure per 25 acres once every three years. The following year I'll put on the recommended prescription blend. In the third year I'll bring in compost.

Has your soil improved?

When we did our first soil test back in 2005 we had a pH of 4·6, a CEC level of 10·5 and a calcium/magnesium ratio of 2:4. Manganese levels were excessive. The organic matter was 6·6%. In 2009 we had lifted the pH to 5·4, improved the CEC to 14·9, changed the calcium/magnesium ratio to 3:1. In 2008 we were still low in silicon, boron, copper, zinc and molybdenum. The good news is that manganese has come back into balance. The trends are in the right direction, which is good.

How do you sell your pecans, Geoff?

Well that's an interesting story. In 2007 the price of pecans dropped dramatically. Up till then we were getting $4 kg but in that year the price halved. We looked at exporting to China but they weren't interested in just 20 tonnes. I phoned a few other pecan growers and we decided to pool our nuts. In total we had 60 or 80 tonnes. Now we had the Chinese interested. The price they offered was $3.30 so the farmers were pleased.

The following year the price was still low and we realised we had to put in a sizing plant and silos, because the Chinese hand crack their pecans, put them into a solution of secret herbs and spices and then roast them. Pecans vary a lot in size and if those different sized nuts go into a roasting oven at the same time, they cook unevenly.

Once we had the sizing plant and we could offer sized pecans we had 6 or 8 companies chasing us. We did 100 tonnes in the second year. This year we could reach 150 tonnes and we've got 30 or 35 farmers in the area working with us.

Do you have any advice for anyone who would like to do what you have done?

Don't take anyone's word. Do the research for yourself. Find out the facts and be clear on where you're going. It doesn't take long to see the changes. The benefits come immediately but you have to obtain the knowledge and know what you're doing first.

I'm fairly passionate about what I do and excited by what is happening. Tomorrow we have our first truckload of nuts for the season being picked up at 5.45 in the morning to go off to China. That's exciting. Things are getting better and better all the time. I look forward to every day. I watched the sun come up this morning when the river was coming up after last night's storm. It was magic.

Yours is a lovely story, Geoff. Thank you so much for sharing it with me.

Martin Brook
Macadamia grower and manufacturer
in Byron Bay, NSW

Brookfarm is a family business run by Martin and his wife Pam and their two sons. Martin Brook asked his farm manager Peter Barton to be present during our interview and the answers to the questions asked come from both Martin and Peter.

Martin is obviously involved in the day-to-day decisions about how the farm is being run but is not a hands-on farmer. In fact, he is more a farmer by accident than by design. In making the transition from conventional farming strategies to a more sustainable organic approach, Martin has discovered a passion for eliminating chemicals and agricultural poisons from the farm and a real understanding of the reasons why it is so important to do so. This understanding comes not just from the science that supports sustainable farming practices but also from a very practical evaluation of market trends: people world-wide are looking for agricultural products that are high quality and chemical free.

Marin and Pam, his wife, and their two sons are totally involved in the manufacturing and marketing aspect of an international business, which has been developed as a "value added" component to growing macadamias. It is the amalgamation of a successful agricultural enterprise and a brilliant manufacturing and marketing business that has won Brookfarm wide recognition in Australia and overseas.

Your background as a film producer is an unusual one for a farmer. Tell me how you come to be growing macadamias in Byron Bay.

You're right about me having had no practical experience as a farmer prior to moving to Byron Bay, but my forebears were farmers in southern England. I did do quite a lot of the physical work on the farm when we first moved here, particularly the regeneration of the creeks. Now I leave most of the actual farming work to my farm manager, Peter, whose background is farming, but I would like to emphasise that we're working together on this new road that we're travelling. I share with Peter a real excitement. I can see, just walking around the orchard and looking under the trees, just how much our soil has improved. The general health of the trees has improved. I love being able to dig around and see the activity in the soil.

Tell me the story of how you come to be doing what you are doing.

My wife Pam and I came to Byron Bay for a holiday and we bought a 98-acre farm. It was an impulse buy rather than the result of a well thought out plan. We had dreams of moving to Byron, working and having a farm to come home to but hadn't thought through the practicalities. That was back in 1988. What we bought was a run down dairy farm full of camphor laurel and lantana and boulders. There was a very small area of remnant rainforest.

What we hadn't taken into account when we bought the farm was the fact that the economy was about to take a nosedive. That meant we had to continue living in Melbourne and working incredibly hard to keep the place going. I was a TV producer and Pam was a dentist.

Shortly after buying the property we had a notice from Council requiring us to get the weeds under control and the only thing we could think of that would do that was to plant trees. A friend of mine in Melbourne, was a surgeon and he actually owned a macadamia farm. We turned to him for advice and settled on growing macadamias, even though I knew absolutely nothing about them.

For 10 years we were absentee landlords. A farm consultant ran the farm. He did the work. We just worked incredibly hard to pay the bills while we dreamed our dreams for the future.

We had the land cleared soon after we bought the property. We planted 4,500 macadamia trees and about 30,000 rainforest and eucalypt trees along the creek bed and in the areas that were too steep for macadamias. What this reforestation did was to slow down water run-off, and the creek, which previously only ran intermittently, now flows for 12 months of the year. We have continued to develop more rainforest areas and plant 1,000 trees every year.

Our permanent move to Byron Bay coincided with our first commercial crop. That was when the steep learning curve really began.

What sort of farming practices did the consultant use when he was looking after the farm?

His method of farming was very traditional. At that stage we had no insect monitoring. It was just a matter of spraying on a rotational basis. He had an extensive spraying regime for all the bugs and used a range of different chemicals. He sprayed for husk spot on the nuts and there were issues with spotting bugs. There were problems with nut borer and lots of rats. In 1999 every 10th tree was baited for rats.

What's changed in your treatment of insect pests and diseases?

We did away with spraying copper about three years ago because we thought it was impacting on our earthworm colonies. We also decided to stop spraying chemicals because we thought they were ineffective. They didn't do what they were supposed to be doing. Eliminating copper sprays made a real impact on the soil micro-organisms. When you dig into the soil now there are earthworms. Just doing away with one fungicide made a huge difference.

We haven't been able to get rid of husk spot on some of the trees and rather than treat it, we've decided to remove the trees in the areas that are affected. We don't want to use fungicides any more.

Planting the sub-tropical rainforest areas got rid of the rat problem. For one thing it is a home for owls that kill rats. The second thing is that where the sub-tropical rainforest has been planted the floor is clear and there is absolutely no place for rats to hide. Rats love lantana and grass. We used to lose 7 - 8% of our crop every year to rats even with the baits, which cost a fortune because every 10th tree would be baited. Even worse, it didn't work. Now we lose only 0.3% to rats. That's an insignificant loss.

We haven't sprayed for nut borer for the past five years because we've introduced trichogramma wasps to control it. Richard Llewellyn from Nambour is the person who supplies the wasps and the Department of Primary Industry comes and does a survey each year to test the effectiveness of using wasps to control nut borer. Wasp eggs hatch and kill nut borers. The damage now compared with the damage that we used to have when we sprayed is much lower.

We're also one of six farms taking part in a DPI study that has planted rows of different species of trees and plants that are hosts for spotting bug, near the macadamia trees. The bugs go to those trees in preference to the macadamias. They've also found a parasite that attacks the spotting bug eggs. Three insects lay their larvae into the eggs and hatch there. They haven't found a way to breed the insects yet but it looks promising.

What are you doing in terms of maintaining soil fertility?

Our soil is predominantly kraznozem. It's a red volcanic soil. It has a cation exchange capacity[5] of 16 and an organic matter level that used to be 12% but we've built that up to 16%. That's extremely high in comparison with other parts of Australia. Our pH is between 5·8 and 6·2. It's difficult to take it up higher because of the rate of leaching and the very high rainfall. We're happy with the current level. Australian macadamias seem to like a range between 5·8 and 6.

Up till last year we've had soil and plant analysis done by a soil scientist. He tested all over the farm and provided a "per tree" chemical fertilization programme. The question we started to ask was: "Do we need soluble synthetic fertilizers of the sort that we've been buying, or is there another option?" It was this question that has caused us to change our approach to fertilization during the past 18 months and now we're going in a totally different direction. We've committed to being 100% organic. For my manager Peter, who comes from a very traditional way of doing things, this represents a 360^0 turn. My view is that there is no long-term sustainability relying on synthetic fertilizers for agriculture.

Because we are going down the Biological Farmers of Australia (BFA) organic path they will be doing the soil testing. It's a much more scientific approach than the one provided by the fertilizer company.

On the mineral side we struggle with calcium levels. The calcium / magnesium ratio is less than 3:1, which is low, and we've been addressing this by putting on lime at the rate of 5 tonnes per hectare in the past few months. That's about 10 kg per tree. We're also low on boron so we're applying that as well.

Nitrogen levels are low and our magnesium is too high and we're hoping to address this by building up the soil biology. If we need to put on trace elements we get them from Superior Fertilizers. We're using rock phosphate to build phosphorous levels. The fertilizers we're using work more slowly than the ones we've used before so we might find there's a bit of a gap before everything starts to move through the system.

Rainfall is our biggest problem. In the past three weeks we've had 350 mm of rain and we had the same amount last May. Because the property is hilly we have to slow down the flow of surface water. We use mulch and grass. We've got a special slasher that directs the grass under the trees. We also use the husks from the nuts. We chop them up, add some chicken manure and leave them for a while, then put them all back under the trees where we're building up a terrific layer of humus. In the bad old days we used to have a blower and we would blow all the leaf litter away from the trees to make it easier to harvest. Now we've got a beautiful bed of organic matter and it's a firm bed to harvest from. In the past few years we've really come to understand how absolutely crucial organic matter is for proper soil function.

Because of the rain we don't grow any crops between the trees. We also believe that the weeds are an important way to slow down water runoff as well as being a habitat for beneficial insects and as aerators of the soil. Weeds provide a habitat for lacewings to come and breed. Lacewings attack bad bugs. The assassin bug is another predator that kills unwanted insects.

Weeds hold soil structure together. We don't have a major weed problem. We remove cobbler's pegs by hand. Cobbler's pegs have become resistant because of guys spraying RoundUp on them over the years.

We've dismissed inter-row cropping but realise that it is vital that we start to consider the nutrition level of the area between the trees. It's absolutely critical because that's the area that feeds all the roots. We're starting to understand that weeds aren't the problem. They're just an indication that something is missing within the soil and it's this imbalance that's triggering weed growth. The real problem is under the top layer of our soil and it's our job to identify that and fix it. Removing the weeds doesn't solve the problem; it only gets rid of the symptoms of the problem.

Are you doing anything to improve soil biology?

If we have an imbalance of critters in our soil it's because we haven't got enough organic matter to provide a food source for them. We no longer disturb leaf litter in the off-season when we're not harvesting, and we pile up the green manure under the trees. We're not inoculating at this stage but it may be something we'll do when we get more involved in developing the correct level and balance of soil biology.

I have looked into compost tea. Certainly we're using a lot of compost and that may well do the job.

We do a soil health test each year. It's a test that was produced specifically for the macadamia industry by Tuckombil Landcare, which we're working with. We have a look at what's in the soil. We count the soil bugs, nematodes and identify the fungi and check the level of diversity. We count the individual insects and check what's munching the organic matter and breaking it down so that it goes back into the soil. Doing the soil health test shows us how we're travelling.

The Tuckombil Landcare group formed a member-based company called Soil Care and we're members. They're based in the Lismore / Alstonville area. What we get from that organization is brilliant. It's made up of a group of farmers who are passionate about soil. We get together and discuss things. If someone has a problem, we work together to find the solution. The idea is that you don't isolate yourself as a grower. Tuckombil Landcare has been hugely significant for us on our journey.

Have yields per tree risen since you changed strategies and moved away from chemical fertilizers and poison sprays?

We've only stopped using synthetic fertilizers 18 months ago and yields fluctuate each year. We produce 50 to 60 tonnes of macadamias a year. We're expecting that as we build our soil health our yields will rise dramatically but it's too early for us to state categorically that there has been an improvement.

Peter, Martin has told us that the approach you are now following represents a total turn-around for you. Have you done any training to support the changes you are making?

I'm fortunate that our local TAFE is only 25 km away, so last year I did an organic / biological farming course called "Biological Farming Incorporating Climate Change". That was brilliant. I've also done another course on the use of insects as biological deterrents which opened my eyes up on what you could achieve using beneficial insects rather than going out and spraying and killing everything, good and bad.

Has the manufacturing side of your business influenced your thinking, Martin?

I guess because we're a fairly large manufacturer of macadamia products we have a real passion for eliminating chemicals. That's what our customers want. As a consequence of this I've developed a real desire to be able to produce the raw materials for our food products that are chemical free.

My personal view is that there is no long-term sustainability relying on chemical fertilizers in agriculture. More and more, there are going to be pressures and concerns coming from consumers, which will determine what we produce and how we manufacture it. I'm seeing and meeting many farmers who are doing the same as we are because they realise this is what people want.

Tell me about the manufacturing arm of your business.

During the first 10 years, when we were absentee landlords with the farm being run by someone else, we had plenty of time to think about future possibilities. Our plans for developing a food manufacturing business came from watching people sending their macadamia nuts overseas where other people did clever things with them. We decided that we wanted to add value to the product we were producing on the farm.

Learning how to grow macadamias was difficult but nowhere near as difficult as it has been to develop the manufacturing and marketing side of the business. The first eight months were spent developing a mayonnaise that didn't work. We were more on the right track when we developed macadamia muesli, but even so it took 18 months to develop. We started selling it at the Bangalow community market and through the local post office. We eventually found a supermarket in Byron Bay willing to give it a go. While all this was happening Pam had to continue working as a dentist to finance the development.

In the beginning we worked from home to develop the concept and test it. We'd make the muesli at home, put it into food grade bins on the back of a farm utility and take it to the local bakery. Often we had to work strange hours to fit in with the bakery's bread baking schedule. When we started selling the muesli we hired a factory in Ballina and that was where we started.

It took 3 years working in this way before sales were sufficient to justify building a small factory. I really believe we could not have made the progress we did without the support from our local community. Then we had the challenge of meeting demand, which grew at the rate of 20% per year. Nine years after we built our first factory we had to upgrade. By then we were exporting to Europe and America and supplying airlines with our muesli products and macadamia oil. Our new factory enabled us to treble production, introduce a range of new products and bring our sons, Will and Eddy, into the business.

We can no longer produce all the macadamias we need so we have to rely on other local farmers to provide much of the raw ingredients we need and we work with other farmers to ensure quality control from the ground up. This has boosted the macadamia industry in the Byron Bay area.

That's a fascinating story, Martin. You've obviously been highly successful.

Yes. We've won lots of awards, both in Australia and overseas including the Telstra "Australian Business of the Year".

Congratulations. I have just a couple of final questions for you. The first is: Where do you see agriculture in Australia heading?

We have to go back to before the 1950s when the chemical companies gave us these wham bam chemicals and sprays and said: "These will solve all your problems." Not only haven't they delivered on this promise, they've created a whole range of other problems in addition. Mind you, they are trying to develop safer products now but I think we need to go back to what our grandfathers were doing: maintaining the biology in the soil.

But it's not just about going back. As a result of what we've done, we've gained a huge amount of knowledge in the past couple of decades, so we're actually a lot more knowledgeable than our grandfathers were. Now we understand what works and why it works. From here on in we need to question every aspect of what we're doing and look at the impact of everything we do on the whole of the farm. The information is available and is accessible. All we need to do is to be sufficiently open-minded to investigate alternatives.

We've also got to take into consideration the carbon footprint issue. Chemical fertilizers have a very heavy carbon footprint. As farmers we're going to have to become more and more embroiled in these sorts of issues.

Finally, Martin, if someone who is thinking of going into farming were to ask you for advice about what they should do, what would you tell them?

My advice would be to put as much organic material as they can into their soil as they can get their hands on. Buy it if they have to. Get organic matter back into the soil. That's the crucial first step. We chip our eucalypts and put the woodchips under the trees.

Thank you, Martin and Peter.

Jim Velehris

Almond Grower from Renmark in South Australia

Jim Velehris farms in one of the marginal farming areas in Australia. He is totally dependent on the Murray River for his livelihood and is extremely aware of the problems that have been created along the Murray in terms of soil degradation, soil salting, water degradation and water shortage by over-use and misuse of this valuable resource.

Jim has already lost one orchard. In 1979 he started growing oranges in Renmark, but he pulled them all out 9 years ago when oranges became financially unviable.

Jim is now growing almond trees. He is immensely proud of the quality and productivity in his orchard and of the gradual improvements he is seeing in his soil and the health of his trees.

You're an irrigation farmer on the Murray River, Jim. Can you tell me a little about your farm?

We have 100 acres. We irrigate from the Murray River. The soil is red and not very fertile. It's sandy, similar to drift sand. It doesn't hold moisture, nutrients or carbon. It has a pH of 8 and has a 2% carbon level. It's very low in selenium and it locks up phosphorus. The calcium / magnesium ration is OK.

How long have you been growing almonds, Jim?

I bought the first property in 1978 and the second one in 2003. We have 100 acres of almond trees. That's a total of 6,000 trees. I grew all of them from seed. I planted peach seeds, grafted almonds to them and grew them to the point where we could take them from the nursery and put them out in the field. I've nurtured them right from the very beginning to where they are now.

Have you always been an almond farmer?

Back in 1978 I was growing citrus using conventional overhead irrigation systems with the sprinklers higher than the trees and using only synthetic fertilizers like ammonium nitrate, urea and superphosphate. Twice a year we used to put out 300 kg of synthetic fertilizers to the acre in two applications. I never used pesticides at all. In the early days I couldn't afford to use them and then I began to realise what they do. That was when I decided to stay right away from them.

Why did you change from citrus to almonds?

I wasn't making any money with the citrus. Half the reason I wasn't making any money was because I was flogging already depleted soils with synthetic fertilizers. The trees went into a real decline. I didn't understand the effects of under-irrigating, or of using excessive amounts of fertilizer in one big application. That really sent the trees into a downward spiral and then the commodity prices dropped. Concentrates were being sourced from Brazil at ridiculously low prices and it got to the point where I wasn't making money with my trees, so I pulled them out. That was in 1997.

Why did you choose to grow almonds?

There are a lot of products grown on the land that are very labour intensive. I saw that in my family and in my wife's family. Everyone worked very hard for very little return.

I had some ideas about how I could market almonds and because they have a long shelf life there's no pressure to sell them quickly as you have to do if you are growing something like apricots.

What was your motivation for moving away from chemical fertilizers, Jim?

I started making small changes about four years after I began to grow almonds. We started using composted chicken manure under the trees.

There was a salmonella outbreak in a smallgoods factory and the government changed the rules for farmers. There were certain things we weren't allowed to do and using composted chicken manure was one of those things. They started monitoring everyone and regulating us. People came out to check whether we were doing the right thing according to the new laws.

Instead of using the chicken manure, I changed back to using the synthetic fertilizers and I could see the trees start to decline almost immediately. They had no vigour, no new growth and we weren't getting the yield from the trees. The almonds had no taste or flavour and didn't look appealing to consumers. Also we started getting 2 small nuts in one shell. I noticed that a lot of the trees were aborting nuts at blossom time and we were having big problems getting zinc into the trees and there was no new growth.

I was dealing with a customer in Melbourne at that time and when we started back with the chemical fertilizers he told me that doing that meant my product was no longer better than anyone else's. Without a competitive edge I found the almonds hard to sell.

It was important for me to see the effect of that change and it spurred me on to making even bigger changes. The reason we weren't allowed to use the composted chicken manure was that when almonds are harvested, you shake the trees to make the almonds drop off and then you just pick them up from the ground. It was the harvesting method that was the reason for banning the use of chicken manure. You can get chunks of manure on the ground and these can harbour salmonella.

It was around that time that I heard of someone in Adelaide who was doing some exciting new things. His name was John Norton and he ran a company called BioTech Organics and he sounded as if he knew what he was doing. He's a distributor for NutriTech products. It took me a while to track him down and I caught up with him one Sunday afternoon. Our telephone conversation lasted till almost 11 o'clock that night. He told me about how the soil works and what he told me left me absolutely speechless.

He came out to see me and suggested a programme to follow. In the first year I started seeing differences that were truly unbelievable.

I went back to the food safety people. If I put the manure out earlier than I was doing, it's all used up by the time we harvest. Just by changing the timing, we were able to solve the salmonella problem. I am now using composted fertilizers, about 2 tonnes to the acres, and I put that out once a year when the trees are starting to flower.

Whilst I haven't stopped using synthetic fertilizers completely, probably the major reason I've been moving away from using them is because they're basically a salt. We're building salt levels and they're getting progressively worse. When we get a big rain event it pushes the salts down into the aquifers in the soil and they find their way into the waterways. The more we do that the bigger the problem gets downstream. It will ruin our waterways and the whole environment will suffer. Saltpans are not a natural phenomenon. The whole salting problem is because of the fertilizers.

The problem isn't just with salting either. When we put herbicides into the soil they get into the waterways. Fish eat them and die. Blue-green algae grow. My generation won't see too many problems but I'm fearful of what we're going to leave for future generations.

Do you have salt problems?

No.

Do your neighbours have a salt problem?

Yes. I believe so.

So what are you doing now in terms of building soil nutrients?

We're using the NutriTech products and getting good results in terms of the health of the trees and the nutritional value of the almonds. We're not getting split fruit where you get two nuts in the one shell and the amount of fruit abortion at flowering has dropped. We're still not achieving big yields and we've gone back to using some chemical fertilizer inputs in conjunction with what we're already doing.

We're using sulphated products that will help adjust soil ph and we're using very small amounts. The Almond Board recommends using 800 kg of ammonium nitrate fertilizer per hectare per year. We're using just 200 kg per hectare and getting great results.

Natural fertilizers don't go into the ground and get swallowed up by the root system and sent straight up to the leaves to give the tree a growth burst like chemical fertilizers do. Theirs is a much slower release and they go into the ground in a form that the tree will accept. The natural fertilizers we're using include fulvic and humic acid and boron. We spray on silica and selenium. We spray 2 or 3 times after flowering and a total of 4 times during a year. We know what to put on because we do a soil and leaf analysis every year.

What we're doing is putting a lot of micro-organisms into the soil about three times a year to make the release happen continuously. We brew the microbes. We're using Bio P that helps release phosphorus from the soil and Bio N that fixes nitrogen and another nitrogen produce called Twin N that helps lock phosphorus into the soil and gets the nitrogen into the plant. We put on active carbon. We could use brown coal but it takes about 30 years to break down. The carbon we use is effective immediately.

I've heard of one farmer who's using the exhaust from his tractor as a carbon source and he's getting great results. Instead of sending carbon into the atmosphere, he's putting it into the soil. I don't know how he's doing that.

What changes have you noticed in your soil?

The top inches of soil in a hectare amounts to 10.000 tones of soil, so to make big changes, you need huge amounts of inputs. What we're finding is that we're getting the nutrient levels slowly building up. Our big problem is that carbon levels aren't building. They're being sustained, but not building, probably because the carbon we're putting on is being used up by the trees. We grow a ground cover every year. We grow clover and we're constantly cutting that so that it goes into the soil. It takes years and years of mulching to build carbon levels.

The soil has improved considerably in terms of balance. It improves a little every year. I'm noticing nice, but subtle differences.

What's happening in terms of productivity?

Productivity has become very consistent. We're not getting the huge production levels that growers in the synthetic world are getting. They're force feeding their trees on a weekly basis and the trees have no choice but to produce big crops. They're also getting all sorts of disease issues and it's costing them thousands and thousands of dollars, so they're actually losing out financially. Also, what they're doing will seriously impact the life span of their trees. It's a bit like putting someone on steroids. It creates problems.

The yields chemical farmers get hover around 1·6 tonne per acre, but to get this they're using absolutely huge amounts of fertilizer. Often they use as much as 1 tonne to the acre of potassium nitrate, calcium nitrate or ammonium nitrate.

We're getting around 1·2 to 1·3 tonnes per acre. It's a reasonable yield of uniformly average to good-sized nuts. The other guys are getting smaller kernels and lots of size variation.

Have you done a lot of education to help you make this transition?

No. I get advice from John. We work together. He knows how the soil biology works and I know what's needed at different times of the year to make the crop happen. We're constantly adjusting things and working to come up with improved results.

What do you do about weeds?

For 9 months of the year we mow the mid rows. We get close to the trees. We leave a metre on either side of the tree and then we have to go in with glyphosate and burn the weeds out. We use a control droplet application using a unit that puts out something in the vicinity of 5 litres of solution per hectare. The solution goes out in a very fine mist. We use only about 1·2 litres of glyphosate per sprayed acre because we dilute it with fulvic acid. That helps the glyphosate get into the plants that we're trying to eradicate. When the fulvic acid gets to the soil it helps to dissolve the product so that we don't get residue build up. We use 100 grams of glyphosate per 100 litres of water and 100 grams of fulvic acid to every 10 litres of water.

Do you have disease problems?

The higher the nitrate nitrogen in a plant, the lower the plant's pH and the lower the plant's pH the more susceptible the plant is to disease. Most cancer patients have a pH way below neutral and it's exactly the same for a tree or a vine.

Because we don't use nitrates at all, we don't get diseases. However we do protect the crop with cover sprays such as copper.

We do have problems with mites and we use an organic product that smothers the mite eggs. It's an oil spray and it suffocates them. We can't control them completely. Mother Nature is awesome and they're part of the natural scheme of things. When we get a build up and too many eggs get laid, we go in and smother the eggs and reduce the numbers.

We also get mites from the soil, so we have to be very careful we don't raise any dust. That's another reason why the cover crops are good. When we grow cover crops we don't have dust.

We also have earwigs. They eat new growth and it was becoming quite a problem but this insect only has a four-week life cycle so we can live with that. There's no long term damage done.

How reliable is your water supply?

We water weekly. The quality is OK but the quantity is a problem. We buy the right to use a certain amount of water per year. We also pay to pump that water onto our properties.

Before the drought we could buy a permanent allocation of water for $1,200 per mega-litre. Since the drought we are paying $1,200 per mega-litre just for the year's supply.

The authorities have told us that they have grossly over-allocated the water from the Murray-Darling system and that they need to take a lot of the water from us. If we want extra water we can go into the temporary market for the year. It costs a lot of money to do that. It nearly sent us broke.

Since the drought, the price has gone down considerably. The government has been buying big amounts of water and a lot of investment companies that encouraged investors to plant huge areas of land have all gone broke. Also, we've been getting a little more rain.

Agriculture on the Murray River has declined and will continue to decline. People here cannot survive financially. The debts they have incurred, trying to keep going during the drought, are now just too big.

How and where do you sell your nuts?

We've been fortunate to have 3 very good years from 2004 to 2007. During that period there was a big demand for almonds. People found us. We developed good relationships with those people. We sell to some companies that value-add. Some go to retailers and some to wholesalers. They know our product is consistently good and every year is the same. We've built relationships with several people and we still deal with them.

I wouldn't deal with Coles or Woolworths even with a gun pointed to my head.

I talk to the people at the Almond Board a fair bit and I tried on several occasions to buy some almonds from one of the chemical farmers so that I could do a nutritional test comparison with my nuts. I just wanted to find out how my nuts compare in terms of nutritional value with nuts grown using conventional methods. The Board won't sell me any product from another grower so that I can get a comparison done.

I deal with the Waite Institute in Adelaide. They test for e-coli, salmonella and all sorts of toxins. We do this as part of the regulation requirements and I just wanted to send them the two samples and see what results we got. It would help me market my product but I actually wasn't even thinking of doing it for that reason. I just want to know. Pure curiosity, I guess.

Thank you for sharing your experiences, Jim.

Chapter 4

Fruits of the Season

Six fruit growers, each specialising in particular fruit types, demonstrate a variety of strategies in order to produce high quality fruit, which is grown without chemical fertilizers, pesticides or insecticides.

They are:

James Fernley	*apricots*
Heinz Gugger	*persimmons and nectarines*
Dennis Angelino	*apples*
Malcolm Heather	*avocadoes*
Ian Smith	*apples*
Mike Ottone	*pineapples*
Kym Green	*cherries*

James Fernley

Apricot grower in Western Australia

James and Michelle Fernley are apricot growers. James Fernley came from a background in mining and absolutely no knowledge of farming. In twelve short years he has turned a run-down small farm into an extremely productive apricot orchard. He has had to work hard to do this. He has researched extensively and worked with a variety of strategies to find some that work well for him. He has been open to a variety of new and sometimes fairly radical ideas.

None of this has been achieved without setbacks.

James has planted 6,000 trees but after 12 years has only 3,000 in production because 3,000 of the trees he planted were the wrong variety for his district and didn't produce fruit. He had to pull them out and replace them and this has set him back over 7 years. He is not yet at full production capacity.

James likes the idea that every year he's trying to break new boundaries and he has found the project of establishing and maintaining a productive apricot orchard incredibly exciting. At the same time he has found it frustrating because of the mistakes he has made, some of which have been horrendously costly.

Young farmers like James provide the hope for the future of Australian farming, which demands people who are intellectually curious, hardworking, innovative and enthusiastic.

What led you to what you're doing, James? Do you come from a farming background?

I'm country born and bred but not from a farming background. My parents had a general store in a small wheat belt town. I went to Perth to school and when I left school I studied accounting and hated it. I threw that in and went overseas for 12 months. I came back broke and got a job in mining and stayed doing that for 10 years. I was in gold mining and ended up doing a lot of different jobs ranging from prospecting in the bush to pouring gold bars.

Michelle and I were married while I was still in the mines and when we decided to have kids I left mining because it's not a family-friendly occupation with the long shifts and long hours. I came looking to buy a business in Bunbury and ended up buying this property. It wasn't what I had planned but it was just how things turned out.

When we first saw it, the place was stripped of trees except for the apricots. We arrived in the middle of summer and decided to pick the apricots. Up until then I'd never even picked a lemon.

We ended up with about 4 tonnes of apricots. The fruit was heavily diseased and we were surprised that anyone would pay us for it when we sent it to Perth. That was when I made the decision that if we could send poor quality fruit to Perth and get paid, we could do it properly and grow good fruit and then we'd be paid lots!

We went around asking people about apricots and couldn't find anyone to give us advice. Most people said: "We used to grow apricots but they ripen at Christmas and that messes up the family time." A lot of the orchards around Donnybrook are mixed fruit. There are some very big apple growers and they pick apples for four to five months of the year and don't want to pick for longer than that.

Since we started, things have changed a bit. A lot of smaller guys are looking to find areas where they can get a good return and apricots will give you that. When we started there was no one else in the area.

Tell me about the physical environment of your farm, James.

We have a two small blocks on the edge of Donnybrooke. One is 10 acres and the other 5 acres. A 5-acre block separates the two farms. It's heavy clay country that was used for potatoes and asparagus in the early days. On our blocks we have river loam through to heavy clay and it gets sandy the closer you get to the top of the rise. We're right on the edge of a river.

After potatoes, the area was planted with apple trees. The person who owned the land before me basically ran it into the ground. As the trees failed he just pulled them out. He didn't fertilize.

We arrived here about 12 years ago and there was still a small block of about 50 mature apricot trees and another block of pear trees that the previous owner had planted. He told us they had never had any fruit. During the 2 years after we arrived we knew he was telling the truth about the pear trees. They produced a total of one pear and it wasn't even a nice pear!

The pears were useless but we did see some promise in the apricots. We decided we'd plant more apricot trees.

We're on the Preston River and there's a lock further up river from which water is released and is purchased by farmers downstream. It's like a mini irrigation scheme. It's very small scale. The lock holds about 1,800 mega-litres. The water has a little bit of salt in it, about 350 - 400 ppm and it can get up to 800 ppm at times during the year. We monitor the water very carefully so that we don't use water with high salt levels on young trees.

We get about 40" of rain a year, generally in winter. About 10" of it falls in spring. By the end of November it starts to dry off. Temperatures in summer sit around 32^0 - 33^0C, though we do get 40^0C days. We don't get many frosts in winter, which is just as well because when we do get them they tend to come towards spring and can cause damage to the flowers. Our chill scale is at the bottom end. For fruit to set you need a certain amount of time below 7^0C. If you get one hour at 1^0C it's equivalent to 5 hours at 6^0C. Places like Batlow and Young, where they grow cherries, get really cold nights for a long period of the year, and they're said to be high on the chilling scale.

We're in a place, which has a borderline chilling scale. If it were any warmer a lot of the trees we grow wouldn't set fruit. When we're looking for new varieties, we have to select from the ones that have a low chill tolerance.

We lost a fair bit of our crop to hail last year. It was the worst hail in 54 years, according to our neighbours.

Our soil has a pH of 5.7 in some areas. There were major deficiencies and imbalances in the soil when we first arrived here. The obvious one was too much copper. Zinc and iron were very low. Boron was non-existent. Sodium was a little high because of the irrigation water coming from the river. Nitrogen was low. Phosphorous was very, very high, but since the soil test was a standard one it didn't show that the phosphorous wasn't being taken up. The guy that was here before us made the mistake of thinking that because there was lots of phosphorous in the soil he didn't need to add any. It was totally locked up. In the ten years he was here he never applied any phosphorous, which was a major mistake. Calcium was low and after we did the first Albrecht test we bought our first truckload of lime. Magnesium and manganese were low, but not excessively so. The level of organic matter was 1.6%, which is also low.

What have you done to bring the organic matter level up?

We made a lot of fairly costly attempts to try and improve organic levels. Since we've been here we've brought it up to around 3%. We've still got a long way to go. My target is to get to 5 or 5.5%. After all this time we're just getting a handle on the quickest way to get there.

Initially, we tried compost but the cost meant we couldn't put very much out and we were spreading it so thinly that we weren't getting any benefit. We used it as a trial for a couple of years then gave it away. We then tried just using compost when we were planting trees: putting it in the holes so that at least there'd be some underneath the trees. We didn't see any difference between the trees where we'd put compost and the ones where we hadn't.

Our next strategy was to mulch. We got some green waste mulch and put it under the trees but that mulch, which was partly composted, also contained a lot of eucalypt in it, which meant that we ended up with a lot of non-wetting mulch and that made it very difficult to put the irrigation water through. It just slid off to the side. The mulch had quite a lot of nutrients in it and the trees grew roots into it in spring and then, because it dried out in the summer, all the nice new roots that had grown in the mulch zone also dried out.

We then tried mulching with hay and that worked very well. We were very happy with hay but it needs to be re-applied yearly. The cost of the hay was quite cheap and very cost effective. We were paying about $16 per 100-metre row using big round bales of "seconds" oat hay that we bought for about $60. We'd go out when people were cutting hay, put it on our trailer and bring it home. That meant they didn't have to store it.

We were keen to do mulching but as we planted more and more trees the cost of buying in mulch became prohibitive and we had to come up with a way of achieving the same effect at a lower cost. That's when we decided to do inter-row cropping. We've done trials for a couple of years and this year will be the first one we've done it on the whole property. We've sown rye, oats, lucerne, vetch, lots of different varieties of clover and peas as inter-row crops. We grow things that give us a lot of bulk. Now all our tree rows have a layer of whatever has been grown there and mowed down. We have very little bare dirt. When we mow we end up with a straw layer across our orchard floor and then, as soon as pruning is finished, we mulch all the prunings and spread a liquid or granular fertilizer containing organic minerals and a lot of silica. Then we rotary hoe all of it in, but only to a depth of 1 - 1 ½ inches deep. We just turn the straw and the wood chips and fertilizer and incorporate them into the topsoil. I also spray microbes into the mix. This year the crop will be a mixture of vetch, rye and millet and we'll spread that down the row with a few chains to incorporate it.

At one stage I did a biodynamics course. Part of that was about cow-pat pits. Rather than do it the normal biodynamic way we decided to just buy some cows. We run an electric wire down the rows so that they can't touch the trees. We bought Dexters, which are good because they're so short they can't reach the trees but they can put their heads under the wire and reach to the trees without being able to lift their heads and eat them. We leave the cows on each row for just one day. If we do that the crop is able to recover quite quickly. Once the crops get to flower we mow them down.

I got the idea for inter-row cropping when Graeme Sait from NutriTech came over and showed us some photos. I like NutriTech. They've done massive amounts of research and they provide a really good resource. I don't like the way they keep introducing new, you-beaut products, but I'm going to do their 5-day Certificate of Sustainable Agriculture programme in July.

You've come from a mining background with no experience to being a very knowledgeable and successful farmer. How did that happen?

When we first arrived we just started cleaning up the old orchard and we did that for about five years. One day a guy by the name of John Korn turned up. He told us our trees were unhealthy and we needed to use a better fertilizer. Because of our inexperience, we were willing to listen to anyone who came in and told us anything. We did a soil test and found out that everything was out of balance and that the copper was excessive. It was 8 times the recommended level. The people before us had sprayed copper to keep down disease levels and they'd used a lot of copper sulphate, which is cheap but causes a build up of copper levels in the soil. The new copper fungicides are actually quite low in actual copper. You get a lot of carrier but just a little very fine copper.

At that time most of the people here were getting their soils tested through CSVP and they just got them tested for nitrogen, phosphorous and potassium (NPK). There wasn't even any testing for zinc or iron. CSVP is the biggest importer and supplier of fertilizer in Western Australia. They supply all the wheat belt guys with muriate of potash, superphosphate and urea.

We knew we had problems because our soil test showed us everything was badly out of balance. I was a bit lost and not sure what to do, but a guy called Brian McLeod came over from South Australia to give a talk about soil and what interacts with what. I went to that talk and said, "My goodness!" This guy ran a laboratory that did Albrecht testing in South Australia, which was radically different from what other people in the area were doing. I thought that if we could do some of the things he was suggesting, we could really change things and improve them.

Now I had some fairly strong motivation for making a change away from what we'd been doing. We had small children by then and our house is right in the middle of the orchard. What we were spraying on the trees was ending up on our roof and being washed into our tanks. I wasn't happy about using chemicals, but until we turned up on this farm I was probably as far removed as it is possible to be from the organic world. Neither Michelle nor I had ever been to a naturopath. We went to standard GPs for anything connected with health. We'd never bought a vitamin. We'd never even thought about alternatives to mainstream chemical farming practices. We used pesticides and insecticides as a matter of course.

After hearing that talk I did a training programme and, as you know, in a lot of these sorts of courses the people who run them normally include a small amount of information about the relationship between soil health, food quality and human health. I thought this was interesting, so when I came home I said to Michelle, "This is something we need to do."

How did you get your soil into balance?

We did more soil tests. We did what people recommended. We're not a big jump away from the soil being balanced and nutrient dense. Some minerals are a bit low, but we're now starting to worry about the molybdenum, cobalt and selenium rather than the major elements like calcium and phosphorous. We've solved most of the major problems. Now we're fine tuning and that means we're on the home run.

The hardest thing has been finding the right product to correct the imbalances. A lot of companies will do a soil test and say: "You're low in zinc" and will then sell you some zinc sulphate to correct the deficiency. Then a couple of years later you'll do another soil test and you're still low in zinc. The problem hasn't been solved.

Calcium in our soils is sometimes quite low. We have really excellent calcium levels in our fruit, which means the fruit is getting it, and perhaps that's why the calcium levels in the soil aren't going up as fast as I believe they should.

Calcium spraying is used quite a lot by some of the orchards around us, but people are using calcium chloride, which doesn't give them the results they expect. Because they don't get good results they poo-poo calcium spraying. We know why they're going wrong and we would tell them but of course they aren't going to listen to us. We're the new kids.

When we first started we did a calcium correction based on lime. Someone suggested that we should put it out every year and others said, "Don't put too much lime out, you'll have a whole lot of problems if you do." So we waited a couple of years and did another soil test which showed that we needed to put out another 1000 kg per hectare. We put that out and someone else told me that even though I was using a very good, finely ground limestone product, it would take 10 years for it to become available to the trees. So we decided to put out 250 kg per hectare every year and start using products like Calsap through the irrigation when we wanted to stimulate microbial activity in the soil.

We put high-grade calcium products through the irrigation system and make sure we do a good foliar programme with calcium. I spread the equivalent of 60 litres of 26% lime in a mixture I make up myself. To the lime I add humates and powdered humic acid and break it down to a ratio of 6:100 water. I spray at the rate of 200 litres to the hectare.

I think we're getting a handle on calcium. I certainly know it has got to be put out in some form every year and it is probably worth while buying Calsap, which is sold by a fertilizer company called Optima. They sell high quality bagged fertilizers and fish/kelp fertilizers but their core range is lime products. They buy limestone and process it right down to fine powder. There are also some new calcium products that have been pre-mixed with humates and others that are a calcium/boron mix.

We stopped doing the 250 kg per hectare lime application because of advice from Optima, but their solution to our calcium deficiency is a lot more expensive than the strategy of putting out lime, which we were happy with. They said, "You don't need to do that. Do this." And we did what they said. In retrospect it may not have been the right way to go.

I want to know why there are deficiencies in the soil the first place. I'm always looking for products that will correct deficiencies and stay in the system. I've been able to do that for boron. Western Australian boron levels are very poor and for a long time I couldn't get the boron level up. Every year I used to spread borax, but it didn't make a long-term difference. I spoke to a guy down the road who was using boron humate granules and we put that out and now we have a good level of boron. I only did it one year and that was about five years ago. To fix the problem meant finding the correct product. Now, to maintain boron levels I mix boron in that spray and we also do a boron spray just before flowering.

Boron is a really important mineral. I found that out one year when I was mixing up the boron /calcium spray. I made a mistake and put a litre of boron into the mixture when I should have put in calcium. When I realised what I had done I diluted it and threw it onto some grass and by accident, over a metre high citrus tree. A week later that tree was covered with flowers. Every bud was initiated. Immediately afterwards the beetles came in to attack the tree and the leaves fell off. Any that remained had yellow blotches on them. That showed me the power of small amounts of that stuff.

You started with just 50 old apricot trees and now you have 6,000. That must have been a major undertaking.

We've actually planted 6,000 trees but we don't actually have quite that many producing yet. Unfortunately half the trees we planted were new varieties that didn't work. They were nice looking trees but many of them didn't actually produce any fruit. Those that did produce fruit grow beautiful big apricots. The trees had been developed to produce large sized fruit with a great appearance but little flavour. They don't suit the market we have, so we've classified them as failures as well.

Three thousand of the trees we planted were failures. That caused a lot of financial hardship for us, but we're coming out the other side now. We've pulled a lot of them out and we're still in the process of replacing them. From the time we decided to plant those varieties till the time we'll get fruit from their replacements we'll have wasted 7 years. We could have pulled them out earlier, but we just didn't have the resources to do that when we realised they weren't going to be any good.

Since apricots aren't grown in any volume in Western Australia our problem was finding someone we could go to and say, "Hey. We've made a mistake. What should we do?" Now, because we went through that, people are coming to us to ask us for advice and we've only been here for twelve years. We've broken new ground as far as new apricot varieties are concerned.

There was one time when we had over 40 varieties planted as a test, and out of those varieties we found only 3 that worked as a good commercial crop.

Nine-five percent of all varieties available in Australia are developed overseas and the vast majority of them are developed in California. We just don't have the chill factor that these varieties need to set fruit and also, I think, we've fallen into the American trap that "appearance is everything". Eating quality is low down on the American selection criteria.

In hindsight our experience has had benefits as well as the downside. New Zealand, South Australia and Tasmania are selling the fruit varieties that we couldn't get to produce. They sell their fruit in Western Australia in huge volumes. In South Australia when the dried fruit market dried up because it was so much cheaper to import dried apricots than to produce them, the South Australian government supported growers who had to replace their old varieties. That was when all the new varieties were coming in from California. Huge numbers of apricot trees were replanted and they're the ones that people don't like to eat. They arrive onto our market earlier than mine do, so when ours are ready we get a really good price.

The old varieties are the only reason we've survived. When we arrived we had trees that were 30 or 40 years old. We had varieties like Telidha and Gravatt and one called Newcastle, which is tasty but produces small fruit. Those trees set fruit every year. People like the flavour but the apricots don't look as good as the new varieties of fruit. They stay green until they're almost ripe. When people come to the shed to buy we give them some to eat and they're surprised. We tell them to take them home and leave them in a fruit bowl for a few days or even a couple of weeks and they'll turn a nice orange colour.

With those varieties we never have a failed crop. We've had failed crops because of disease problems but that's caused by too little fertilizer input, never by the trees not producing. The new varieties we've planted that have worked are Golden Sweet, Solar Nugget, Solar Glow and Solar Flare. They're fairly good varieties and they have the nice orange colour that everyone wants and they give a good yield. I only know of one Australian-developed variety and it produces huge fruit but has a very small yield.

We have about 3,000 trees producing at present. We produce about 30 tonnes of fruit a year and have the potential to produce about 60 tonnes. It's a very large production out of a small area, but even so our trees don't set a really high yield. We probably produce about half the tonnage of orchards in better locations.

Is your orchard organically certified?

No. I don't see the value in organic certification and we are still using some chemical sprays.

I have tried to reduce fungicide applications. We had a couple of years with the old trees where we had fairly good results not using fungicides but really, we didn't know what we were doing.

Once we moved into the more alternative methods of growing we found out about a lot of different suppliers of product. Everyone comes knocking at your door once they discover they might be able to sell you some snake oil.

That was a minefield. It was very difficult to work out what was rubbish and what wasn't.

We plodded along with the new trees and had a bit of disease. Towards the end of our seventh year we came to the conclusion that we needed to use fungicides in spring. We came to this decision after a few attempts at trying to use organic sprays to control fungi and losing a lot of money because we were getting potholes and freckles on the fruit. Spring is when our first varieties come into flower. It always rains. It rains right through the period until the outside of the flower falls off the fruit and so the fruit sits inside the flower, wet, for the first 2 weeks of its life.

We figure we'll have disease until we get to the point where our soil is super nutrient rich and we're not there yet. We do a fungicide spray at flowering, which is when the trees are under a degree of stress. We don't spray after that. We don't need to.

We've got rid of brown rot.   When it did occur it was at the end of the season and was the result of nutritional deficiency. Now that we have a handle on the nutrition we don't see brown, rot but people who are our neighbours have it right through their orchards. They spray regularly with a brown rot programme. It's not terribly apparent in their trees but when they pick the fruit it starts to break down. We have fruit sitting in our cool room for 6 weeks with no breakdown at all, even though apricots aren't well known for good long-term storage and ours just sit in boxes.

I know we're farming the right way or getting towards farming the right way. We use only 10% of the chemicals other farmers in the area use on stone fruit and we get the same results in term of cleanliness.

With nutrition farming you can do it at the same price or cheaper than conventional farming. That's something that annoys me about organic accreditation and price premiums for organic produce. To me, getting a premium price is probably the last thing I think about when I farm. My aim is to get my production costs down. If I get the same price as the guy next door, I'm actually better off. That's the premium you should be getting for changing the way you farm. It's about being smarter. Either you get a better yield or you have reduced costs and if you get the same price as everyone else, because that's where the volume of buying is, then you're pocketing more money.

In the beginning I didn't look at things from a financial point of view, but now I have to look at that aspect of what I do. I have to justify my decisions. I may pick the same volume of fruit as I would if I were farming conventionally, but the fruit will have a higher nutritional level, which means it stores better, handles better and I have much more saleable fruit.

Someone might pick 30 tonnes, but the important figure is how much of that 30 tonnes is Grade 1 saleable fruit. If out of the 30 tonnes you get 10 tonnes of stuff you have to give to the cows, then your production is really only 20 tonnes. If you can do things differently and reduce wastage down to 5 tonnes, the 5 tonnes you save would pay for a 30-tonne apricot fertilizer programme. By just improving the percentage of good fruit, you get your fertilizers for free.

We get quite a lot of fruit that's second grade, but because the flavour is so good and we sell seconds direct from our shed, every year we sell more and more of what would previously been classed as "waste". That makes good economic sense to me.

What damage is caused by birds and other pests?

When we bought this place, it had 60 apricot trees. When the fruit was ripe the parrots were everywhere. I used to go out and pick for an hour and shoot parrots for 15 minutes, then pick for another hour. I'd be picking one tree while they were busy eating the fruit in the next tree. Actually, they weren't even eating the fruit. They were just pecking at an apricot and then doing the same to the next piece of fruit.

When I started nutrition farming the birds started eating the fruit rather than just pecking it. It looked to me as if they'd bite into an apricot and go, "Yes. That's a good apricot," and they'd sit there and eat the whole fruit. Actually no, that's not quite right. They'd actually only eat half the fruit. The size of a parrot's stomach is such that it can eat only about half a 40-gram apricot in one sitting. It can't fit any more in. He'd come and get half way through and be full. What happened then is what was really interesting. After the parrots left there'd be half eaten fruit on the trees, but by the end of the day, all those half eaten fruit would be gone. They come back and finish them off. The pieces of fruit on either side of the eaten one aren't damaged except occasionally the parrots poop on them.

If there is a drought we get lots of parrots but now we're also seeing a much greater variety of birds. The nectar birds do cause damage because they're only getting juice out of the fruit.

We probably lose about 5% of our production to birds but I haven't shot a bird in more than five years. We wouldn't see more than 100 parrots in a day. Some days we might get only 10. I think birds are a lot smarter than we think they are. When there's fruit available they spread themselves around.

We do still have a couple of older trees that I didn't pull out and I do tell the birds that they're allowed to have the fruit on those trees. They tend to stay in those trees till the fruit is finished. Now I don't know whether that sort of thinking makes any difference at all, but I think it gives me a mental framework, which means that when I see birds in the orchard it doesn't worry me that they're there. If it doesn't worry me, then I don't go and upset the birds or interfere with them. I just allow them to fill their bellies and fly home. If everything in the system is less stressed, then the damage is negligible.

Because we run our sugar levels quite high we don't have any mite problems. Mites are bad in stone fruit generally, but not in our orchard. We do get weevils and we spray them with a target spray rather than all through the orchard. The spray also cleans up the paper wasps, which tend to build up their populations at the same time weevils do. We use 'Avatar' which is a "soft" chemical spray and it doesn't kill the lady beetles or lacewings or the green tree frogs in our orchard. We probably do have aphids and mites but we don't see them because the lady beetles clean them up.

The weevil larvae stay in the ground and as we get a bigger microbe population the microbes tend to feed on the larvae so it's becoming less and less of a problem. We may get to the stage where the numbers are so low that we won't have to spray at all.

Are you using fungi and bacteria applications?

Yes. I did a microbe course with Elaine Ingham and I also did a three-year programme with the University of Western Australia. They came and tested our microbes and I went in to do a few short courses where they'd go through their findings and research to improve microbe levels.

As soon as I finish our fungicide programme I wait till the leaves have developed and then I inoculate with beneficial fungi to re-establish the micro-organism population. I don't know whether it does any good because I don't have a microscope to test it. I mix up the microbe inoculant with the fertilizer that I spread over the orchard.

When I'm putting stuff out with the sprayer and it's not under a lot of pressure I use microbes and I do one or two applications once I've got a good leaf cover on the trees.

I use freeze-dried trichoderma but I really believe that if you're going to use these products you really should invest in a good microscope. I believe that when you apply anything live, you should take a leaf that has been sprayed and put it under a microscope to see if the microbes are alive. I fear that a lot of people are spraying a lot of dead microbes over their orchard and not getting the sort of results they think they should be getting. Then they're saying: "Microbes don't work." Some of the stuff comes with a warning not to put microbes and fungi through spray gear with a lot of pressure because you get a very low success rate.

We combine microbes with dried kelp prill, which we buy as a powder. We buy the microbes at Bunnings. They're sold as compost starters. I'm planning to do my kelp the way the bio-dynamics guys do it. They put herbs and preparations in a drum and leave it for a year. The liquids that come from that process are really good. I've got a couple of 200 litre drums saved up for that.

I've been very interested in brewing my own microbes, but it's been a lot easier to mix the freeze dried microbe powder which contains a range of microbes that are typical of Western Australian soils. I get them from Western Minerals. I strongly believe you should use microbes that occur naturally in the area you are farming.

Do you use nitrogen?

We started using calcium nitrate as a starter spray about three years ago because we couldn't get any size in our fruit. We got the size back and we're weaning off the calcium nitrate and replacing it with a couple of liquid nitrogen products that are available.

How do you know what to do?

We do leaf testing. I go out and collect a leaf or two and then squeeze it and get the sap out. Then I look at the brix levels and look at whether it's cloudy which is an indication that there's calcium in the sap. I do pH tests so I know if there's a problem. I did a workshop with Bruce Tanio and he gave a bit of a list as to what the missing elements might be when the pH isn't at the right level. I do potassium testing on site and I want to do nitrate tests as well but I don't have a kit to do that yet. With those 4 tests I've got a lot of information about what to put on the trees. In Western Australia we don't have access to good testing facilities such as leaf testing. If you can't get a 3-day turnaround it's useless.

I don't sugar test my fruit. If the fruit is not sweet by the time it's due to be picked it's too late to do anything about it anyway.

You appear to have done a lot of research and a lot of training courses with different people.

I did. During the past two years I've been a bit slack. That's why I want to go to Queensland this year and do Graeme Sait's Sustainable Agriculture workshop.

In the early days before we had the children I really worked hard. I was able to put a lot more time into research and learning and we were able to spend every cent we had. I had the idea that it would repay us further down the track. When we needed money I would go and do a stint on a mine site. We were lucky because we had a low debt level and when we had bad years we were able to survive. I could just go out and work as a loader operator at a mine. That's what got us through the bad years. Now, with three children, I have to be a bit more realistic.

I did a couple of days with different agronomists who came over from east. I've done about five days with Graeme Sait, Jerry Brunetti and Gary Zimmer. I did radionics courses with David von Pein. That was a big jump in the learning curve. I haven't bought a radionics box yet. I've done training programmes with Arden Anderson and Dan Skow. I did a Microbe Testing course with Elaine Ingham. Most of my information has come from reading and the Internet.

Everyone's got heaps of ideas but there's no one saying, "This is what you need to do now and this is what you'll do next year." Most of the people who are dabbling in nutrition farming see the benefits but they don't know how to take the next step. They either have to pay people to help them get where they want to go or buy a lot of products that they think will get them there. For many of them it's just too hard and they give up. People who are giving advice generally don't have a broad enough level of knowledge.

For example, most people don't realise that applying fertilizer at the wrong time can be quite detrimental to the tree and it will take a while to recover. An application of the same product at the same volume at a different time can be quite beneficial. Our trees need high nitrogen and low potassium at the start of the season and as the stone hardens, the potassium level has to be well above the nitrogen level.

Where do you see farming in Australia heading?

In Western Australia I think we're in a downhill spiral. They're promoting liquid nitrogen as the new "magic" product and it's very acidic. Where there's no organic matter its effect is disastrous. The big farmers are all moving towards no-till farming. Our soils need to be tilled. The organic matter and the microbe levels are so low you need to till to incorporate the organic matter into the soil after the first rains. If that is done, the microbes can break down the carbon and digest it. With no-till the organic matter tends to sit on top and when the soil dries up it just blows away.

We need to become carbon farmers and the best way to do that is to work the soil. To make no-till successful you need chemical input and the chemicals that are being used are further depleting the organic levels. There's not one guy I know of that has had any increase in organic matter levels in the past 5 or 6 years. The argument is that if you don't till you don't oxidise the organic matter but there's none there to oxidise. It's all sitting on top and it has to be put underneath so that the microbes can look after it.

Corporate farms aren't getting it right. They adopt a minimal cost approach with lots of chemical inputs.

The smaller farms that are hanging on are embracing nutritional farming. A lot of people are seeing that this is the way to solve problems. They've seen the success some of us are having with nutrition and are starting to do foliar applications of things like kelp and fish and chelated fertilizers.

We've seen a couple of success stories around here. A nectarine farm in town was taken over by someone new. In his first year he picked 90 tonnes. He started using a high nutrition programme and in the second year he picked

90 tonnes but in the third year that went up to 360 tonnes. That's the sort of thing that's making people take a second look.

Do you have any advice for people who are looking to make a change from conventional farming?

When I talk to my brother, who's a conventional farmer, I say to him, "You're using muriate of potash because it's cheap. Don't use it. Use potassium sulphate instead because it's much kinder to the soil and you'll get better results." He'll reply, "It's too expensive." That's when I explain to him that it's not more expensive because you spend exactly the same amount of money on the potassium sulphate as you would have done on the muriate of potash. You may not get as much volume of potassium sulphate for your dollar, but you'll end up with more potassium and a higher yield.

That's the advice I'd give everyone. Don't spend more than you're already spending; just spend it differently and be selective. Take small steps rather than rushing and trying to do everything all at once, because if you have a bad year, the first thing you'll cut out will be the new expensive fertilizers.

The other thing I would tell people is that farming this way is incredibly exciting because every year you're breaking the boundaries you set the previous year.

It's been fascinating talking with you James. Good luck with your orchard.

Heinz Gugger

Persimmon and Nectarine Growers in Gympie, Queensland

Heinz and Angela Gugger were born in Switzerland, owned a business in the USA and then moved to Australia to become farmers because it was something that presented a challenge and they were bored doing what they were doing.

They bought a 72-hectare farm just south of Gympie on Queensland's Sunshine Coast. The farm was producing a variety of fruit including mangoes, lychees and persimmons. They received a crash course in farming from the son of the people who had sold them the farm so that they had a basic idea of what to do. In six years they have created a miracle, making the transition from conventional farming to a mixture of biological and biodynamic farming strategies to which they add a touch of radionics.

They now have an 11,000-tree persimmon orchard and export the fruit to S.E.Asia.

It has taken Heinz and Angela 5 years to make the transition from conventional farming methods to biological farming. Within the first 2 years of making the transition production went up by 30% and, even more importantly, fruit quality, shape and size improved markedly. They believe they could export three times as much as they're now producing but don't have the supply.

Heinz says that they're still in business so they must be doing something right. He is now mentoring others and speaking to groups about his experiences.

Where is your farm, Heinz?

We're 20 kilometres south west of Gympie and about 10 minutes from the Bruce Highway. It's a very hilly area and it looks a bit like Switzerland, which is where Angela and I come from: rocky and green and covered in forests. The farm is 72 hectares in size and we've been here for 6 years.

What do you grow?

When we came here there were mangoes, 50 lychee trees, and persimmons. The previous owner had quite a lot of different fruit but not much of any of them. We decided to concentrate on persimmons, with nectarines as a second crop. We replaced the mangoes with persimmons when we discovered that persimmons and mangoes ripen at the same time. We've now got 11,000 persimmons planted and 2,200 nectarines.

Persimmons aren't popular on the Australian market. We export them, mainly to Asia. In Australia people remember the grandma tree in the back garden where the fruit had to become really soft and mushy before you could eat it. Our varieties are different. They're seedless and quite big and you eat them like apples. Asians can't get enough of them. They call them "the fruit of God".

How does someone from Switzerland, who had a business in America, come to be growing and exporting Australian-grown persimmons?

Angela and I were born in Switzerland. We have business degrees and an MBA. We moved to the USA and set up an import/export business selling dinnerware and glassware to restaurants and hotels in New Jersey. We had a very successful business but we got bored, so we decided to sell up and make a change. We found the farm and came to

Australia with our two kids, Mitchell who was 5 and Leslie who was 9 years old at the time.

We had no idea about farming. After we purchased the farm, the previous owner's son stayed on and helped us. He taught us what he knew. He showed us how to pick and when to pick and how to pack. He told us when to prune and how to prune and what sort of fertilizers to put on and when to put them on. He had to teach us everything.

The former owners didn't use a whole lot of chemicals like some people. On a scale of 1 - 100 I suppose they would have scored about 50. They used the traditional sprays, endosulphans, fungicides, insecticides and herbicides. We didn't know any better so that's what we did too in the beginning.

Whilst we didn't know anything about farming, we did know about business. We started exporting and we organised boxing and labelling and marketing. We streamlined the packing operation

I think the "great awakening" came when we employed an agronomist and did some soil samples. The agronomist looked at them and said: "Add such and such." I said, "How much?" He didn't know. From that moment on I thought: "We've got to go and find out for ourselves." That's how we found NutriTech. Their office is only 40 minutes away. I went to Graeme Sait's 4-day workshop and after the first day I thought, "Holy Moly! Farming is not just about throwing a bit of calcium around. There's a whole relationship between all the elements and a lot more besides."

During the Seminar I was beginning to understand how everything works together and that you cannot just fix one thing, because if you do that, everything else is affected. I even started to see the bigger picture but the information was just too much to absorb. I didn't know where to start. I didn't know what to do to make the changes that I was beginning to realise were possible.

When I came home from that seminar I told Angela, "We can't do what we've been doing any more. We can't use that. This has to go. That spray is no good."

You needed to know where to start and how to do it, because if you have a farm and your livelihood depends on the production from that farm you have to be careful. If you damage your crop, or don't even get one, you're done. You can't change everything in one year. It's too big a risk. You have to put some plans together and decide where to start and what steps to take.

Now, when I go and talk at Graeme's seminars I provide the link between the theory and the practical. Having the theory is one thing. Putting it into practice is something totally different.

So how did you start and what steps did you take?

We continued to use the chemicals but we added fulvic and humic acid and cut down on the amount we were putting out. It was the same with glyphosate. If you lower the pH of the water you put with glyphosate, you can halve the amount of the chemical and get the same effect. To lower the pH to around 3 or 4 you just use citric acid.

I also had to change my attitude towards weeds. When we bought the farm it looked beautiful. It was neat and tidy. The ground under the trees was bare. Do you know what happens when ground is bare? It grows weeds. The first thing that happens after you spray herbicides and kill all the grass is that the cobbler's pegs come up. They always come back so there must be something wrong with this approach. There's no point poisoning them because they keep coming back bigger and stronger than before. You have to work with them and you have to ask, "What are these weeds telling me?"

What I didn't realise about weeds is that they grow best where the soil is unbalanced. Their job is to help bring the soil back into balance. Weeds with deep roots are going deep into the soil and bringing to the surface the elements that are missing. Weeds with broad leaves and long leaf nodes are bringing up the calcium. Blue-topped weeds bring up phosphorous. Duckweed grows where calcium has been leached due to compaction and where oxygen is lacking.

The first thing we did was to start using fulvic and humic acid. This was a small step but when we did it we saw that the leaves on the trees where shiny and healthy and the fruit was tastier. It was a great confidence booster to see that. We were then able to go to the next step.

We put granular form humic acid out under the trees in winter. We also put it out twice a week through the fertigation system. A bag of humic acid granules makes up 170 litres of liquid fulvic acid. I used 5 litres per hectare of this strength for each fertigation.

I also used fulvic acid every time I sprayed herbicide or a leaf spray. I used 4-5 litres of the fulvic acid liquid and 3 litres of herbicide to 400 litres of water and this was sufficient to do 1 hectare, and then I started putting in citric acid to lower the pH of the water so that I could cut the glyphosate amount by half. The fulvic acid acts as a buffer. It sucks up the glyphosate and the bacteria and fungi can digest it. I used RoundUp till a year and a half ago in the back but I'm not using it any more.

I started off using an enormous amount of fulvic and humic acid and I continue to do this because the soil tests are showing the benefits. My CEC (cation exchange ratios) have risen from 24 to 29. The organic matter has increased from 3·2% to 5·5%.

What we did next was to change the soil nutrient level and get the various elements in balance. We did another soil test and put on a prescription blend to bring all the elements into balance. You need the balance because they work together and if some are missing, then things don't work properly. Zinc and iron work together. Calcium and magnesium work together. Boron and calcium work with one another. We corrected the deficiencies and imbalances of the major minerals with the prescription blend. We correct small imbalances and trace element deficiencies with leaf sprays.

We've put out a prescription blend every year for five years. The composition of the various components that are in the blend differs, depending on the results of the soil test. Each time we do it, the investment is less. In our first year we put out 1 tonne of prescription blend to the hectare. We put this out during winter. Last year we put on 750 kg per hectare. The more we let the biology of the soil evolve, the less we have to put on.

When we tested the soil in the front area of our property we found it was deficient in calcium zinc, iron and magnesium. The nitrogen level was extremely high, even though it had never been added. The back area of the property was deficient in phosphorus, and was low in calcium but very high in magnesium. The soils in different parts of the property were different. It was all over the place.

Now, after 6 years of soil testing where we take soil from the same areas each time, the soils are almost identical. We still have some small imbalances. The nitrogen level has come back down and calcium is in the same range everywhere.

The third thing we did was to stop using artificial nitrogen so that we could get away from using fungicides. When we started improving the soil we saw from our leaf tests that there was an increase in silica in the leaves.

Silica is the defence force for the outer part of the leaves. Someone did a test with silica-rich leaves and little insects that eat the leaves and the insects actually broke their teeth. Trees that grow in well mineralised, balanced soil where there is lots of available silica don't get fungal diseases. The theory is that if we get the soil right, then we wouldn't have to use fungicides, so we stopped using them and watched to see what happened.

Everyone promotes NPK and it is still the most widely used fertilizer but I think it is the wrong thing to use. When you do a bit of research you realise that soluble nitrogen is not good.

Water is taken up into the trees by the big water roots. The smaller feeder roots take up the food. The feeder roots get it from the humus colloids. Artificial nitrogen is taken up by the water roots and makes fruit tasteless and watery and it has a very short shelf life. Food that is boosted with artificial nitrogen also affects the health of the people who eat it. It causes cancer and even Alzheimer's disease, I believe. So if you use artificial nitrogen you have to ask yourself, "Why am I poisoning people?"

If you use artificial nitrogen it's virtually a calling card for disease and insects. The nitrogen attracts insects. If you've got the soil balanced and have plenty of silica, then you've got in place a defence force against pests and fungus. The trees just don't get attacked any more. We had to stop using artificial nitrogen before we could stop using the fungicides.

Finally we started monitoring the soil life. I did a fungus and bacteria test in November 2009 and the bacteria levels were good. I still need to build up the fungi and I'm doing that by putting on a fungi tea that I brew up. I do that every 6 weeks. I can back off when the fungi is all established, but because we used RoundUp in the back until relatively recently, I think the biggest thing I can do is to feed the bacteria and fungi in the soil by adding fungi food to the surface.

I could have done the micro-organism test 3 years ago but I felt it was better to get the soil balance right first and then work with the bacteria and fungi. It wasn't till I started doing that, that I needed to know what the active soil life level was.

That's what we did. How we did it was to start with one really bad area and go 100% organic straight away on that area. We knew we were risking 800 trees but they weren't much good anyway.

In our test area we immediately started using organic sprays. Actually we hardly sprayed that area at all from then on. We even left the cobblers pegs. We used a whipper snipper to cut them down. We had 1½ metre tall cobblers pegs when we started. When we stopped using herbicides the grass came back and we kept whipper snipping. The cobbler's pegs were still there but they were now only 30 cm tall. We mulched them under the trees.

This year, after three years converting to organic growing, we had one of the worst seasons in regard to poor weather, fruit fly and birds, and that starter patch had the biggest fruit and hardly any fruit fly. That's the best proof I could ask for.

The hardest thing to get rid of was the herbicides, because as soon as you stop poisoning the soil the weeds come back. There will be different weeds and they all tell you something. Cobbler's pegs tell you the soil has too much nitrate nitrogen. So you let the weeds grow and cut them down, mix them with humic acid and fulvic acid and mulch them down and the weeds give you beautiful fungus food for the trees.

Five years ago, when we looked down at the trees from the highest point on the property we could see lots of yellow, dying trees. Those trees have all come to life again. This year when we looked down there was only one yellow tree. All the others are healthy. It's almost a miracle but it didn't happen overnight. Our farm isn't like a machine where you can just tune things up a bit. It takes time to get everything into balance and working.

I've got a good inner feeling that I'm doing the right thing by not putting chemicals on the trees. I'm producing "proper" food and I'm not here just for the profit. I've done my research and now I have to ask, "Why would I put the stuff out that I used to put out when I know that if I do, my fruit is going to be soft and watery and have no flavour?"

So, to summarise you started by adding fulvic and humic acid, then you got the soil minerals into balance, then you stopped using artificial nitrogen so that you could also stop using fungicides, insecticides and herbicides and finally you've started working to build the fungi in the soil. Is that what you've done?

Yes, that's what I did, and after that I started investigating biodynamics and incorporated that into my programme and that's also given us a boost.

We use all the fertilizers and sprays that NutriTech provides. Nature is organised and biodynamic inputs cause a reorganization of the structure of the soil. I use a range of biodynamic preparations from 500 to 508 and some other things as well. Biodynamics is like using homeopathics for plants and the soil.

Their 500 is a small amount of what is basically cow manure which is energised over the winter by burying it in the ground in a cow horn. It energises the soil when you put it out. Generally I put it on four times a year. Twice in spring and in autumn. Maybe I put it on three times, depending on the moisture levels.

501 provides basic silica polarity. It works with the etheric forces and brings light to the trees. If you have a lot of rain and the soil is too wet for a long period, the 501 brings light to the trees and balances the excess of water. You can also use 501 for flower setting but if you put on too much it kills the tree, which tries to produce more fruit than it can carry.

502 works with sulphur, potassium and copper.

503 involves calcium and amino acids which are very important when you have high levels of nitrogen. Under normal circumstances the tree doesn't take up nitrogen from the soil. Normally, nitrogen has to be converted into amino acids and then the tree can take it up. The best way to get nitrogen is to get it from the air. Every hectare of land has thousands of tonnes of nitrogen in it. If you get the soil balance right it pulls in the nitrogen in an amino acid form and the tree can take it up. That form of nitrogen is free.

504 works with calcium, protein, magnesium and iron in energy transactions. 505 works with calcium and carbon to reduce nitrates to amino acids. 506 works with silica and potassium. 507 works with phosphorus. And 508 is fluid silica for the cell walls.

Biodynamics provides a very inexpensive way to get the soil right, but you can't avoid the initial step of putting in all the minerals and trace elements, and you can only use biodynamic preparations if you've eliminated all the poisons and chemical fertilizers, because unless you do that, they interfere with the process. You can only take this next step if you're already farming organically. Once you've done that you can start getting the relationships moving and becoming organised.

An inexpensive way to get started with biodynamics is to use a radionics tower. The earth is laid out with energy grids. You put a tower in a really good spot, one which has a good flow of energy, and at the bottom of the tower you put your homeopathic preparations that go into the ground and on the top you put out the ones that go into the air. If you put in calcium, the tower broadcasts the energy force all year to your trees. It's a sort of continuous homeopathic treatment.

I've done this and I think it works very well. It's not something that you can measure. You just have to look at what's happening and realise it's part of a much bigger picture.

In business you make decisions based on clear-cut information. This is the cost. That will be the price. When I got into farming I thought, "You put out a bit of fertilizer and that's that." I was so wrong. Nature is not a machine. Every year is different. Every season is different. You have to let go and basically you have to learn to trust yourself.

What have been the comparative costs of doing this compared with what you were doing before?

My inputs in the beginning were high but now we're using less. It's a bit like running a marathon. For the first 10 kilometres you think you're dying but then, the more you do it, the easier it gets. You can't run in a marathon without working towards it. I think we're on top of our investment marathon now. You can overcome the investment hurdle by starting with just a small area and doing it right.

Everyone's investments will be different because the starting point will be different from ours. I would suggest that it's about a 3-year investment programme in time and money. We did everything by hand. We cleared the weeds under the trees by hand. Now we have a slasher that we designed ourselves that will go under the trees so we've solved that problem now.

Has the investment been worth it in terms of increased productivity?

In the first 2 years we had a 30% increase in productivity. That's steadied. This year was more or less the same as last year but the fruit we're getting is much sweeter.

Customers used to call us about problems with soft fruit but we don't get calls like that any more. The export people want our fruit. We could probably sell three times as much as we do, but we don't have any more to sell.

When we started, we discarded a lot of fruit because the shape was wrong. Now the fruit formation is perfect, and when you look at the trees, the fruit is growing all over the tree. This is different from before when there were clusters of fruit on one side and none on the other.

We still have rejects, depending on the season. This year the late harvested fruit was useless because of all the rain. Generally the amount of rejects from the packing shed is getting less and less. I don't know the numbers. I do know that we have fewer seconds and the amount we throw away is negligible.

Many farmers complain about the difficulty of getting labour. Do you have any problems?

We employ three people permanently. With Angela and myself that makes a total of five. At picking we employ 25 or 30 people. They're all locals. We also have wwoofers.

The first year we had trouble getting pickers, but now people that have worked for us keep coming back. We've built a shelter shed for them for when it rains and we provide flexible hours. We treat them fairly, and these are people who want to work and they know that we pay them the right amount and we pay regularly on Monday morning so there's no discussion. It's an easy working environment, but if you make it hard, they talk around the town and they don't come back, and that makes it hard to get others.

When you started making the transition to organic farming, were you concerned?

Yes. If someone had told me what he'd done or if I'd been to a field day and seen what someone else had done, it wouldn't have been such a big step. It would have been easier if someone had done it already, and I'd been able to look at their trees or crops. I would have known it was possible for me to do the same because I would have seen the evidence. But there was no one in the area with a large farm for me to look at.

My biggest fear was that I would screw everything up and we'd have no fruit. I was afraid I would do something catastrophic to the soil and the fruit would all drop off.

The humic and fulvic acid I wasn't too afraid about because they're substances from the earth and I was just putting them back into the earth. There was nothing dangerous with doing that. I was more afraid when we stopped using pesticides and fungicides. I had nightmares that we'd have an overnight pest attack and I'd go out in the morning and everything would be ruined. Angela and I would go out and look and everything seemed fine. We'd go out again and look and there was still nothing wrong. I did a leaf test and everything was in balance. Then we realised that the natural predators had come back. We were standing in the orchard in May and there were ladybugs all over. I'd put my hand out and there'd be 10 ladybugs sitting on my arm. The wild life that has come back is amazing. We have spiders everywhere as well as wallabies and kangaroos. The vitality of the whole farm has lifted.

Do you think you had an advantage in not having a background in farming?

Yes. Definitely. I'm talking now to people who've grown up on farms and I tell them they need to change their fertilizers because what they're using is poisoning the soil and what they're doing isn't sustainable. They don't want to change. Even so, they're interested to see what I'm doing. I tell them to make a start and do something, even if it's just using fulvic acid and humic acid, because they'll see what happens when they do this and it won't involve any risk.

Some of them are interested and they want to do what I've done but they're afraid of losing everything. What they don't realise is that they're putting on more and more chemicals to get the same results and they'll end up losing everything anyway because the soil will be dead. I think you've got to be able to see that there's something wrong when you spray with herbicides and the problem you're trying to eradicate just comes back worse than it was before.

I talk to scientists. They still think that the biological approach is just for the greenies.

What are you going to do with your nectarines?

We grew persimmons chemically free for the first time this year. The persimmons are our bread and butter. We've changed over to growing organically and we'll take the same approach with the nectarines. We've already taken some of the steps, but we had to step back again because we had fruit fly loss. I think our work towards getting the soil right will go a long way towards getting rid of the fruit fly. Everything is easy by comparison with getting rid of fruit fly.

I used pheromone lures for male fruit flies. I put out an organic yeast spray that they lick up from the grass. We put out inexpensive biodynamic traps and I use biodynamic fruit fly attractant, which is just 20 litres of water, 10 cups of sugar, 5 ml of vanilla essence and 400 ml of cloudy ammonia, which you can buy at the supermarket. It all goes into a bottle with four holes in the sides and you hang them out.

Even with all this, it didn't succeed.

I'm going to continue working with the soil as the primary focus. It's not going to happen overnight, because I need to get the balance right and lots of silicon in the leaves. When I achieve that, the fruit fly won't dare come here.

Obviously you've worked extremely hard and done a lot of study to get where you've got to in only six years. Where did you get all the information?

I started off with Graeme's Sait's 5-day Sustainable Agriculture workshop. That opened my eyes and I thought to myself, "Whoa. This is something about the future, because the way we're going is not sustainable any more."

After that I had great mentors in Hugh Lovel, Cheryl Kemp and Tom Priestley. Hugh is an American psychologist. He's also a radionics guru and he's based in northern Queensland.

I'm using radionics at a certain level. If it's raining and I want to spray something out and can't do it because of the rain, I use radionics.

What advice would you give someone who wants to make a transition to more sustainable horticulture?

I'd tell them to stop thinking like a farmer and start to think like a horticulturalist or at least a grower.

When we moved onto the farm here and I went into town, people would ask me what I did. If I replied, "I'm a farmer," they would start to talk really slowly as if I'm slow at understanding. After that happened, when I went into town I'd tell them I was a grower. Once they heard this they spoke to me at a normal speed. If I really wanted to get them going I told them I was a horticulturalist. Being a horticulturalist puts you above everyone else. In truth, these are all the same profession. People have a different perception, depending on the label you use to describe yourself. It's the same with farming.

There are some people who are farmers. They aren't open to change. We've found that farmers won't tell you what to do but the growers really open up. When I talk to growers I tell them to get as much information as they can. I tell them they need to find someone to give them some guidance. At the very least they should make a start to reduce the chemicals they're using. They need to talk to people. People in the organics and biodynamics industry will help them. There's so much information out there.

Where do you think horticulture in Australia is heading?

People in government don't get it yet. They talk about carbon storage but they've totally missed the point. If we start improving soil carbon levels across Australia, we'll reduce carbon levels. They don't understand that if we improved nutrition and living food across Australia we'll have far fewer people in hospital. If people have enough calcium and potassium and all the trace elements in their food they won't get sick.

I think the people are ready. Last year we took our nectarines, even the little ones, to the local market in Gympie. We sold out by 10 a.m. They loved the taste. They'd buy a tray and be back a little while later because they'd eaten them all. At that market the first question they would ask would be, "What do you spray?" People are aware. This is the way it has to go because the ways we've been using are not sustainable any more.

You have a really valuable story to tell, Heinz. Thank you for talking to me.

Dennis Angelino

Apple and stone fruit grower in the Granite Belt in south-east Queensland

Dennis Angelino is second generation Australian. Dennis' father bought a 28-acre farm in the Stanthorpe area in 1946. Between 1955 and 1958 he planted 2,700 trees, mostly old apple varieties and a variety of stone fruit: peaches, plums, nectarines and pears.

Dennis' mother still lives on the farm. She has vivid memories of the early days when she cooked for the men who worked on the farm and helped plant corn, cabbages and other vegetables. They used draught horses until 1955 when they bought a tractor, which ran on kerosene. Dennis recalls that the draught horses were really good at pulling the hand scuffler when they were growing cabbages.

Dennis has worked on the farm all his life and most of his knowledge has come from his father's teaching. He left school at 13 to work full time because money was short and his father expected his two children, Dennis and Lorraine, to help. Dennis learnt how to prune and how to pick to ensure the fruit is not damaged and still prefers to do these jobs to make sure they are done right and the fruit is not damaged. Dennis is proud of awards he has won for fruit packing.

According to Dennis his Dad was not a good farmer but he certainly did well to establish and run an orchard under extremely demanding conditions. When his father died of prostate cancer in 1985 Dennis started to change how things were done on the farm. His story is about these changes and what has happened because of them.

Tell me a little about your farm, Dennis.

I've got 25 acres under fruit. I grow a whole variety of fairly old types of apples and some stone fruit: peaches, nectarines, plums and some pears. There are 2,400 - 2,500 trees. We've got lots of varieties: Stanthorpe Belle, Red Stark Risom, Imperial Gala, Royal Red Delicious and Crofton. I've got an old Delicious they call Lala Delicious. Even though it's 60 years old, the old Stanthorpe Belle is still going strong. I've never put any artificial fertilizer on the ground around that tree and maybe that's why it's still producing.

In the days when dad was alive we grew vegetables, but I just concentrate on the fruit. I've got enough to do looking after them.

What sort of climate do you have?

It's been very dry these past few years. We've been in a severe drought. This year we didn't get much rain from Christmas onwards and it was really hot for this area, around 33^0C - 34^0 C. That's very unusual and it was a bit too hot for the fruit. We normally get some rain in summer. Winters are really cold. We get frosts right up to September sometimes. I don't worry about the frosts earlier in the year, but the trees come out in flower in September and that's when I worry. We had three frosts in a row this year and it got down to -5^0C. I don't know what the annual rainfall here is. I've got dam water but I don't use it. There's good underground water too.

I don't irrigate. The real problem is that I don't have a big enough pump to do the job properly.

I don't like trickle irrigation. Trickle irrigation is definitely no good for trees. All the roots clump up into a tangle. With close planting trickle irrigation would cause a real mess because all the roots would be all clumped up together.

Hail is the worst problem.   Between 1983 and 2009 we had hail damage on nineteen different occasions. Not total destruction, except in two or three years, but something like 50% damage. When you lose the whole crop that's kind of a setback. The good thing is that I can sell my apples even when they're marked because people know what they're eating.

What's the soil like, Dennis?

It's fairly sandy. It's a deep loam sandy soil and very fertile. We've got deficiencies in phosphorous and calcium. I hardly put any dolomite or lime out for a few years because I was short of money and cutting corners and that's the reason for the calcium deficiency.

You tell me that your father wasn't a good farmer, Dennis. What were some of things he did that you didn't agree with?

Dad gave the trees heaps of fowl manure and chemical fertilizers. He was putting a bag of chicken manure around each tree. That's far too much nitrogen. Cow manure would have been better. With all the fowl manure we were getting bitter pith in the apples. He was using Nitrophoska, Crop King and Sulphate of Ammonia. One thing he did use that was really good was borax. He used to spray that on the trees. We put boron in the foliar sprays we're using now.

He was using lots of poisons to keep the insects under control. We had codling moth, red spider, black spot, woolly aphids and brown apple moth. I remember that vividly because I was the one that had to work with the sprays. We put on Metasystock, Parathion, and Arsenic of Lead as well as DDT. Metasystock used to give me really bad headaches.

All the farmers around here have used Gramoxone and now they're using RoundUp under their trees. Around here, lots of the farmers have nets to protect their fruit. They put on a chemical called Retain, which retards the crop so that it doesn't mature as quickly as mine does. They use another chemical that even retards the growth of the trees and another one to colour the apples and they're still using pesticides for the insects. Because a lot of the farms have netting, the chemicals are trapped in the nets. When it rains all the stuff they've sprayed out lands back down on the apple. That's a lot of chemicals because they spray between 10 and 14 times a year.

I don't use any of these chemicals any more. Before Dad died the problems were getting worse. With all the sulphate of ammonia he was putting on he was ruining the trees and I couldn't control the pests. They just got worse and worse. The pests were always there. The fertilizers and sprays were expensive and I wasn't getting the results I needed to pay for them. I started cutting back on the fertilizers. I pruned the trees hard and made them work harder. I didn't water them when it was hot and dry and they responded beautifully. Trees need to work because that's when they produce the best-flavoured fruit. You shouldn't make life too easy for them.

Now some of the trees have mites but it's not really a big problem. We don't have a problem with fruit fly. The codling moth is the only pest I'm still trying to get rid of. With the heat this year I got caught with codling moth. You can get baits to put on the trees but you need to put 3 or 4 on every tree and it's a very expensive procedure.

This year with the dry weather we had more trouble with parrots than with insects. I had to pick some of my apples a bit earlier than I would have liked because of the damage the parrots were causing.

I was treading really carefully with the chemicals. That was around 1985 to 1988. At the time I was taking apples up to the Mackay Base Hospital. Sister Grey was buying apples for the patients and she thought mine were much tastier than the ones other people were growing. They did some tests in the hospital laboratories and compared my apples with other peoples, and mine had far fewer chemicals in them than the other ones.

I got a bit of knowledge of how to do things from some organic growers I met so that I didn't need to use poisons and chemicals. It was about then that I met David von Pein. That was about 8 or 9 years ago, maybe longer, and David became my mentor. It was because of what David told me that I switched over. David told me that most of the chemicals we'd been using were no good and that there were other ways of doing things. He taught me that the problems I was having were because of the deficiencies in my soil and I thought he was right.

What are you doing that's different from what your Dad did?

We're putting on phosphorous soft rock, to improve the phosphorous levels, and organic compost. It helped a lot. David made up a mixture, which we spray on the fruit before the frost season. The mixture's got sea minerals, fish fertilizers and kelp in it and lots of trace elements. It helps a lot so I definitely know there is a way to minimise frost damage.

David makes up different mixtures for me depending on what the leaf tests show. They contain different trace elements and I know he puts vitamin B12 into some of the mixes. I put out agricultural lime and some organic compost. We apply the minerals before the full moon. That's helped a lot. I also spray with organic cow manure.

I put on the minerals with a hand piece. It's a pretty heavy application. I put on 3,000 litres onto 400 trees. I spray it onto the trees as a drench and it falls down on the ground and you get a double reaction through the leaves and through the roots. I spray once a month before the full moon. I go by the moon. That's when the tree takes it in best. If you put it on at night it's even better.

David has been getting me to put out ground applications in the winter. We've had good results. One year after we did that the Red Star was really good.

I test my brix levels. This year I had problems with parrots and I had to pick my apples earlier than I did last year. They were starting to take on a yellow tinge, which meant they were ripening. I would have loved to keep them on the tree for another week, but I think they'll be OK this year. The apples I had ready tested at 11 in February, and 11 is a good reading. Poor quality apples have a brix level of 6. A reading of 11 showed that there were good sugar levels The Red Stars tested at 9 so I had to start picking them because on a dry farm the fruit matures more quickly than it does under netting and it takes me a while to get all the apples picked.

What changes in the soil have you noticed, Dennis?

I didn't do soil tests 10 years ago so I've got nothing to compare the 3 or 4 soil tests that we've done in recent years with what we had before. I know that the soil is softer. We've still got deficiencies but this year I had a really good crop until the hail, and I'm satisfied with what's happening.

What do you do about weeds, Dennis?

I just let them grow. I work all my land between the trees. I disc it and turn the grass and weeds into the soil. This allows the moisture to penetrate the soil if it rains. If I don't disc the soil it gets too hard.

Under the trees I just let the weeds grow. I don't touch under the trees because if the soil is bare and you get a heat wave and no rain the ground gets rock hard. The roots can't breathe and they break. I could mow the grass into mulch under the trees but the ground isn't level enough to do that and we don't have enough rain to create mulch. Having grass and weeds doesn't hurt. I never use weedicides under fruit trees.

How do you sell your fruit, Dennis?

I do the marketing myself. I don't wax my fruit. Here in Australia the big growers wax their fruit to make them shiny. They're best left natural.

For 22 years I took my fruit to Townsville. I've been driving the same truck for 38 years without a major breakdown on the road. I probably shouldn't have done what I did, because I didn't get enough money for my fruit in Townsville to justify the time and the expense of going all the way there and back.

Now I've got a lot of private customers who want my apples. I can sell a Number 2 grade apple and get a Number 1 grade price because my customers know my apples taste really good. Having customers who respect what you do makes a big difference. When I was driving my fruit up to Townsville I got to know the people who run the Big Orange at Gayndah. They sell their organically grown oranges and mandarins to a community supported agricultural distribution network called Food Connect in Brisbane and they suggested I contact them. I've been selling my fruit to Food Connect for the past 8 months and they always comment on how good it is. Wade Dillon, who looks after ordering, has been to visit my farm to see for himself how we do things. They're very nice people at Food Connect and they're very honest. I really like dealing with them.

Do you have help on the farm, Dennis?

I employ people now and then. I like to do the picking, particularly if we've had hail, because some of the apples have to be thrown away. Inexperienced pickers aren't careful.

The pruning and the thinning I do myself. Pruning is an art and you have to go by the tree. With the old type delicious I did a summer prune so that the apple colours up in the sunlight. It's better for the apples to get natural sunlight. The Department of Primary Industries people taught Dad in the 50's and I learnt from him.

What advice would you give to other farmers who wish to make the transition from conventional farming to a more sustainable farming system?

For a lot of the farmers around here it's too late. All their trees are contaminated and their soil's ruined. They could fix things but it would take a long time.

My advice would be to find a mentor that you can trust totally. Also you have to get to know your soil because that's where problems start. When things go wrong, it's because you've got a problem with your soil.

What do you think the future holds for Australian farmers?

Farmers aren't getting the income we should be getting because the chain stores control the market. They have high mark ups so that they make a huge profit and the farmers get very little. They demand perfect, unblemished fruit and a lot of big farmers have got Quality Assurance programmes established. Even so, they're not going to be able to compete against imports from countries like

China where the wages are really low and they can land their apples here really cheaply. If they keep doing that there won't be many farmers in Australia in 5 or 10 years. We don't get any help from the government and we can't compete.

I'm really pleased to have spoken to you. Thank you.

Malcolm Heather

Avocado grower on NSW central coast.

Malcolm Heather describes himself as a "simple" man and it would seem that simplicity is the key when it comes to running a successful farm under conditions that would frighten most people away. Malcolm is absolutely passionate about what he is doing and is a really strong advocate for using microbe teas to inoculate micro-organisms into the soil and for lifting carbon levels in the soil to maintain soil bacteria and fungi populations.

For many years, Malcolm was ridiculed as the "the muck and magic man" by avocado growers in his district, but he now has their attention. At the last growers' meeting they passed a resolution to get Avocados Australia to investigate the application and benefits of compost tea to avocados.

The son of a stone fruit orchardist in western Sydney, Malcolm now farms near Kempsey on the NSW central coast. He successfully grows 1600 avocadoes in what he describes as "beach sand."

What caused you to move from Sydney to Kempsey, Malcolm?

I grew up on a farm in western Sydney at Orchard Hills near Penrith. We grew peaches and grapes. I did my apprenticeship as a fitter and machinist and left at the end of my time to run the family farm with my cousin. I bought property here in Kempsey because it was cheap. Developers wanted our land in Sydney so my parents moved to Kempsey before I did and they managed the property for the first few years.

The property was originally cleared in the late 60s and early 70s. Originally, Amatil owned the land. They had plans to grow asparagus. I don't know whether it was poor management or lack of knowledge of how to deal with the extremely porous soil conditions but they couldn't make a go of it. The whole place was sold to farmers here. I bought 75 acres. That was back in 1983. I planted stone fruit trees and my parents were up here managing it for me until it got too much for them. I planted more trees when I moved here but it was a bit of an exercise in frustration.

The majority of the properties were used for potatoes and my neighbour still grows potatoes but he's also planting avocados. Whilst in the beginning I was growing stone fruit, I was also the first farmer to trial some Hass avocados when I moved up here back in 1990. I've got a total of 1600 trees but the total in the area here now would be well in excess of 30,000 trees. Avocados have really caught on.

Tell me about the conditions on the property

We're just 1 kilometre from the sea and I believe that at one time this was all beach. I dug some soil profiles and about

14 inches down the sand starts to go light grey, and if you keep digging you end up with white sand. There's a lot of shell base as you go deeper.

The nature of the sand is such that there's very little humus. The soil carbon levels were residual from the bush that had covered the land before it was cleared and the farming methods that Amatil used to grow asparagus caused it to be almost totally depleted. Artificial nitrogen does that. It causes the carbon to change into gas and blows it off. When I started here the soil carbon level was 0.7%. We're currently sitting on 4.7%.

Our water comes from an aquifer. It's very high in calcium and it does present us with a bit of a problem because we do have around 85% base saturation of calcium. We suffer from a high pH. Currently it's around 6·9 - 7 but I have had it up to 9. I've just had to learn to change my inputs to include more sulphur and I've also found that building the soil biology has made an enormous difference to stabilising pH.

The aquifer sits 5 metres below the surface and the water contains a high level of iron as well as calcium. I've dug a hole into the sand and exposed the water table so that the water interacts with oxygen at the surface and the oxygen changes the nature of the water and causes the iron to drop out. That was important because once I'd dug the hole I no longer had to worry about iron building up in my irrigation pipes.

We have frosts every year and sometimes we can have a week of -5⁰C. We've had it down to -7⁰C even though we're right near the sea. Avocados can handle temperatures down to -6⁰C but when it gets any lower than that the stems freeze and when that happens the fruit starts to ripen. It happened back in 2003 when the trees were in a weakened state and we had this enormous frost. We were in big trouble. We had to do 12 weeks of picking in a week. It was terrible. The fruit was OK but we had to get it off quickly.

Since then I've made some changes. I find that keeping high levels of potassium in the leaf is critical if you want to stay on top of frosts. I also studied the movement of air around the place and discovered that I was damming the air in by having windbreaks. I knocked them down and it's made a significant difference. That goes against all conventional thinking.

Because the soil here has such a huge level of positive cations, it gives the anions very little space to lodge in the soil. They tend to bounce around like ping pong balls in the soil profile. Anything with a negative charge just disappears through the profile very quickly, so that makes keeping things like potassium in the soil very difficult.

How do you overcome the soil mineralisation problem?

I fertigate. I use straight potassium sulphate as a boost. Then there's a naturally occurring form of potassium, which is sold as K-mag. That's my base fertilizer for potassium and magnesium. Since it's natural I find it's a lot slower to dissolve so that it stays in the soil profile a lot longer. When I use that I don't need to put such high doses of potassium though the fertigation and then at critical times I top up with potassium sulphate. I do put out about 40 litres of molasses per hectare per month through the fertigation system. I also buy soluble humic acid, which I mix with the molasses and the nutrients. The molasses feeds the micro-organisms. Doing what I do slows down the leaching process, because it encourages fungi growth and makes the nutrients far more available.

I boost with manganese and boric acid. I put on a little bit at a time and I do it often. I fertilize every week. It's not as if the trees are getting huge amounts. What I put on are top ups that allow the trees to feed steadily. I'm not bombarding the soil with huge concentrations of salts because I believe doing that is very detrimental to the soil biology. Using the "little but often" approach allows the soil microorganisms to remain at a healthy level.

Are the strategies you're using now very different from what you did when you were farming conventionally?

When I was farming in Sydney and in the early days here when I grew stone fruit I was basically using a standard chemical regime. I did use some fowl manure but most of the inputs were chemicals. I used an NPK mixture that was blended specifically for our farm. We followed a Department of Primary Industries schedule using the chemicals they recommended for pests and diseases. We'd use Super Size for thrip and aphids and we'd basically be spraying from bud swell all the way through to fruit ripening. We'd spray twice for aphids then use copper sprays every two weeks through the winter. Post bud swell we'd use Diathane, Sumisclex or wettable sulphur. We had to be careful with the temperature when we used the sulphur spray. Sulphur can burn the leaves on a hot day. Actually, we had to be quite vigilant with all the sprays. Winter spraying was critical because you had to attack the spore counts in the winter to make sure that the bud swell was clean. Sometimes we'd use lime-sulphur.

Monolepta or red-shouldered beetle was always a problem and still is but we also had to get rid of thrip and aphids. Fruit fly was the really difficult problem. We used Senthion. The common name for that is Lebaycid. That has been the only spray I've not been able to get around when I stopped spraying for pests.

I've always had an interest in doing things naturally. I used to look at the bush and say: "Well, no-one's fertilizing that. Why is it doing so well?" I was trying to do things that were as biologically friendly as I could. I was working on ways of getting around using harsh chemicals. Fungal rot in stone fruit is a serious problem and I was actually starting to get on top of that by spraying compost teas on the fruit. That was having a better effect than the chemicals I was using.

I'd actually been doing trials with the stone fruit to see if there were alternate ways to control some of the pests and diseases, and I transferred some of that knowledge over when I started growing avocados. There's a particular spray I was using that's made of eucalyptus and tea-tree oil and it even has distilled chilli in it. It's called Envirospray. It worked brilliantly on aphids and thrip and I did some tests on monolepta beetle and it was reasonably effective on that as well.

You obviously didn't like using the poisons.

I think farmers are in more trouble than the actual end user when it comes to poison sprays. The farmers are actually handling the concentrates. I was trying to get to using a much more friendly regime. Basically now I'm down to just having some copper hydroxide in the shed. I use paraffin oil for sucking insects. I do use some Carbaryl when I get monolepta beetle but I'm also doing trials on some stuff from Ray O'Grady. He's got a product called Panda, which is pyral acetate. That's the condensate from making charcoal. It's sort of like a concentrated smoke. I've been spraying that on and finding out that it's turning out to be a reasonably good deterrent for the monolepta beetle, so that could end my use of Carbaryl.

What started you on the path you're on now?

Back in 2003 my trees were skeletal. I wasn't using any compost or compost tea and I hadn't woken up to just how important the biology of the soil is. Basically I wasn't paying any attention to soil biology.

I was fertigating without molasses or fulvic acid. Up to that time in 2003 phytophthera hadn't been a huge problem but it suddenly became one. Perhaps the trigger was that it was quite wet that year or maybe it's that with phytophthera you tend to get a compounding effect once the disease is present. At some point it becomes unmanageable. I hadn't been buffering the soil with any kind of organic amendments and basically the phytophthera had free reign.

I could have injected or sprayed but at the time I was looking at soil biology and I decided to go down that path instead.

I'd gone to a seminar on soil biology run by Elaine Ingham and it really opened my eyes and filled me in on the science behind what I was trying to achieve. Subsequently I developed a deep interest in soil biology and started experimenting with compost, then getting on to compost teas, and I ended up friends with Ray O'Grady and that friendship has taken me even further. I went to Ray to buy a brewer from him. I'd been trying my own brews before then, but not with a lot of success. Just learning to use the brewer and experimenting with different kinds of teas and then learning what the timing was for putting on the microbe tea in order to get the greatest effect involved quite a journey. I actually discovered that putting out compost tea just as we're coming out of winter and just as we're going into winter has the greatest effect. Then I had to learn how to sustain the microbe and fungi populations that were there.

Part of the picture is the soil carbon, and that's been my major aim here - improving soil carbon levels. There's a waste management place down at Port Macquarie called Re-Earth. I started getting compost from there. They mulch green waste and they also get biomass from the local sewage treatment plant. They use the sewage residue to initiate the process by adding this to the green manure. They have a massive composting facility. They use tunnels and they pump air up through the floor so that they're not turning the compost. The process is very fast. I've actually been there. They open the doors up and it smells like mushrooms. It's a sweet smell. Their compost is not organically registered because you can't use human waste because of heavy metals when you're growing organically. That's a bit of a drawback.

Twice I put on 20 cubic metres per hectare and now I've got grass and clover growing between the trees. I use a side throw mower to throw the grass under the trees. As the trees get bigger they tend to mulch themselves with a lot of leaf drop, which converts to carbon.

I now make my own compost in a concrete mixer. I use a method of stripping the microbes off the compost. I use one of Ray O'Grady's aerating brewers. You mix ½ compost and ½ water and aerate it quite violently and it strips the microbes off the solid material. I screen it and that leaves me with a liquid compost inoculum. I add a portion of that back into the brewer and heat and aerate it for 24 hours. That's how I make compost tea.

During spring I put about 4 brews on at the rate of 400 litres per hectare. I've got a 3,000 litre brewer down near my pump shed. I brew it and suck it straight into the line and water it on. It's the best way because you're putting it into a living environment with plenty of moisture. I find the spring application is critical. At 16°C the pathogens wake up and are active, and it's not till it gets to 18°C that the good microbes start to increase in enough numbers they can keep the pathogens in check. It's a critical time to inoculate. You get an instant hit of good biology in the soil and you're keeping the bad guys in check. The whole system is really simple.

I got the picture of what to do basically as the result of a lot of observation. I was just picking up ideas and learning the nature of what I was up against. I was doing trials and seeing what I was getting. The first time I inoculated against phytophthera in spring I saw an amazing turnaround in the trees, and realising that there was this temperature gap confirmed that there was a good reason for it.

I'm even doing trials on compost tea spraying for control of anthracnose. I've been spraying the compost tea on some blocks and using copper on other blocks. I think compost tea has the potential to eliminate the use of copper and I'm finding pyral acetate condensate at certain dilution rates is quite effective in preventing fungal diseases.

Where does your information come from?

I look on Google. I read and research. I'm not a trained horticulturalist. I've just been raised on a farm.

Some of my information comes from Ray O'Grady. He's done some trials down here and I'm interested in his charcoal-making process. Charcoal provides housing for micro-organisms. There's been some interesting research done in South America and there's a documentary called "The Secrets of El Dorado" which tells the story. Apparently there were reports that in the 1600s there was a huge population in the Amazon jungle. Scientists went in looking for evidence to prove the stories. To support such a large population you need a robust food supply and the scientists couldn't see any evidence of this. As they were travelling along the rivers they noticed that in some areas, the soil on the riverbanks had a rich, dark loam layer, which was very different from other areas along the river. They investigated and dug down into these areas and found pottery shards in the soil. More testing caused them to realise that the Amazon Indians had developed a charcoal making process and it had enriched the soil so much that it became fertile enough to support heavy cropping. They did some trials. They planted corn into these soils and found that the corn grew three times as high as it would normally be when grown in Amazon jungle soil.

Are you using charcoal?

I'm doing trials. The first thing I have to do is to get a large volume into the soil. It's early days yet and it's too soon to tell if it's making a difference. What I want to do is incorporate enough charcoal into the sand to really affect the profile and I'm planting more trees in the near future so I'm hoping to get a whole lot of charcoal to work into the soil. I'll do some trials and make some detailed observations on what happens.

I'm impressed by the potential that charcoal offers. Basically charcoal houses beneficial soil organisms perfectly, and the ability to keep soil organisms in place and breeding successfully depends on the interrelationship between carbon levels and the micro-organisms. If you increase your soil carbon levels, then the soil biology levels also increase, and soil organisms are so important for interaction with the trees.

Are you trying to develop particular strains of organisms?

It's more about diversity than developing different kinds of strains. You can go down the path of selecting and looking for particular strains, but in doing that you're starting into what I call "chemical thinking". You're looking for a silver bullet to fix a particular problem. I think you can get the balance wrong when you think this way.

I tend to try and go for more variety and diversity and particularly native species if possible. I'm using some of the inoculum Ray O'Grady is making. That contains 12 different strains and I'm finding it quite effective. I'm also making some inoculum from my own compost to help boost the diversity. Every area has its own particular set of organisms that have developed and are beneficial to the plants in that area. That's why it's important to have local input.

Where do you get your soil tests done?

They're done at Soil Food Web laboratories at the University at Lismore. I do them every year. I also have Mark Percival help me interpret the soil analysis. He's a horticultural advisor and he's done the Soil Food Web course that I did. He understands both sides of the picture and he's given me some very valuable input. He advises me on fertilizer inputs. We're trying to tailor the fertilizer inputs to make them biologically friendly. I'm using soft rock phosphate, K-mag and Twin N, which is a specific variety of bacteria that fixes nitrogen from the air and makes it available to the tree. Twin N is an interesting concept. I think farmers have to wean themselves right off artificial nitrogen inputs, and adding these microbes might be the solution. I believe artificial nitrogen is very destructive. Any nitrogen I put on goes on in a sulphur form – I use sulphate of ammonia. I'm very careful how I use that. I mix it with humic acid and molasses, which tends to slow its release and buffer any bad effects it has on the soil.

Do you test brix levels?

Yes. Our brix levels are currently sitting around 16 to 18. We still need to improve the health level of the trees because, when we do that, the trees will be more robust and disease and insect resistant. Microbes are helping build the brix levels, but that's only one thing that we need to look at. We need to look at the whole picture and try and mimic the natural system.

Where are you going from here? Are you planning to gain organic certification?

I don't think organic certification is for me. They have very strict rules and particular methods and systems for apply the nutrients that your soil is lacking. That's not something that suits the nature of my soil profile.

There are some interesting things happening in America. They did a trial selling fruit and vegetables with brix reading and they found that even though food labelled in this way was more expensive, people gravitated towards it because it tastes better. Perhaps that's the way to go. In the meantime I'm just selling through the normal wholesale system.

Where do you see horticulture in Australia is heading?

If fertilizer costs keep spiralling upwards as they're doing, conventional style chemical farming is going to be in trouble.

I think there is need for a shift to more holistic type farming. It's not necessarily a case of chucking the baby out with the bath water: you're organic or you're not. I think there's a need to understand the role of soil biology and the nutritional benefits that food gains when we enhance soil biology levels. Using techniques like the ones I'm using gives yields that are every bit as good, if not better, than the yields from conventional farming methods, and costs are reduced. I've been able to reduce the number of hours I irrigate because soil moisture stays a lot higher. I've been able to reduce my fertilizer inputs because I've been able to hold what I put on the soil a lot longer.

I think there's a fast moving groundswell occurring. At the avocado meetings they used to poke fun at me: "Oh there he is with his muck and magic yet again." At the last meeting we actually put forward a motion that the Avocado Australia start investigating the application and benefits of compost tea.

Finally, if you could give some advice to people who want to make the transition from conventional horticulture to something more sustainable, what would that advice be?

Choose your land very carefully. Plan very carefully how you plant and what you plant. If you're growing avocado on heavy soils, do soil profiles to find out what layers are underneath the trees. Make sure you have good draining by mounding. Do your homework. Learn as much as you can. Investigate the soil biology. When you have problems find answers by testing and trials. That's how I look at all problems of farming. You've got to be able to find the answers if you look hard enough. I do testing and trials before I introduce anything new and I recommend that approach to everyone.

Thank you for sharing your experiences, Malcolm.

Ian Smith

Apple and Cherry grower in the Huon Valley, Tasmania

Ian Smith is a fifth generation apple grower. He can trace the history of his property back to the early settlement in

Tasmania. It is situated in the Huon Valley, which was gouged-out in pre-historic times by glaciers.

Ian and his son Andrew have a 35-hectare apple and cherry orchard. They grow Gala, Fuji, Pink Lady and Sundowner apples and a few granny smiths. About 10% of their orchard is planted with cherry trees. Apart from the orchard they run about a dozen cattle, basically as lawnmowers to keep the land cleared and usable.

Ian and Andrew started converting to organic growing about 12 years ago and for the past three years have been totally organic. Their apples are sold throughout Australia and some are exported overseas.

Ian and his son Andrew have searched the world to discover apple growers who are, in their opinion, the best in the world. These people have been their mentors.

Tell me about the farm, Ian.

We have 140 acres, but not all of it is usable. The farm is on the Huon River which runs through the bottom of the valley and gives us drinkable water and water for irrigation. The river supplies us with most of the water we use on the farm. We pump it from the river and use it for our sprinklers, and some of it goes into dams. We take some water out of bores.

We've got third class soil. There's no depth to it. It's not suitable for high-producing vegetable crops. This soil has about 8 inches of topsoil, a cement pan underneath and clay underneath that. The only exception is along the river. Most people call that soil alluvium. It's valued very highly and it's not bad, but it's basically pulverised ironstone from the glacier.

We've just had the wettest winter in 50 or 60 years and we've also just had the warmest February. Generally it's a temperate climate with summer temperatures around 25°C but we can get four seasons in just one day. The rainfall averages 32 inches, but we had a metre of rain last winter.

We're extremely vulnerable to frost, particularly at blossom time, and for that reason we have overhead irrigation. We use that to combat frost damage.

The soil pH is generally between 6 and 7 in the orchard area, which is within the right range for apple growing, but it wouldn't be if we hadn't put lime on it. When we were growing conventionally we needed quite a bit of lime. We'd put on about a tonne to the acre every 4 or 5 years. Since we've gone organic the pH is in the right range and we don't put lime out directly, but we do add it during the composting process along with molasses and fish emulsion.

The soil has trace element deficiencies, including manganese.

When we were farming conventionally, most of the inputs to the soil were quantified in terms of how much nitrogen, phosphorous and potassium the tree extracts, and we'd put on so many kilograms of NPK, depending on the yield. It was comforting to know exactly what to do.

Now we've virtually no knowledge of what is needed. We use composted fowl manure, which is very high in phosphorous and very low in potash. Under the organic regime, any chemical that is mined naturally is permitted as an input. We do put on quite a lot of potassium sulphate when it's required.

We're really interested in developing the soil, and our emphasis has changed from just adding the elements to building levels of bacteria. We think the fowl manure has been a major influence there. It's composted before we apply it, therefore it doesn't contain nitrogen. The thing we're really interested in, but don't yet know the full story on, is photons. Since we've gone organic the composition of the soil has improved. It's difficult to give a quantitative assessment but it's got a lot more organic matter in it now and its water holding capacity has increased dramatically. Those are the major differences.

Logically, the increase in water holding capacity should have reduced our watering costs, but we're probably irrigating more now because when we do that we get higher yields. The time when the apple tree wants moisture is when it's hot. Everything, including growth, speeds up when it's hot. If the tree doesn't have enough water it goes into stress and shuts down. The fruit gets sunburnt. We water overhead to keep the trees from being stressed and they respond dramatically in terms of growth and yield. One of the unexpected results that's come from becoming organic and changing the emphasis to improving the soil and increasing watering has been the increase in productivity.

The science of organic farming is very different from conventional farming and, in my opinion, still fuzzy. That puts the onus back on the farmer to make it work. The farmer needs to be able to handle the nutrients. His skill might be in reducing the crop load, or putting in more irrigation, or watering the trees on a really hot day so that they're not sapped down and stressed.

What was your motivation for making the transition to organic growing?

I have a son who's actively involved and we've spent a fair bit of time trying to be better at what we do. This eventually led us overseas, because the technical knowledge is easier to obtain overseas.

I went away and worked when I was young and came back enthused. When I first went overseas, Australia's methods of growing apples conventionally were about 15 or 20 years behind what was going on in other parts of the world, especially in Europe. They understood tree physiology and tree-training. They had systems that produced high yields from small acreages because the land was so valuable that they had to do it better. Each country was doing its own research, but it was only 2 or 3 hours' drive from one country to the next, so the research was available to everyone.

My son did the same as I did when I was young. He was working in England and trying to decide whether or not to return to the farm, so he spent time with European growers. When he came home he'd been talking to some of the best apple growers in the world and he had more technical knowledge than I did. He had lots of bright ideas and wanted to start growing organically. By that stage he had a good enough grounding in what was going on to make the assessment that going into organic production would open up marketing opportunities that weren't available to us as conventional growers.

In the early 90s I was on the national Research and Development Committee for the Australian Apple and Pear Growers' Association. The conventional industry was in big trouble deciding how it was going to market fruit without it being tainted by the chemicals that were being used.

After seeing my son's enthusiasm and hearing about the things he'd discovered in Europe, I decided, "It's time I went again to have another look." It was 30 years after I had been away the first time.

After travelling around the world looking what others were doing, I realised that it was possible to produce organically grown apples and survive in an industry that's in big trouble.

We thought that by transitioning to organic growing methods we could market a different product, one that was safer for the consumer. We thought we had a chance of marketing directly to supermarkets and clients without having to compete with every other grower in Australia who was stuck with fruit and wanted to move it by discounting.

I'm basically saying that the conventional apple market is over-supplied and growers fight for their share of the market by discounting all the time. Supermarkets also fight for any price reduction they can get.

We converted some of our trees and it worked. We found that there were people in the municipal markets that wanted to specialise in organic products and shops that wanted to buy them. After we converted some of our trees and tested the market, we gained sufficient confidence in our own skills to do it properly. We started converting more and more of the farm over to organics. Now it's 100% organic.

But we've not been successful just because we've transitioned to being organic. Our success has come because Andrew and I are both sponges for knowledge. We believe that if you look at the global apple situation you find some countries that are better than others at producing apples. They've got a network of intellectual property that's behind the improvement. Generally speaking, we've gone to those countries to check out their planting systems. I go to England, Holland, Belgium, France and Italy, and by the time I've done a trip like that I think I've got a fair handle on what the farmers that are outstanding in various ways, are doing. The only country I've neglected is New Zealand, where there are a lot more organic producers than there are in Australia as well as an excellent semi-government research organization.

We found a fellow in Holland. He's a conventional grower but he's an expert in tree training and structuring orchards to make them more efficient and to improve yields quite dramatically. He knows how to get trees with enough frame so that you can produce a yield of between 40 and 60 tonnes per hectare. That means changing planting density.

When I first started we planted trees 18 metres apart. You had to wait 7 years just to develop the frame of the tree before you could start to crop it. Now we plant trees 1 metre apart and when we do that we can be in production within 3 years. There are ways of pruning and training that allow you to get sunlight on the tree, which allows it to keep producing.

When I came home from Europe after my father died I was 22 years old. At that time there were 11,000 fruit growers in Tasmania. Now there are 20. When I first started farming we were exporting all our apples to the northern hemisphere. Later we sent it to South East Asia and then that became difficult because we were competing with South Africa, South America and New Zealand. With the advent of controlled atmosphere storage we were able to extend the life of the fruit in storage. That was when we re-grouped and started marketing all our fruit within Australia, because with controlled atmosphere storage we could keep the apples for a long period of time.

How do you do that?

Brix levels change depending on the ripeness of the fruit. We can pick apples when they reach a brix level of 12. If we delay picking a fortnight, the brix levels will be 14.

If you want the optimum apple, you leave it on the tree until it is fully ripe and eat it immediately. Apples left on the tree to ripen are best.

If you want to store your apples for a long time and have them ready for the Christmas market, you have to pick the apples early. If you harvest them when they're at optimum eating quality they won't last till Christmas. The important thing is to make sure the apple has good brix levels when the consumer eats the fruit, and harvest timing has a lot to do with that.

Our apples might last longer than most and be firmer for longer, because they have a higher mineral density than most apples, but even so, when you put them in a cold store you're just delaying the ripening process.

What has been your biggest learning during the transition process?

Something that keeps it all together very simply is the concept of balance. We've had to learn how to keep the apple tree in balance with its support systems. It's a matter of: "How much growth is needed?" "How much crop load is needed to get a return bloom?" An apple tree likes to be kept in balance. When we used artificial fertilizers we gave the trees a gutful of stuff that they reacted to very quickly. Organic science says, "Keep the soil happy. Keep the nutrients in the soil in an available form so that when the tree needs them it can access them."

I agree with the theory behind organic growing. It means that what we put onto the soil keeps it working and alive. When the tree needs something, it's readily available and we're not chasing quick fixes of minerals and trace elements that the tree suddenly runs out of. Fertilizing the soil is like putting money in the bank. It's there when you need it.

What has been your strategy in making the transition?

We use dry fertilizers. There is a range of commercial people in the fertilizer field who will sell you organic fertilizers. It's up to us to evaluate what we're getting and decide whether the fertilizers are giving us the results we want.

Basically we went back to using the simpler chemicals that were natural products. We had to rely on our own ability and experience to make them work. Growing organic apples is a bit like growing apples with one hand tied behind your back, because you can only use certain products and they're generally old ones, and at the same time you need to achieve the same results as you do using modern inputs. The older chemicals have to be operated with skill and they need to be used with correct timing and diligence.

Because we can't use artificial nitrogen we get reduced vigour in the orchard. We're not getting massive water-shoot growth, which is what we need. The apple tree has to develop a frame that will support the crop. You make this happen when you put nitrogen on the ground.

The problem is that what we're now putting on makes the tree want to crop apples magnificently but not increase in size very much. In most of the organic orchards I've seen in other parts of the world, the level of vigour steps down quite a bit when you don't have the nitrogen inputs. We combat that by increasing the bacteria numbers in the soil with compost. It works because, when the bacteria die, nitrogen and protein are released back into the soil.

Compost tea would probably also work but we've got to be careful what we spray on the trees. We have considered it and it's not out of the question. We don't want to damage the fruit we're going to harvest so we've concentrated on the soil up till now. We're using a natural protein instead of compost tea and we've been doing that for five or six years. It's doing some marvellous things but there are negatives as well.

We're moving into fertigation and we're moving into composted fowl manure that's high in microbial action, and we expect that it will have the effect of increasing microbial activity in the soil and releasing the nutrients that the tree requires.

We microbe test our soil, the sap and the compost and we've gone to a lot of scientists to give us some rules that we can base our system on, in the same way we could when we used NPK fertilizers. I'm looking to getting all the information quantified and translated into a process that we can use, but that's nearly impossible without a lot more research and development. My son Andrew has been to Elaine Ingham's courses, but she's a league above us at the moment. We don't doubt her science, but getting it into a practical farming operation is not as easy as it looks. It's proving very difficult. We're finding there's not enough data to tell us whether we're above or below the average, because the levels we get vary from orchard to orchard and depend on the time we do our tests. All we have is the understanding of what's going on in the trees so that we're able to judge whether we're getting the result we want.

We went from using very expensive and very modern fungicides with a whole range of properties for killing spores that were on the apple trees. They're called "kick back" chemicals. As organic farmers we weren't allowed to use those so we went back to older chemicals that are natural. These are ones that the industry has been using for 40 or 50 years. Powered sulphur is a classic example. We've got to keep the trees as clean as possible to get a good pack-out (the percentage of the pick that will be acceptable for sale). We do this by monitoring the insect population and having a strategy for controlling black spot fungus.

We use lime or powdered sulphur for that. Our worst problems occur when we get periods of wet combined with high temperatures. Fungus multiplies rapidly in conditions of heat and humidity.

We control some of the insect pests using pheromones. These are hormone attractants, which confuse the male moth so that it can't find a partner to mate with, and you don't get grubs that damage the apples. Pheromones come in little strips and we put them through the orchard. It's an expensive exercise. We probably spend about $20,000 on pheromones to do 40 hectares.

The incidence of damage has increased but not, except in exceptional circumstances, by a lot. Normally we're looking at a pack-out of 70%, which compares with 80 - 90% previously. If we can achieve 70% we're happy. We do things to try and improve the situation, and sometimes they work and sometimes they don't.

We're developing a large beneficial insect population in our orchard. Earwigs are a very good predator. They eat anything that moves or crawls. We didn't introduce them.

The principle behind insect infestation is that there's normally a balanced population of insects in an area. When it gets out of balance for any reason, you get damage. The insect that's out of balance provides a food source for another type of insect that comes along, has plenty of food, so it's also able to multiply and get out of balance in its turn. Once you have one problem it tends to cause the next one, and the next, and so on.

The rest of the insects don't cause damage. They probably just reduce growth and yield. Insecticides kill the whole insect population, both beneficials and baddies. Once you stop spraying, the orchard gradually comes into balance and you don't have a problem.

We had to be capable of creating an environment with sufficient predators and organisms to stop the destructive ones taking over and wrecking our crop. It's a high risk because if we don't get it right we could suddenly have all the apples with black spots, and not be up to market standard. Alternatively, we could maintain the standard and not have enough volume for our operation to be economical.

Coming from a conventional farming background, weeds are my biggest bugbear. They make the orchard look very scrappy but actually do very little damage. There are various methods of controlling weeds that we could adopt. At present we're mowing them with a swing arm mower, but sometimes they get higher than we'd like. If we were still conventional farmers we'd be using herbicides down the strips and we'd be trying to stand the trees in a weed free strip with no organic matter in it and probably the worst soil in the row. When you let the weeds grow back, you start to get life back into the soil but it does have the problem that it looks unsightly.

We mulch pruning clippings and grass and that all goes back into the soil. We put pasture in the sward between the rows of trees and we try and have as much clover in the sward as we can. We could have mucked around with particular grasses that will influence our insect population but we haven't seen the need to do that.

In your opinion, has the transition worked?

Yes, it has. The chemical costs are slightly less. Fertilizer costs are about the same and labour costs are higher. Our pack-out is lower but our productivity has increased.

It's a moving target and the target is still moving. It's not working with the cherries. We're not getting a good enough product. The cherry trees are the last ones to be converted and this is probably only their second year since the change. The reason it's not working is that we're not good enough cherry growers to address all the problems. We've elected to continue and try and solve the problems, but on a horticultural farm you only do things once or twice a year and you have to wait 12 months before you see the results. Only then can you modify what you're doing. It becomes a long-term project, which is difficult in a modern business environment. Most businesses change very quickly. I think that's one of the reasons why large corporations aren't successful in horticulture. I don't think you get a lot of synergy with increased size. You just get bigger costs. We think we're just about the right size as a producer to maintain some sort of cost efficiency.

The health of the trees and the productivity of the trees are now as good as any conventional orchard, so we're looking to a future that's pretty rosy unless we stuff it up with our own inexperience. That's why we're on a quest for knowledge all the time.

From a business perspective, going organic has been successful. The organic label has a lot of kudos with a lot of people who really don't know too much about food. When you grow conventionally, you have to operate within acceptable residue limits that are imposed by governing bodies in Australia. These limits aren't set at zero and zero might be the only acceptable level of agricultural spray content for some people. It's those people who are our market target. When people buy my product at the store, they do so because they get a fuzzy feeling because it might be healthier for them. They don't understand the difference between organically grown apples and conventionally grown apples and they haven't got time to appreciate the arguments on both sides.

Where do you market your product?

We probably export 10%. We deal with an organic wholesaler that has outlets in Sydney, Melbourne and Brisbane, and we're a national supplier to Woolworths. Because we're a certified organic grower we get a price premium for our apples. The premium isn't large. There needs to be a premium, because our production inputs are higher than if we were growing conventionally.

In the past, the market has been more forgiving in terms of blemishes, but as the volume of organic produce increases, standards for colour and blemishes will rise and we'll be expected to produce fruit of the same standard that's required of conventionally produced apples.

Is growing organically more interesting than conventional farming?

It certainly is! We're constantly trying things and monitoring whether it's effective. As a farmer, I'm still having trouble getting my head around the science.

I guess we said to ourselves at some stage that there were too many question marks about the chemicals we were using. We decided that, in the long term, organic growing had more business possibilities than continuing to grow conventionally. During the time we've been doing it we've got a lot greener, but so has the conventional industry. Their problem is that they don't have a label they can use to promote their products. They're reducing insecticide usage and switching to pheromones. They're still chasing their tails with broad-spectrum insecticides, which wipe out the predators and the beneficials. With organic methods you can get a better balance, but the risk factors are higher. It puts a lot more pressure on the farmer who has to make sure they do things at exactly the right time to be effective and also has to do a lot more monitoring of insects to get the timing right.

Do you like being a farmer?

Yes. I think there are so many facets to being successful as a farmer that you end up acquiring skills throughout your life. It's never dull. It might be hot, cold or wet at times. I like working with the land.

What I don't like is government regimentation, which is a part of doing business. Workplace health and safety is based on correct principles but application of the law is very "hit and miss". Anything that is run by government is basically poorly administered, but it has clout behind it, which can come and bite you at times. It's a full time job just keeping up with legislative changes. People are unrealistic about farmers' ability to run a business according to a set of very demanding requirements, and this unrealistic expectation extends into the quality assurance scheme. The principles aren't wrong, but there's an awful lot of paperwork for not much gain. Years ago, if anyone had told me that we had to be extremely computer literate just to operate the sort of accounting system that meets the requirements of various government bodies and quality assurance schemes, or that we would have to have specialist staff to administer our operation, I would have told them they were crazy. But that's what's happened. We're implementing systems that have been dreamed up by people who really don't understand the impact of what they're asking. Making sense of it is sometimes very frustrating.

As a large apple grower you've provided lots of information about apple marketing in Australia, which has been very interesting. I thank you for sharing that, Ian.

Mike Ottone

Pineapple and sugar cane grower
in Tully in northern Queensland

Mike and Jenny Ottone's farm is located south of Tully. Farming has been Mike's whole life. He's the son of a farmer, the grandson of a farmer and the brother of a farmer. Mike's father purchased his own farm in 1972. Previously, he'd looked after his mother's farm. The new farm had a shack on it, an acre of cleared land and a couple of fruit trees. The rest was rainforest or blue gum forest. Gradually the forest was cleared and Mike's father planted pineapples. Pineapples have been grown there ever since. Today, twenty-five hectares are planted with pineapples and there are 100 hectares of sugar cane.

Mike went to school in Tully. He did an apprenticeship as a boilermaker at the Tully sugar mill. When he finished his apprenticeship in 1981 he came to work on his father's farm with his brother, who had just left school. They grew bananas for 24 years and since then have grown pineapples and bananas.

What is the climate like where you live, Mike?

Tully is one of the wettest parts of Australia, where rainfall is measured in metres rather than centimetres. This is Queensland rainforest country. In summer it's hot and wet. In winter the temperature can fall as low as 4⁰C at night, but by 9 o'clock in the morning you're sweating again. Climate like this is associated with major pest and disease problems

What are the biggest problems with the physical environment, Mike?

I suppose the biggest problem is the grub that looks like a little centipede that eats the roots off the pineapples just as fast as they send roots out. You need a chemical to control them. Then there's the problem with phytophthera or root rot. That's one of the biggest problems we have with the pineapples. Getting good root growth is the thing we aim for.

What about the economic environment? What's your biggest problem there?

Freight costs are high. Not getting a fair deal in the market place has caused lots of problems.

There were quite a lot of small banana growers in the area 7 or 8 years ago. We were one of them. A lot of the bigger growers sold direct to the major supermarket chains. The supermarkets got the good produce and the inferior stuff was put on the central market and this destroyed the price. The big growers didn't have to do this for very long before quite a few of the smaller growers, who up to that time had been making a reasonable income, had to move out of bananas and do something different because they just couldn't afford to pay wages. Many of them left their farms.

Are prices still a problem?

Things are better with bananas now. They still have price fluctuations but the prices have increased to such an extent that it's a much better proposition.

In pineapples the same things happen. The reason we're still growing pineapples, as small growers, is that we've gone in with other small growers and we have our own packing shed. We're all partners. By combining all the farms we have a reasonable amount of volume and we get volume rates for freight and cartons. We supply the packing shed and the shed sells direct to agents and some of our pineapples go direct to Woolworths and Coles.

What was the motivation that caused you to make the transition from conventional farming?

I suppose it's finding something that really works. Chemicals are expensive. Some of the ones we were using have an S6 or S7 poison rating. They can damage your health. We're always looked for ways to save costs and we knew using chemicals was very expensive and the chemicals didn't always work. Because we'd grown bananas for 24 years we were pretty experienced. We used to fumigate our soil because that's the recommended strategy to keep the nematodes down. When EDB (ethylene di-bromide) was banned we sat down and looked at what other chemicals we could use. I spent about $200 on a course to learn how to use different fumigants. After seeing how poisonous this stuff was to the person putting it on, I decided I wasn't going to use it. We started growing crops without fumigation and searched for alternatives. That was about 10 years ago.

Initially we only stopped using the ethylene di-bromide. We were still using other fumigants to control the pests in the pineapples. I went to a couple of seminars with Graeme Sait of Nutritech Solutions to find if there were other ways of handling the disease pressures. Graeme talked about compost teas and I was convinced this was the way to go. From that beginning it's been a sort of slow progression.

I started using some liquid fertilizers that came from Vital Resource Management in Townsville. Those fertilizers were supposed to have microbes living in them but I wasn't sure that this was true so I bought a microscope and used it. The trouble was that when I looked through the microscope, I didn't know what I was looking at! That's when I decided to do a course with Elaine Ingham at Soil Food Web in Lismore. Now I can identify different microbes and fungi.

We were also using compost teas at the time and having only limited success with it, partly because some of the product we were using had gone off and we weren't putting on as many micro-organisms as we could have been. It wasn't until I got the microscope that I found that out! I'd just been given a recipe and I was following instructions. Until you know what you're looking at, you don't really know what you're doing.

In October of that year I had a field day on the farm. I'd only been using the compost tea for a few months in a small area. I showed some of the field day participants the pineapples and told them we were using compost tea treatments. One bloke pulled out some of the plants from the compost tea area and they had better roots than the conventional bay pineapples. He said: "That's not bad!" That's all we got out of them.

We kept plodding along, doing our compost teas following the recipe I'd been using: kelp, humic acid and fish emulsion. I was trying to grow fungi, checking it out with the microscope, and I wasn't happy. It wasn't growing as fast as it should have been doing. I got in touch with someone I'd met at Elaine Ingham's course, organized a new brewer to replace my home-made one, because I was thinking that the problem might have been insufficient oxygen, and I also got him to send me some of his food. He told me to use molasses in my brew. Even before the new brewer and food arrived, still using my home made brewer, I had more fungi that I'd ever seen before. It was the molasses that made the difference.

I continued using compost tea on and off for a while and then the year before last, I separated two bays of pineapples and did a controlled experiment to seriously test how effective this treatment was.

I planted all areas normally. On the control bays, I started using compost tea after we'd done our basic fertilizing programme. I didn't use any fungicide or any other chemicals, which was a big change because normally when we plant we use Ridomil for phytopthera. We put it on and hoe it in. We also used Lindane. We used Ridomil for our first and second post-plant spray and then we sprayed again about three months later. We sprayed regularly with phosphoric acid. We sprayed Dimethiate four times for red mite. Then of course we had to spray to get rid of ants. We used Diazanon for that. It was a pretty intensive spray programme.

We didn't use any of these sprays on the two control bays.

What happened?

The control pineapples were growing just as well as the ones we were spraying! The colour was different because we weren't using any urea. We were putting on urea in the conventional areas.

The results were pretty exciting. The red mite wasn't wiped out but it was under control. There were no obvious symptoms of root rot, even though we went through what was probably the wettest year for over 30 years. It rained all January and February.

This year I've done our whole farm without the Ridomil and without the fungicide.

You know, I should just shut up about what's happened. Every other farmer is a competitor after all! But I think we've all been pushing shit uphill for a long time between trying to get a good price for our product when all the supermarkets want to do is screw down the prices tighter and tighter. The chemical companies keep putting prices up and changing the formulations, telling us they've got better chemicals coming along. We farmers have been stupid enough to keep buying them, and when we buy them we only have limited success with them.

The trouble is that the chemical companies aren't the ones who are using the sprays. We're the ones putting it out on the paddock or we're asking our workers to do it.

Sure, we've got chemicals that will kill the phytophthera but then we have to another chemical for this problem and another chemical for that problem. You don't have to use chemicals to get rid of phytophthera. I've absolutely no doubt of that. We're the wettest place in Australia, and if we can do it anyone can. I know I can control phythophthera on my farm and it doesn't take much to do a trial.

There was another field day last year in October. I took some of my pineapple plants down. They were the ones I had grown with my compost teas. We visited several farms where the farmers were using conventional methods and none of them had pineapples with root systems as good as mine. There were reps from DPI, Golden Circle and some top agronomists who are pineapple industry representatives – blokes that have been in the pineapple industry for years. I showed them my pineapples and told them what I'd been dong and it just went right over their heads. I spoke to one bloke before the meeting and said, "Look. This pineapple has been grown without any Ridomil and without phosphoric acid. Compost tea is causing this pineapple to be as good as it is." He said: "That's good!" Wasn't the slightest bit interested! As soon as they hear the word compost tea they think of long-haired hippies wearing sarongs.

The conventional farmers find what I'm doing a bit much too accept so I have to demonstrate - and keep on demonstrating.

I've spoken to the DPI (Department of Primary Industry) and they just don't want to know about what I'm doing. They're too busy getting funding to register new chemicals. I suggested they do a trial of compost tea and I'd supply the product. I wanted someone independent to do a trial to show how well it works. They said, "How much money can you pay us?" They wanted me to pay for the trial. This is something that could make a huge difference to productivity but all they're looking at is genetically engineering sugar cane.

What they're not realising is that plants that don't have chemical fertilizers to keep them going, take up nutrients from the soil and therefore they're more nutritious to eat. You don't need genetic engineering to get a better product!

What fertilizers do you use?

I use a product call K-Pac, which is organically based. I also use rock phosphate and chicken manure, potash, and then there's the stuff I put into my compost tea: fulvic acid, fish emulsion, and molasses, and the inoculant which contains different sorts of bacteria, including trichoderma bacillis. I get it from Ray O'Grady, a very switched on guy whose company, Smart Bugs, is in Lismore.

Do you do soil tests?
I did my last soil test in May last year on two compost tea blocks and the bays alongside them The compost tea blocks had more available phosphorous than the conventional blocks, which shows something is working.

Is there anything that stops the compost tea working?

I've found you get much better results when you don't add nitrogen fertilizer. Nitrogen attracts insects and diseases. I'm working with five growers at present. These blokes are growing taro and getting a lot of rot in the plants. It's hard for growers to change when they've been taught, "You've got to put on loads of nitrogen otherwise you won't grow a crop." Compost teas don't help much if you're still putting on lots of nitrogen. You'll still have disease pressures.

What's the relative cost between conventional growing methods and using microbe teas?

I've done an approximate costing. Conventional methods cost in excess of $1,000 per bay. Compost tea costs $200. It's a big difference. In the area I didn't use fertilizer as well as the compost tea, the production was down a bit compared to what I'd normally expect. When I used the compost tea and did two fertilizer sprays using nitrogen, potash, iron and zinc, the production was similar for both areas.

Are you also testing these methods with your sugar cane?

The year before last I applied compost tea to 2 hectares in the sugar cane. For the first six months I could see a difference in the sugar cane. Plants were taller and there were subtle differences. It only cost me $15 per hectare to do this. With such a low investment you wouldn't expect to see any differences, but I did, so that was encouraging.

That trial showed me that even if you don't change your normal fertilizer programme and use the compost tea, there is an advantage. If you assist the microbial health in your soil, something's got to happen.

On those 2 hectares I could see the difference but it wasn't enough to document. This year I've done about 90 out of my total 100 hectares of sugar cane. I probably did one spray overall but it would have been even better to have done more while the cane was still small. It'll be interesting to see the result.

What are your plans for the future?

After I found I could control phytophthera, I thought I could grow organically. I've leased a block that's really sandy. I cleared it in March, fertilized it with rock phosphate and planted 4 acres in May. I've registered with the BFA (Biological Farmers of Australia) to get it certified. My only problem with growing organically is how to get rid of the grass. Grass is a hassle. We've had to pull grass out by hand. Our neighbours have had a laugh about that!

How are the organic pineapples doing?

Better than the conventional ones on our own farm. It's probably because we've just gone though the driest planting period we've ever had. It didn't rain much for four months. In the sandy block, where the organic pineapples are, there's moisture a little way down in the subsoil.

Do you have some advice for anyone who's thinking of changing over from the conventional ways of farming?

I think one of the big things is that, as farmers, we've been taught to feed the plants and not the soil. NPK fertilizers feed the plants. If you've got trouble with disease and soil health, learn how to feed the soil.

I think my advice would be that people shouldn't be afraid to do trials of new methods on their own farm. It doesn't take much to do a trial, and the benefits when you change your farming systems are there for a long time. If you're planning to still be farming in 10 years time, you can start making a change to improve your soil health and you're going to see the benefits. It's not going to cost much. Microbe teas cost about 15c per litre to make and you put out 100 litres to the hectare.

My second piece of advice would be to talk to the people who are getting results. Then once you start getting results, don't narrow what you're doing down to just one crop. If it works for one, it works for all of them. The more we talk about this sort of thing, the more people we'll convince to do their own trials. The DPI doesn't want to know about it, but they'll come round.

Thank you for the thoughts you've shared today.

Kym Green

Cherry and apple grower
in the Adelaide Hills of South Australia

Kym Green is a fifth generation apple and cherry grower who has broken the mould and introduced a large variety of innovative ideas to a farm that he and his brother work. Kym's neighbours have yet to be convinced that Kym's methods of controlling insects, pests and diseases are worth investigation.

Kym has been making the transition from conventional farming to not-quite-organic farming since 2000 when he was first introduced to the idea that soil biology is a vital part of the world of agriculture.

Kym is a very deep thinker who's looking at the real causes of problems rather than looking for superficial explanations. His explanation and solutions for codling moth damage are fascinating and provide easy solutions to a very difficult problem.

Tell me a little about the physical characteristics of the area where your farm is located, Kym.

Our farm is situated in the Adelaide Hills about 30 km east of Adelaide. The farm is in steep, rough, wooded terrain. It's a fairly high rainfall area. We get 1,000 mm rain a year but we also have large dams and bore water.

Our soil is heavy clay loam. When we got our soil report about 10 years ago the soil was about 5·5 pH. We've brought that up to 6·3. The soil is naturally very high in magnesium so it's very hard to work and the water is also high in magnesium. The organic matter was only 2% but we've now got one block that's up to 5·5% so we're making changes. All the people who talk at workshops stress the importance of improving your organic matter and your soil biology. That's basically the most important thing you have to do.

We have 15 hectares of cherries and the same area in apples.

I farm with my brother and we're fifth generation farmers on the same land, which means we carry a lot of entrenched baggage about the way we've always done things. I came straight from school to work on the farm and I've been here ever since. Actually, I had planned to teach biology and history. I came home for the holidays after I finished school and never left. I've been here on holidays for 35 years!

My father is still involved in the farm but these days he gets around on a four wheeler and when I'm not looking he sneaks out and puts RoundUp on everything because, in his eyes, the mark of a good farmer is to have everything looking immaculate. In my father's view the area under the trees has to be as bare as a baby's bum and the area between has to be mown like a bowling green. Getting him to stop doing that has been a real challenge.

I was very fortunate in that I was awarded a Nuffield Farm Scholarship in 1993 and I went away to look at apple and cherry production throughout the world. The Nuffield Scholarship makes you hungry for excellence. You look at what others are doing and you want to know more. Initially I did a 6-week trip with other Nuffield Scholars and we looked at all sorts of different farming environments as well as the agri-politics of the world. One day we could be looking at silos and the next day we'd be looking at pig farming. We were hosted by farmers, which gave us a great opportunity to get to know them and find out how they do things.

At the completion of the six weeks of generalised study, I then did an additional six months, specialising in my own area of expertise, which was apples and cherries.

From that experience I learned to stand up and ask questions when I need answers. I telephone people for information. From my Nuffield experience I learned that there are really useful networks around the world and the movers and shakers of this world are really pleased to share their knowledge and help others.

When we started making the transition to more sustainable forms of farming that was a really important thing to have learned, because when you're making the transition you have to be receptive to a whole range of new ideas. You have to be open to picking up new information.

You started making the transition to a more sustainable form of horticulture about 10 years ago. Before you did that, what sort of farming regime did you practise?

We used ammonium nitrate as our soil conditioner and we sprayed constantly with fungicides and pesticides. This is still the norm for the district. We put on four sprays for brown rot at flowering, products called Tilt and Sumiflex. After that we put two sprays of Captan through the growing season to protect against the possibility of brown rot. Immediately prior to harvest we put out two more sprays. We had black cherry aphids and cherry slugs, so we sprayed about 4 times per season.

What was the trigger that sent you off down the sustainable horticulture track?

In 2000 there was a notice in the local newsletter. Elaine Ingham was coming to give a 1-day talk in the Barossa Valley, which is about three-quarters of an hour from here. The talk was about soil life.

Now I knew there were worms and stuff in the soil but that was the limit of my knowledge. Elaine spoke very basically on soil life and how important it is to build up soil life by using compost and compost teas and I was quite suprised to learn that compost could do so much good in terms of encouraging soil life. Up till that day I thought compost was in the same category as woven jumpers and dreadlocks worn by people in hippy communities.

It was practical, down-to-earth sort of stuff. I thought, "I'm going to have a go at this".

I think it was the following year that Elaine teamed up with Arden Andersen and did a four-day workshop at Roseworthy, which is an Agricultural College in Adelaide. Arden was hard work. He was right into chemistry and physics, ratios and atomic weights and I didn't do that sort of thing at school so I had to battle with it. Elaine got us grounded because she used very simple analogies and gave us examples.

At the 4-day seminar Elaine spoke about a "zone of adequacy," which meant you have between 300 and 1,000 milli-something units. I sent off a soil sample to Elaine's Soil Food Web laboratory in Lismore. Instead of 300 we had 55. We were doing all right at this level but we could see the potential if we could get the numbers up. We built a compost tea brewer and did four sprays of compost tea onto the ground and sent off a second test. This time, the numbers had crept up to 138. I was flabbergasted that we could actually change the level of soil life in our vast soil area with just 4 tea bag brews. We were just spraying out something that looked like coloured water. The next time we played around with some lucerne tea. That shot the levels up to 400. That was in 2002 and I haven't tested since because I knew we were going in the right direction.

After a while I realised that we were putting these teas under the tree line where we were also putting on herbicide. On one hand we were working to build soil life but at the same time we were destroying it with herbicides. Our orchard is planted in double rows and you can't put an outrigger mower in the double row. Our orchard mowers cut the grass and threw some of it under the trees but the machines couldn't get in under the trees because we had sprinklers and poly pipes and the mowers would have destroyed them.

After that realisation, we converted our irrigation system from sprinklers to drip irrigation so that we could allow the area under the trees to have weeds without causing problems for the watering system. Weeds stop the sprinklers from working.

We gradually started moving away from using RoundUp because it's really deadly for worms and mycorrhizal fungi. We reduced our herbicide treatment to once a year. Hugh Lovel is really adamant about not exposing soils to sunlight so we've come up with a solution that's not ideal, but is the best we can do at the moment. We allow the winter grass to finish and the summer grass to start growing and then burn it off a with knockdown spray. We knock down the grass and use it as a mulch. The stiff grass stays standing. You should see the slaters and the worms under the mulch. I don't apply any herbicides directly to the soil.

I'm now looking to natural sprays as well: acetic acid and pelargonium plant acid.

In some ways Arden Andersen scrambled my brain. He told me that we can't keep farming the way we were doing because the chemicals we were putting on were bad for the soil, bad for the plant, and bad for for the health of consumers. I hadn't heard of that connection before. He told us that a lot of illnesses are caused by chemicals and poor soil nutrition. I'd never heard that before either.

A lot of people will argue with what he says but I thought it made sense. He told me that there was another way to do things.... and then he went back to the USA!

Two years later he came back and spoke at an Apple Conference in Tasmania in 2004. The apple industry was and still is a very heavy user of chemicals and most of the delegates attending that conference just didn't want to hear Arden's message. He's a bit of an evangelist and he got a lot of criticism. At that time he was travelling with Doug Murray from Michigan, who I'd met while I was overseas.

Doug had become my mentor. The negative energy directed at the two of them at that conference was amazing. I said to Arden, "It's not going too well. There's a lot of negative feeling." Arden suggested I give a presentation as part of his segment. Well, that just alienated me from everyone else as well!

Things have changed since then for many people, but there's still a lot of vested interest in holding onto the old ways. For many people it feels safe to keep doing what they've always done. I know when I first started making the transition I didn't have anyone to talk to. I'd go to the agronomist, but he was only interesed in promoting chemicals. My dad belongs to the old school so he didn't understand where I was coming from. It really wasn't until I met up with a guy called John Pannon, who also attended the four day workshop at Roseworthy, that I started to make real progress.

John would explain the chemical reactions that caused certain weed species to grow in particular soil conditions. I'd never thought of that before.

John also suggested that I work with radionics. I did courses with Arden and with John back in 2001 and 2002. That was amazing. You're in a room with 40 others who might be cotton farmers or dairy farmers. They were just "normal" people learning some pretty way out stuff. I went with two mates, which was great because you need the moral support of your friends when you venture into something as new as this. I just went through the motions without really understanding what we were doing, but as a result of it all I decided to take a machine home and try to understand this mind-boggling concept. I also took home a book that comes with the machine that deals with human health.

Let me tell you about something I did in the early days using the radionics equipment that really blew me away. Using it I identified what was causing a particular problem and what I needed to do to fix it. From that time on I've been a total convert and I've been using radionics techniques ever since.

On a radionics machine you can dial up a number for something like calcium. I was having real problems with my cherries at that time. They were producing wads of gum from the trunk. I thought I could use the machine to find out what was causing this to happen. I asked the question "What is causing this problem?" The answer was that the trees had "diarrhoea". They were trying to purge something out through the bark and in the process great gum globs, the size of tennis balls, were being formed. The next step in the process was to identify the contents of the gum balls and I discovered they contained all the nutrients we were putting on. My next step was to identify what I needed to do and the answer came back that we needed to give the trees "milk of magnesia," which is what you give someone who has diarrhoea. Now remember, I was working with a human health book to get all this information, so then I had to translate the human health information I had, into something that was relevant to trees. I put on epsom salts and the trees stopped producing gumballs. Epsom salts contain magnesium, which we discovered is also a great remedy for bacterial canker.

When we were starting to sell our cherries in Western Australia, a requirement was that we use copper to stop bacterial canker and early rot. The Western Australians didn't want fruit with these diseases to come in from other states for fear of the diseases spreading. The standard procedure is to put on copper hydroxide or copper sulphate. I would have had to put on 6 sprays. At the time we had 40 ppm of copper and the upper limit is 3 ppm so we certainly didn't want to add any more. I'd learned from Elaine that copper kills bacteria for up to 6 weeks following an application. To add more copper meant we were poisoning the soil and it was even more of a problem in that copper doesn't leach so we'd be stuck with it for a long time.

Conventional farm practice tells us that the remedy for bacterial canker is copper but hydrogen peroxide then applications of epsom salts for maintenance works brilliantly. I cleared up the problem and rarely see it now, yet all around us and throughout South Australia it's still a problem.

It's very difficult when the regulations require you to do something that you know is detrimental to your farm and no one wants to listen when you discover a process that works better. Some time after I discovered that magnesium stopped the gumming and the bacterial canker a guy came out from California to speak at a conference. He worked for the Department of Agricultural Research over there. I suggested he do some research on what I'd discovered and his reply was, "Who's going to provide the money?" At the end of the day, if you don't have a proprietory product to sell as a result of research that's being done, no one is going to do the work.

Our industry standard for calcium application is 10 kg of calcium chloride per hectare. In the whole 10 years I've been working with radionics the trees haven't once wanted calcium chloride. I'll use calcium glutamate or calcium nitrate and I'll use it at the rate of 1 kg per tree. If trees don't want something, you can make lots of it available and they might take a little bit up. If the trees need something, they'll take it all up if you put it on.

We have to recognise that we're never going to be able to get away from using inapropriate chemical fertilizers, sprays and methods that are harmful unless turkeys like me get on the soap box and say, "Things aren't necessarily what we're being told." It's one of the reasons I don't plan to become organically certified in the near future. I'll fix the cause of the problems first.

Some of the organics recommendations don't work in all situations, but you don't have a choice. They're very rigid about what you can and can't use and they don't give you any options.

When you first enter the grey transition zone you can use lower rates of chemicals and fertilizers and buffer them with fulvic acid and humic acid. I'm still using calcium nitrate, which the organic crowd think is bad because it's man-made, but the organic crowd are recommending I use copper and sulphur, which would destroy my soil balance. I don't want to go down that path. I think it's more important to get my soil in balance. Mind you, the stuff the organics crowd want you to use is mild compared with the ghastly stuff we were using when we farmed conventionally and which many people are still using.

There are a lot of people who do radionics and work as consultants, but they don't always grow anything. That's the reason I love working with Doug Murray. Doug was an orchard scout for 20 years, so he visited lots of orchards to find out where the good fruit was. He advised a lot of conventional growers as well as some of the organics guys. He came up with a product that's made from orange peel extract. It contains things like malic acid, folic acid, acetic acid and glycerine, and it works as a fungicide in that it drops the pH of leaves and fruit when you spray it out. Black spot and brown rot don't like a low pH environment. It kills them. You can use carb soda which has an extremely high pH in your spray followed by the orange peel extract spray and it causes the pH to swing from high to low and the fungus dies. Now that we're using the orange peel spray we've stopping putting out chemical rot sprays on cherries.

You obviously came in contact with a whole range of different ideas and different people during this period. How did you go about integrating all this information?

When we first started, we ran two programmes in parallel. We kept doing what we'd done previously and in addition we were adding nutritional elements through our spray tanks. We often put humic acid through our irrigation and fulvic acid into into our sprays.

It was interesting in the early days when I started using radionics. I'd ask what my trees wanted and the answer came back: "sugar". Sugar feeds bacteria. I built up the bacteria with raw sugar, then with molasses, then with humic acid which is a bit more complex and also feeds the fungi which are feeding on some of the bacteria. I ended up using fulvic acid, which is the most complex of all.

We tested progress using brix readings. We would do a foliar spray and give everything a boost and the brix levels would go from 9 to 15, but a week later it would be back to 9, which was where we'd started. We could lift the brix levels but the soil wasn't good enough to maintain it. It was because of this that we started using organic manures, which caused the grass to grow, but in the beginning the manure didn't sustain the grass growth for the whole season. We'd get to summer and the grass would just run out of puff.

We kept putting on composted cow manure at the rate of 3 - 4 tonnes per hectare in autumn when the ground is cold. Putting it on in autumn was a biodynamic recommendation. Before we learned that, we used to put it on in spring but we weren't getting the effect of the manure breaking down because everything was too dry. Since we increased the manure levels, the strip where we used to put herbicides is starting to grow grass.

About half way through the 10 year transition period we started using biodynamic preparations and we also started growing green manure crops of peas, beans and oats between the trees and underneath them. Growing stuff that's almost a metre tall gives you a lot of mulch as well as soil organic matter, since tall plants have long roots. Forty-nine percent of organic matter comes from the roots, so with tall plants you get even more than you think you're getting. We grew peas and beans for a couple of years before starting to plant every alternate row with cocksfoot. Cocksfoot grows bulk and it's coarse. When we cut it and put it under the trees it becomes fungal food. If we were growing clover, there'd be no volume in the organic matter. Now we plant green manures under the trees and in the tractor rows in autumn.

We've also started composting the chicken manure and adding lime, manganese and phosphate soft rock into it. We put all the minerals into the compost, depending on what the soil tests indicate.

Cheryl Kemp, who's a biodynamics guru, wants me to back off from using calcium nitrate, and I'm looking now to use my compost regime to replace 95% of the chemical fertilizers I was using. This year I ordered 2 tonnes of potassium sulphate. I went down and loaded it before asking the price. It was going to cost $5,560, so I told them to take it off the truck. I'll rely on putting potassium in the compost instead. I can buy 150 tonnes of composted chicken manure for $10,000.

We had a bad year with our compost application last year. I had the chicken manure delivered in March and it was all dotted around the place and it started raining. That's the trouble with bulky stuff. I had it in the hopper 4 times and had to shovel it out again four times because it was just too wet. We finally put it out this February and now the trees are looking unbelievably healthy. We put out 5 tonnes of chicken compost per hectare.

I find it's important not to overdo things when it comes to putting out compost. The soil just can't handle too much. Moron farmers put out 20 tonnes per hectare. They believe if something is good, then it's a good idea to put "more on".

Have you noticed changes since you started using a lot of organic material and mulch and changed your fertilization regime?

In the last few years we've had serious drought and we haven't even had enough water to irrigate the cherries after Christmas. For the past two years it's also been really hot. Last year we didn't irrigate till late March and the trees just stayed green. We'd never seen the trees look so good and this was with no summer rain and no irrigation.

Our soil is better. The calcium levels are now up to where they should be. It seems it took 20 years to do that, but the reality is that it took about five years and now, with the calcium levels where we want them and the fungi levels high, the calcium won't leach out. The fungi will hold onto it. Last year we put on gypsum at the rate of 250 kg per hectare.

What have you been doing to control pests and insects?

The best stories I can tell you about pest control are about what we've been doing in our apple orchard.

Last year our neighbour had family issues and missed putting on a codling moth spray. Now, our neighbour on the other side is just inundated with codling moth. We're not. We stopped spraying half way through last season with codling moth spray.

- 159 -

What we did was to look at what the codling moth wants out of an apple. The female lays its eggs on the leaves of the apple tree and the baby caterpillars make their way to the apples. It doesn't want the skin, and the flesh is a food bonus as it eats its way through the apple to get to the seed. The seed is what it wants. The seed is high in manganese and magnesium. This is what attracts the codling moth caterpillar. The caterpillars are tuned into the energy frequency of manganese and magnesium because these are essential for their survival.

Once we realised this, we started spraying manganese and magnesium all over the farm. It goes on the leaves, the trunks and on the grass. Now the caterpillars have plenty of magnesium and manganese but they starve to death because they can't find the apples. The apples provided the food for the caterpillars, but the seeds are the reason the caterpillars eat through the apples.

Then there are the woolly aphids. They're dirty creatures. They just love the sappy growth that comes when you apply nitrogen. If we don't spray on nitrogen or put our nitrogenous fertilizers, we don't get woolly aphids, but neither do we get large fruit size! As well as that, I identify substances the woolly aphids don't like. I put those things in my broadcasting tower and spray them out homeopathically or I put them through the spray tank.

Do you think the broadcasting tower works?

Yes I do. My woolly aphid spray went into the top well and we haven't had woolly aphids for two years, though we were inundated with them before that. I often put potentised humic acid in the broadcaster, and when I go back to check the orchard I don't see a need to put anything more on. We cover the cherries with bird netting, and you can't spray after the netting is on, so I use my broadcaster for the orange peel extract.

What other things are you doing for diseases and insects?

The other thing that's stopping insect pests is what we're not doing. We're not putting out the bad stuff that knocks out the predator insects.

This area is very IPM (Integrated Pest Management) friendly. The IPM people bring down predator mites to eat pest mites. We have an independent scout who comes in to test whether we need to spray or not. The last two years, we haven't had to spray because we don't have high numbers of pest mites.

Most of my neighbours use pheromones rather than sprays. The hot weather has encouraged pest mites to breed and they've had to start spraying for mites. I've gone against the trend by not spraying and I don't use pheromones either. I sometimes put on a very soft insecticide early in the season to get the ones that hatch early.

I've been doing really well with disease control on the cherries and I'm not doing too badly with the insects. We do get some losses and I think it's mostly tied up with our use of herbicides. We're continuing to change over more and more to drip irrigation, we're building up the organic matter, and I think we've turned the corner as far as pests and disease are concerned. We're using the orange peel extract and that's all I'm using and we've had very, very good results.

Bacterial canker we've controlled with hydrogen peroxide and epsom salts. Cherry slug is a fly and this year I used hydrated lime and we probably cleaned up 95% of the problem. Our neighbours and everyone around had immense brown rot problem. We don't see any here.

To control insects I've been using diatomaceous earth. We had a garden weevil that got into a block of cherries and ate the skin off them. It was a really good block of cherries so we got into the weevils with Carbaryl Lorsban. It didn't knock out all the weevils but it did knock out all our predator mites and we ended up with defoliated trees.

After this happened, a local agronomist told us that they used to use diatomaceous earth in wheat silos for weevils. We got a silicon product from NutriTech Solutions, put it out as a foliar spray and it worked. Since then I've been using an imported a product called diatomate from the USA and I think it's working very well. We don't have to spray for cherry mite any more.

So, from what I'm hearing, you've got things under control in your cherry orchard. Is that right?

No. We've still got one major problem that I haven't yet got under control.

We've eased most of the problems, even though the market for cherries has become much more demanding than it used to be. People want bigger, harder cherries. Some of the cherries we grew 10 years ago wouldn't be saleable now because they're soft and small.

We prune our trees much more to reduce the crop load. We put a lot more calcium on to make the cherries firmer. We choose varieties that aren't soft. Consumers are asking for something that's really hard to produce. I want to crack it. I think organic matter and soil biology are the keys to doing that.

We're exporting our cherries to Asia, and our exporting agent told us that she was going to stop doing it because of the poor quality of cherries in Australia. Ours were the exception. She thought our cherries were outstanding. That was nice to hear.

One big problem is that for the past three years we've had rain during early summer and our cherries are splitting because of the rain. We've still got the splitting problem to solve and it may be the hardest one of all, but I'm dogged and determined. I'm a bit like a dog with a bone. Conventional farmers would probably think there is no solution. With a biological approach, there's the suggestion that solutions are available and it's just a matter of finding them. That's what we're trying to do. Trying to solve the problems like this one is like having an obsession. It doesn't leave you. I want answers and I'm still looking for them in relation to my cherry splitting problem.

Right at this point I'm pretty unhappy because we lost cherries in December last year. With the cherries we've really taken a beating with the rain and the heat and, as John Pannon used to say, "You can't get a good result if you keep doing the same wrong thing." My tests keep coming back to the one thing: silicon and calcium. We've been putting our potassium silicate in the compost and we've been spraying it on as well for the past two years. This year I'm doing a ground application for the first time. I put this out last February.

I'm starting to think that the silica has got to be applied at or before flowering to get into the cells. Hugh Lovel, who is helping me correct this problem, says that silica is like the mortar that holds a brick wall together, so I'm thinking that foliar sprays are too little, too late. At flowering the cell structure is established, so we need to have the silica available before then. I'll make sure that happens this year and we'll see whether the theory is right.

I'm also talking to Neville Simcock over in Mt Gambier who tells me he's discovered the reason for cherries splitting and has an answer to the problem. He's been over to check out the farm and I'm waiting to hear what he thinks I should do. In the meantime we're doing all we can to ensure that we get a crop next summer. We're looking to trial rain covers, which will shed some of the water during summer storms. There's a system that has been developed in Germany but it costs $80,000 per hectare. Something similar is being developed in India at a fraction of the cost.

The theory says that if we get everything right, we'll get a crop. Theory is fine, but we've not solved all the problems yet, and at the end of the day we've got to do whatever it takes to ensure our crop is able to be harvested and sold, and if covering helps, then that's a good solution.

How do the surrounding farmers view what you're doing?

When we've had field days I've said, "Well, I haven't put on any insect spray." Their reaction? No reaction at all. Total silence. They don't ask any questions.

I think it's because there are established channels of information: the agronomist, the sales organizations, the Department of Primary Industry. I'm the wrong source of information.

If you had advice for someone wanting to do what you've done, what would that advice be?

Don't do it for the money. It's not about money, it's about the challenge.

You can't do it on your own. You need a coach or a mentor, and that's something that goes against the grain for most farmers, who are very indepenent. There are plenty of people who are willing to share. It might be someone who just helps you with your thinking rather than with the technical aspects. Changing is about being receptive to new ideas.

Some companies have their hands in your pockets, so it's a good idea to do your research and find the right people. I've had lots of advisers but few of them have been able to help me with the specifics of cherry growing. Get a good mentor who can help you with the specifics of your farm to achieve environmental balance. Cheryl Kemp helps me a lot.

Where are you going from here, Kym?

Our trees have had many years of struggle when we were farming conventionally. I want to see what will happen when we start from scratch and do things right, from the beginning. We're planting more trees now and that's going to be interesting.

We need to get the organic matter higher. I'd love to get it up to 10%. If we can continue to use peas and beans and possibly sorghum and mow it down, we can put huge quantities of organic matter into the orchard and make that happen. We might even grow lucerne.

Integrated Pest Management theory says that you identify the worst four things you're doing on your property and avoid doing these four things. I think we can use the same principle with what we're doing. I think RoundUp is No 1. Using RoundUp has slowed down our progress. It's been like an anchor dragging us down. It affects the water table, the soil life and destroys mycorrhizal fungi. Perhaps in hindsight we'll look back and say, "That wasn't a good thing to do." Hindsight allows us to learn. Once we do learn, we have to move on.

In the early days Grandpa used to push over the scrub and plant swedes and turnips. They didn't have to water much and there were few weeds. After 2 or 3 years doing that, he had to fertilize. That's when the weeds started to come. The chemical fertilizers he was using burnt off all the humus really fast. I explain to Dad that what we're doing is bringing the soil back to where it was before it was cultivated. He says, "That's good." We're trying to overcome 50 years of bad management because we were sold a lemon. It's going to take time to get things back to how they should be.

Where do you think horticulture in Australia is heading, Kym?

I think we're up against it. I think the cheaper Chinese imports are going to give the supermarkets an opportunity to buy from outside Australia to boost their margins. Growers will be the ones who'll suffer and I don't think the Australian government is into protecting growers.

I really worry about this because I think it's our health that's at risk. I was in China last June. They grow reasonable stuff but their soil's organic matter is 0.5 so that they have to be using a lot of chemicals, both fertilizers, pesticides and insecticides. We're getting dosed up food and I don't think the Australian public realises this. I don't think they realise that clean healthy good food grown at home is far better for us. The problem is that they won't have a choice. The supermarkets will just offer what they can get cheapest and no-one will have any idea what's going on.

People come and buy directly from us. We have shed sales during the cherry season. Sometimes it's hard to get up the drive with all the people coming. You hear them say, "I've never had cherries like this." They get to the end of the drive, turn around and come back to buy more. It's nice dealing with the public when the fruit is good.

It's been an interesting journey because I've been wearing a blindfold and dragging my father along behind me. My dad's hips have gone so he goes driving around and comes back and says, "I don't know what you're doing, son, but the orchard's looking a lot better than the neighbour's."

We don't have blinkers on. We don't believe that just because we're doing things more naturally it's necessarily going to be better or easier. We've lifted the bar and we're still trying to clear it. We get there occasionally, but my aim is to do it consistently. Grandpa did it back in the days before the soil was ruined, so it's definitely possible.

Thank you for sharing your journey with me.

Chapter 5

Eat Your Greens

Vegetable growers from many areas in Australia talk about the complexities of growing vegetables sustainably and share with us the problems some of them encountered in making the transition to biological, nutrition and/or biodynamic farming.

The farmers we interviewed were:

Tony Croft	*mixed vegetables*
Kenneth Keogh	*potatoes*
Ray Palmer	*mixed vegetables*
Wayne Edwards	*mixed vegetables*
David Slacksmith	*corn and pulses*

Tony Croft

Vegetable grower in Swan Hill, Victoria

Tony and Jenny Croft's farm is located 30 kilometres north west of Swan Hill and about 3 kilometres from the Murray River. This is flat, featureless, semi-desert country, which receives about 300 millimetres or 12 inches of rain a year. Without water from the Murray, they could not survive.

Tony is the son of a farmer and, except for a stint when he studied and later worked as a civil engineer, has worked as a farmer all his life. Until he was 25 years old he worked on his father's vineyard and vegetable farm, which was when Tony saw his father give up after hail destroyed his crop three years in a row. "I determined that I'd never be in a position where one event, like a hailstorm, could destroy my whole year's work. It's hard enough to work your butt off for 12 months, and see all your work come to nothing, so that you have to do it all over again for another 12 months. But three years in a row was just too much for dad. It destroyed him."

As a civil engineer, Tony was involved in designing properties, irrigation systems and soil improvement strategies for large farmers and a few smaller ones. When he stood back and looked at what he was doing, he realised that most of these farmers weren't doing things the way he thought was right. He decided there had to be a better way to grow things, so he decided to buy a place of his own and put into practice the ideas he'd developed as a farmer, civil engineer and farming consultant. He purchased his farm in 2001.

You've chosen to buy a farm in a fairly difficult part of Australia, Tony. What made you choose to come here?

It was probably an accident more than anything else. I've actually bought three adjoining properties so that we now have 140 acres, which is pretty big for an organic farm. This first block I bought by pure chance. It was owned for 80 or 90 years by one family and was pretty neglected because the owners were quite elderly. They'd grown grapes for sultanas. It was organic by neglect, which suited my purpose.

We actually bought it to grow lavender. I did some numbers and thought, "Yes. Lavender would be nice to grow". When I looked into it a bit further I realised that was a silly thing to do and we decided to grow organic vegetables, which fitted broadly into our life philosophy, which is "Food for living and nutrition for life."   That's also our business motto and what we try to achieve: good healthy vegetables and nutrition for life, and we're half way there. At least we're on the way. I think we do a very good job.

Initially Jenny and I thought, "What are we going to do to fix the soil and how should we go about it?" We booked a couple of tickets and headed around the world to try and meet people who could help us.

We got as far as New Zealand where I was born and they said, "You've come to the wrong place! Go back to Australia. That's where you'll find your answers." So that's what we did. We came back and met a woman called Elaine Ingham. She taught us about what to do and what not to do. In the early days it was more about what not to do. In my travels I also met up with a fellow by the name of Dr Arden Andersen. He comes to our place whenever he visits Australia. He's our mentor. We try to practise what he and Elaine taught us as much as we can.

Jenny had cancer, which was a major factor in our decision to go organic, and it came back again last year, which caused us to drop the ball for a few months. We're still behind the eight ball with weeds and not much planted.

What problems do you experience because of the physical environment?

This is a semi-desert area. We get 300 millimetres of rain a year, so we depend on water from the Murray River. The biggest problem is getting enough water flowing down the Murray so that we have consistency of water supply. The water was cut off earlier in the year, which cost us a lot of money. That's our biggest concern. We're hoping the politicians don't try and divert too much of it for use in the towns and cities.

We're trying to keep the wind out of our farm. We probably lose 35% of our crops through wind. It's only in the last 10-15 years that we've had major dust storms. We're putting in trees that are native to the area. We've put in 1,500 tree lots around the property, dividing it up. It's a sort of hedge. We're doing it when we can afford to and when we have water available.

When I was designing farms it was one of the things I used to recommend: try and keep the wind out. A few years after buying this place I looked at it and thought, "Gee. Why aren't I doing what I used to tell others to do?" So we started, but it was when we had the water restrictions, so it was an uphill battle.

Another problem is too little organic matter in the soil. We put in cover crops as often as we can, but because we've had limited water we haven't been able to do that as much as we we'd like to for the past few years. We compost a lot of our own stuff to get the organic matter back into the soil. We've cut our water use down dramatically because of the increased soil organic matter and the techniques we use. We've increased our production by 1000% using the same amount of water that we were using when we first bought the farm eight years ago.

What level of organic matter do you have?

We've got 2·5% now and we started with 0·5%. It's a big improvement. We get coal overburden from Yallourn and mix it with compost into the soil. Compost is becoming harder to get as people start to realise it's not a bad way to farm.

What about the mineral content of the soil?

We put on calcium and a bit of sulphur, but we mix that in the compost. The soil is short of sulphur. Any mineral we need to put in we mix it in our compost and then we put it out.

Do you do soil tests?

We do them once a year. We put a lot of foliar sprays on to try and fix any mineral deficiencies.

Do you do leaf tests?

We don't. I just look at what's growing and say, "This is what we're going to do." I get it pretty right usually. We do a lot of testing on the farm with the brix meter. I'd rather put the money I'd spend on leaf tests fixing the carrots rather than doing lots and lots of soil tests and leaf analyses. If we put on a foliar spray we can trace it within the hour just using our brix meter.

We make up the foliar spray mix and trial it on our test plots. We might make up different batches of fish and seaweed and stuff like that and sea minerals using varying ratios and concentrations, spray the different mixes on the test plots and go and check the brix an hour later. We know that the plants have taken up the minerals when the brix levels go up. If the brix level doesn't go up then we change the mix. That's how we work out what the plant wants. The plant tells us. We always test on our small plots before we spray stuff out.

Are sea minerals sufficient?

Sea minerals are fantastic. We put on some humic acid, some humates and an all-purpose sea mineral mix we get from TNN in Stanhope, Victoria. We mix this with liquid calcium, which is a real fine powder. We actually put all our fertilizers out through the sprinklers.

We soil drench a lot. We have a big mister that runs off the tractor that lifts the water 50 feet into the air so it covers a bigger area and we can do the farm in a couple of hours. It sounds like an aeroplane when it's running.

How do you control weeds?

We mainly use backpackers. Weed pressure is getting worse and that's because we dropped the ball a while ago when Jenny's cancer came back. Actually Jenny's cancer is one of the reasons why we're organic growers. Since she first got cancer we've been hell bent on eating right.

We've got mechanical weed chipping implements to do as much as possible. Carrots are very labour intensive as far as taking out the weeds in between the carrots so we use hand weeders. We're looking at getting a GPS so we can get really close to the carrot rows with our machines, but we're waiting for the technology to be absolutely proven before we go and spent a lot of money.

When they cut the water we didn't plant and I don't like seeing soil with nothing in it. This year we've had more vacant land than we've ever had before because of our water problem. We've got rockmelons and pumpkin in at present. We're planting parsnips and we're just putting the last of the beetroot in. We're starting to plant lettuces from seed. We work all year round basically.

What about the economic environment? Do you have any major problems there?

The Australian organic market can be flooded really easily. Finding markets is our biggest problem, even though we're A grade certified organic.

What sort of price premium do you get?

The price is a fair bit more than we'd get for vegetables grown conventionally, but I'm not exactly sure how much conventional carrots sell for. There's a good reason for the price premium. A conventional farmer can go out and spray his weeds and that will cost him $50. To do the same job costs me $16,000. Hand weeding costs a lot more than killing weeds with poisons. The price really should be 50% more than the conventional market pays, but the conventional market is too cheap. They're getting the same or less than they were 5 or 6 years ago. I know that Coles want to put a 10% premium on organic food. That will kill the industry because we can't survive with that sort of price.

We sell all over Australia, using only a couple of agents. There's no point sending to everyone because you only compete with yourself and flood the market.

One of the things we've been trying to make happen is to develop a much closer one-on-one relationship with the people who buy our stuff. We know that people mishandle the produce. They don't look after it and it looks shabby in the shops. That's why we went to the trouble of buying our semi-trailers. We load straight into the truck and take it down to the cold rooms. We've got our own keys so we can put everything straight in. We look after it as best as we possibly can. I've no idea what happens after that. At one stage we were putting a little "How to take care of your organic carrots" leaflet in the boxes to try and inform people how to look after them. Hopefully that hit a chord with a few people.

If we have an economic downturn, there are going to be a lot of people who will continue to buy organic, but there'll also be a group of people who'll say they just can't afford it. I hope that's not going to be the case, but even so, I'd like to see a bigger market.

How much of your land is under crop at any one time?

Not a lot right now. We usually have 5 to 6 hectares of carrots and we pull them out and replace them constantly.

Do you grow the same crops in the same land?

We rotate a bit from time to time but I've been a bit different and a bit controversial when it comes to crop rotation. We're member of the BFA (Biological Farmers of Australia) and according to their rules we're meant to have a 3-year rotation.

I know we've improved our soil a lot. I look at the ground and look at the crops we grow and see how well they hold up all the way through. Since 2001 we've had 7 crops of carrots in the same area. You don't have to rotate if the soil is right. If you've got a healthy soil it will actually look after the pests and diseases in the crop. When we make a mistake, and we've done that, we'll get a patch of carrots, which will show us we've made a mistake. We keep pretty good records, so we know what's we've done to cause the problem. When we cause a problem then we're stuffed.

We don't side dress with fertilizers, we broadcast across the whole field. We use a fertilizer called Seamungus, which is good but I don't like the fact that it is pelletised.

We've got a lot of wide wheel tracks here and we try to keep the same beds forever. Where we drive the tractor is where we always drive the tractor.

Before you started growing organically, what problems did you perceive would cause the greatest problem?

I didn't think about the risks.

What about pests?

I didn't think about them either. It's strange, isn't it, because you've just asked a really good question? I can only answer it by saying that I strongly believe that if you're really healthy, you're strong. Healthy plants won't get sick. We know for a fact that when we stuff up a crop it gets sick and there's nothing we can do to fix it.

We bought about 250,000 seedlings from a nursery and they were sick and just didn't grow. We had to plough them in. That hurt. I think nurseries have to lift their game if they're going to supply organic farmers. The brix level of those seedlings was 1·2 to 2 and it should have been 10. There was nothing we could do to fix that. We tried. I believe we're better farmers as a result of trying but we couldn't bring them back.

This has been the first year that we've had a problem with pests and diseases and I believe it's because we bought sick seedlings. Also the seed we're getting is not as good as it should be either. It's small. Because we're organic we don't get the best of anything from the conventional people. That statement might be absolutely untrue but it's what I perceive sometimes. All the big growers get the good seed and we get what's left. That's why I'm looking into growing my own seeds and seedlings.

This year we're going to grow from seeds, which is going to be a bit more work for us because of weed pressures.

Are you going to plant the seeds directly rather than transplanting?

Yes. If you hear me swearing you'll know it didn't work!

If you were to give advice to someone who's starting out, what would you say to them?

It depends on what they want out of it but I think the most important thing is to go into it for the right reason.

We did it to provide good food for people. We're a full commercial operation. We have our own semi-trailers. We employ 11 or 12 people and sometimes as many as 15 or 20.

It's important to understand that if you're a conventional grower, used to farming out of a can, those days are gone if you want to grow organically. You've got to be a lot more pro-active rather than reactive. You have to have everything ready before you plant and that includes your soil.

What do you mean by "grow out of a can"?

If you've got a problem you go to the store and get a can of something to fix it.

Are conventional farmers taking notice of what you're doing?

Absolutely. There's a change happening. Some commercial farmers are really looking at what we're doing. Others are starting to go down this path. There's no doubt about that at all. When our farm's looking good it surprises people who conjure up the idea of an organic property being overgrown. Ours looks like a normal commercial property that grows vegetables. It looks no different, but the soil is very different.

Is there something you're doing that we haven't yet talked about?

Something I'm thrilled about is that we've got mycorrhizal fungi growing on our farm at present and I don't know of anyone else who's doing that. We found it on some fat hen.

Have you inoculated with mycorrhizal fungi?

We used to but I'm not sure that we can grow it out of a can successfully. We grow mycorrhizal fungi from a powder form. We do our own compost tea brews and spray them out.

How often do you spray compost tea?

We used to do it a lot but we stopped for the last 2 years because it was really hard to manage. Now we're cranking it up again.

When you say "hard to manage", what is it about brewing compost tea that's hard to manage?

If the bacteria level isn't right after 5 hours I don't use it. It has got to be ready and it has to be ready at a time when I can use it. Sometimes it's ready in the middle of the night and there's no one to put it out. All the time we were doing it we were doing a really good job of it and now we've learnt not to be quite so fussy. We put in fish, compost from Jack Waterman in Lismore, aloe vera, fulvic acid, FFS from NutriTech Solutions and molasses

We don't try and get the number of fungi and bacteria in the brew up to the maximum level any more. We get it out when it's close and when we have the time and the daylight to do it. We try and do a compost tea brew once a month and get at least 3 applications on per crop.

Is there anything else you're doing?

What we've also done since we bought the place is to change the width of our growing beds. They used to be 1.5 metres and we've gone to 2 metres because the cost of running tractors up and down the paddocks is lowered. It cost a lot of money to convert over, but I think it's been really worthwhile.

I'd also like to start treating our water before we spray it out. The water quality is pretty good but I'd like to put an energy charge through it. There's a group called Hydrosmart that's just brought a product out. I'd like to try it.

What is it about growing vegetables that you enjoy, Tony?

I love the challenge of growing good vegetables - good quality vegetables that people like. It's a really challenging industry. I love doing what I'm doing. I work really hard but I absolutely enjoy it and our son Sean and his wife Jacinta have just come to join us on the farm, which makes it even better. The thing I really like is that it's so mentally stimulating. Going out into the paddock and finding a problem and then finding the solution. That's the sort of challenge I enjoy.

We're starting to diversify a bit so we don't have to work so hard. We're starting to grow a few table grapes because we've been asked to do it by a number of people in Melbourne. We've put some in but it's difficult for us because we're not geared up for permanent crops. I believe it's a good idea to do one thing and do it properly, but growing vegetables is pretty hard to do.

Your story is really inspirational, Tony. Thank you for sharing it.

Ray Palmer

Vegetable and strawberry grower in the Granite Belt in Queensland

Ray Palmer purchased his grandparents' 120-hectare property in 2001. Mostly remnant bush, the property has about 9 hectares of arable land. Ray and his wife Samantha grow vegetables on about 4 acres of land and have a house cow which keeps down the grass on the remainder. The farm is at The Summit, which is aptly named, being the highest point in the Granite Belt in south-east Queensland. The area, on the border of New South Wales, is a major food producing area where vegetables, grapes, apples, pears, stone fruits and berries are grown

Ray studied horticulture at Gatton College, then worked as a research assistant with the Department of Primary Industry before moving to Growcom, which was previously known as the Queensland Fruit and Vegetable Growers

Association. Before starting out as a farmer, Ray had lots of theoretical knowledge but not a lot of practical experience.

What caused you to become an organic vegetable grower, Ray?

My uncle is a conventional farmer but he has a very strong interest in permaculture and that got me interested in those principles.

When I was studying, I just wanted to find out as much as possible about alternative farming methods. At Gatton that interest wasn't always appreciated. I did one assignment where I suggested that the ultimate goal for integrated pest management was to eliminate pesticides. That suggestion went down like a lead balloon. I felt I was marked very harshly on the assignment. The lecturer didn't like the idea of eliminating pesticides at all.

The Department of Primary Industries was reasonably helpful. I was working under a pathology researcher called Peter Stephens and he was researching organic farming and alternative strategies in between his mainstream projects. There are people within D.P.I. who are interested in organic farming, but if it's just one or two individuals within a much larger organization there's not a lot they can do.

Another significant influence was winning a scholarship to go to the USA to look at organic farms in California and Oregon. The major thing I took away from that was that what happens in the USA is generally followed in Australia not long after. For a long time there's been concern that small farms are dying out, being replaced by huge corporate farms. What we saw in the USA was that there are a lot of small farms that are still doing well. They're organic, diverse and they do all the marketing themselves: consumer-supported agriculture schemes, market stalls, box schemes. Seeing what they were doing was a real wake-up moment for me.

Tell me about the physical environment of the area where you have your farm.

We're just on the western side of the Great Dividing Range, which means we get unreliable rainfall which can come in the form of savage hailstorms. We're very prone to early and late frost events. We've had frosts as late as November and as early as March. The long-term average rainfall is 850 mm but this year it's been much lower. My dams are almost empty.

Soil is sand or sandy loam. It's not very fertile but the pH is 6·2. We're short of all the minerals. Anything the plants need we have to supply. The only thing we've got plenty of is iron. The CEC level is less than 10 and the calcium / magnesium ratio is about 8:1 and it should be 5:1 for a sandy soil.

What do you do to build up the fertility of your soil?

We do soil tests every year.

We're now using a custom-blend compost made for us by a company called Ausmin. They're based in Warwick. In addition to animal manure they add sulphate of potash, natural phosphate, boron, dolomite and lime. I also use a lot of liquid blood and bone and seaweed, which help a lot with trace elements. Liquid blood and bone is good stuff.

I've tried to save money on fertilizers. From time to time I've not put enough out and had poor results because of it. Before we started using the organic compost custom blend our tomato production was extremely disappointing. The difference in yield between the different fertilizing methods is absolutely amazing. We also had a really bad nematode problem, which seems to have resolved itself now that we've changed to a compost-based fertilization programme.

There's a huge benefit to be gained from paying for better quality fertilizer. You don't get anything in return unless you do it right, and that's something I'm learning slowly.

How often do you fertilize your vegetables?

Ideally weekly, with liquid blood and bone, fulvic acid and molasses but I haven't been doing that for a while because my fertigation system became redundant when the dam level dropped to the point where my big pump intake pipe was sitting in mud.

Do you use compost teas?

Not at this stage. My spray gear is not set up to put them out. With my trickle irrigation system I'm a bit worried about putting compost teas through them because they might block things up. I do use other microbial mixes. I use trichoderma to help with powdery mildew as well as whey, which contains lacto-bacilli.

How do you control weeds?

This year I've used quite a lot of bio-plastic, which is a plastic made out of proteins derived from maize. It breaks down when you dig it in and just disappears.

It's expensive. It costs about 50c for a metre in a roll that's about 1.2 metres wide. Laying it is easy. I just hitch it onto the 3-point linkage on the tractor and I can lay it on my own. I can do 100 metres in about 10 minutes. I lay it down with T-tape underneath and when we plant we walk along with a pointed stick and poke holes through it so the plant grows up through the hole. It's no more time consuming than planting in bare soil.

We weed using a wheel hoe or a hand hoe. Instead of planting with a machine we use a tool I designed myself. Compared to a really good machine, it's much slower but it cost me $10 to make instead of $250,000.

Do you practise crop rotation?

My crop rotation practice up till now has been on the principle of "rotation by randomisation". We've got things being planted and things being pulled out all the time. I grow about 2 crops a year in one piece of soil and then it goes into what Peter Andrews calls a "weedy fallow". I've tried to grow cover crops during the winter. We could grow triticale, barley, rye or oats, but because of our location, surrounded by bush and because we get frosts, any green area will attract rabbits, wallabies and kangaroos from miles in every direction. The whole mob would be on my patch of green so I wouldn't get enough to plough in as a green manure crop. I just allow the pioneer weeds that are endemic in this soil to grow.

Do you try to keep these animals out during the growing season?

We have some blocks fenced to keep the pigs in but parrots and wood ducks don't worry about fences so they get in and the pigs get out. We've had to cover our strawberries with wire hoops and hail netting, otherwise we wouldn't get a single berry.

What about other pests?

As far as grubs and insect pests, there are things allowed within the organic standards that help us to manage them. We grow a lot of different crops and it becomes a bit more difficult for pests to find a meal amongst all that. Nearly a third of our production area is under permanent cover and this provides a refuge for beneficial insects and spiders and they help us keep things under control ecologically.

How have you found out what to do to be successful?

The people at Ausmin interpret my soil tests and draw up a nutrition programme for me.

As far as knowing what to do, I don't see any point in re-inventing the wheel so I've just taken what I have seen others do and adapted it to our situation. The initial farm tour I did to the USA planted lots of seeds in my mind and I've spent many years putting them in place. I wasn't sure whether the model I saw overseas would work in Australia.

Last year we went to the north coast of New South Wales for a week away and we caught up with a couple, who have a small farm nestled under Lamington National Park. At that stage we were selling some of our larger lines to Eco Farms and a wholesaler in Sydney. The guys we visited were growing lots of different things and were marketing it all themselves. They showed us that we could make a living growing lots of different things and selling them at farmers' markets.

I became a supplier with Food Connect in Brisbane in 2006 and I'd probably not be farming if we hadn't come across Food Connect. When I started growing I'd had some experience but I didn't grow up on a farm and I made a lot of mistakes. I grew some things that weren't suitable for the wholesale market. Food Connect took them and paid me a good price for them, which helped a lot in those early years.

We also work with a couple of other growers from Stanthorpe and go to the Northey Street Markets in Brisbane. Northey

Street is a really good market, particularly during the summer months. We've started our own box scheme and we sell to a few health food shops and restaurants locally. We haven't sent anything to a fruit and vegetable wholesaler for over two years. When you're a small grower you can't afford to pay middlemen.

If you had some advice for someone wanting to do as you and Samantha have done, what would it be?

It helps to have a routine and stick to it. I'd tell people not to cut corners. When we were short of money I tried to save on fertilizers. I put too little out and had poor results because of it.

I'd tell people to become involved in what happens after their produce leaves the farm. If you want to grow stuff and give it to somebody else to sell, particularly if you're small, you're going to have a battle. There's a massive groundswell of people who want to become connected with the people who produce their food. It doesn't matter how you do it, but get closer to the people who are eating your food. It's important. That's the difference between organizations like Food Connect and farmers' markets and the big supermarkets.

Where do you see farming in Australia going?

Farming is going in two different directions. The conventional agribusiness model where big continues to get bigger looks to be fraying at the seams, but because we've got food distribution systems in place that are so geared up to support this model, it'll persist for as long as petroleum is affordable.

I see a groundswell of change coming from small and fast moving players who are gaining in importance and will continue to do so. Take Food Connect, for example. It's only been going for four years. It's a not-for-profit operation. It doesn't advertise. It distributes boxes through residential homes so it has no costly infrastructure to support and it's winning awards for sustainable practices and for developing an incredible business model. Now it's being replicated though out Australia. Food distribution operations like that are a sign of things to come, involving closer links between food production and food consumption.

Thank you for sharing your story with me, Ray.

Wayne Edwards

Vegetable, avocado and plum grower
From Manjimup in Western Australia

Wayne Edwards is an example of a totally committed farmer who risked not only his own farm but also the family farm to make the transition to organic farming methods.

As a member of a large family-owned vegetable growing operation, Wayne persuaded his parents and his sisters to change from conventional growing methods. It was a long, slow and painful process. He did it because he realised that the farming methods and the acid fertilizers they were using were destroying the structure of the soil they were farming. Wayne's problem was that back in 1998, information on how to work through the transition process was not readily available and neither were the fertilizer inputs that he needed to rebuild soil that had been intensively farmed for several decades. Wayne badly underestimated the investment needed and the time it would take to make the transition. In the beginning he also didn't realise that making a switch to organic farming would require not just a change of inputs but also a total reorganisation of all his farming systems.

Having successfully made the transition to organic growing methods, Wayne is now involved in biodynamic agriculture which he anticipates will take his farm to another level.

Tell me about your farm and where it's located, Wayne.

We're in an area of undulating hills 120 km from Bunbury and 300 km south from Perth. It's traditionally a fruit and vegetable production area. The soil is sand, gravel or loam over clay. It's reasonably good soil. We get about 800 mm of rain per year and it comes in winter. We rely on dams for irrigation water because there's no underground water here.

We've got two farms. One is a family owned farm and the other, which is smaller, is the one I bought in 2008. The big farm is 750 acres. There are about 500 acres of cleared land and the remainder is bush. We crop half or less of the cleared land.

Mum and Dad are still involved in running both farms. My son, Jason, sister Lee, and Darren all work full time. My partner, Anita, divides her time between the farms, depending on where she's most needed. We hire backpackers for picking when the workload gets especially heavily.

Our main production areas are under center pivot irrigation. Each pivot covers about 24 hectares. We rotate between the pivot areas and sow the areas we're not using to lucerne. We grow a variety of vegetables and harvest all year round. We grow onions, cauliflower, potatoes, broccoli, kale, beetroot and three varieties of cabbage. We've also got 30 breeding cows and 300 breeding ewes for lambs.

My property is smaller. It's 40 hectares and it's where I live. I've got 2,000 avocados, 1,000 of which were planted in 1997. I've also got 3 ½ hectares of late variety plum trees.

What's the history of the family farm?

The farm was bought when Dad was quite young. The original farm was much bigger. There were three brothers. They did all the clearing and they started off with cattle. They had a lot of cattle. They grew potatoes on the wet flats without irrigation and then they planted fruit trees. Later the farm was split up and each brother got a share.

We're shareholders in a packing-shed in town that exports cauliflowers to S.E. Asia. In the early 1970s and through the 1980s vegetable growing for export was very profitable because of the favourable exchange rate. We were growing 100 acres of cauliflowers and 60 acres of potatoes on this farm. The potatoes were grown for a potato chip factory in town, which started off being privately owned. Edgells, and later Simplott, took over the factory. It's now called Bendotti's Enterprise. In the 90s, when the dollar became stronger, profits from exporting vegetables declined. Where there used to be 15 packing sheds for vegetables grown in the area, there's now only one.

What sort of cultivation practices were commonly used around the district in the 70s and 80s?

We used super phosphate on the potatoes. MAP and DAP, which were 20% nitrogen and 15% phosphorus, were commonly used, as was muriate of potash. Lime and dolomite were used occasionally. We did use lots of trace elements, including copper and zinc. We sent samples of our soil to CSBP, a fertilizer company, and they'd do an analysis of how much fertilizer we needed. We basically relied on their recommendations. We'd put on about ¾ tonne of fertilizer to the hectare every time we planted a crop and then we'd side-dress the cauliflowers when they were growing. The trace elements were supposed to last for between 2 and 5 years. We used liquid fertilizers as well as foliar sprays and we occasionally made our own which was a complete brew and we'd spray that on the cauliflowers once a fortnight.

How did you control pests and weeds?

We used heptachlor on the potatoes to combat black beetle and white fringe weevil, both of which are soil-based bugs. We used Nemacure for nematodes. Both of these pesticides were very toxic to us and to the soil. Occasionally I'd fumigate the soil to sterilize everything.

For the broccoli we used a very powerful knock-down spray to wipe out everything that was living. Sometimes we'd use Lorsban. We'd spray whenever the bugs appeared. In spring that was probably once a week and in winter we sprayed once a month. We used something called Ambush. Every year the chemical companies would bring out a product with a different name.

We used herbicides, including RoundUp, and then some strong sprays after that to keep the crops clean. There was a product called Goal, which had a residual effect. We could transplant broccoli seedlings into soil that had that sprayed on it.

What caused you to change?

I had a mate, Neville Simcock, who was selling biological fertilizers and microbes and I started talking to him and asking what he thought. Also I was a member of a soil improvement group and we were looking at stopping soil erosion and taking care of the soil. The more we looked at how to stop erosion, the more we realised that the way we were farming was creating hardpans. Our farming methods and the acid fertilizers we were using were destroying the structure of the soil, which should have been like a sponge rather than acting as a barrier that prevented water from soaking into it.

With the soil improvement group we kept hitting the idea that the best way to protect the soil was to protect the surface and have deep drainage. That was absolutely the opposite of what we were doing.

Gradually I moved towards biological farming, which is a mid-way step between conventional and organic strategies. I started in 1998. In the beginning the first thing I did was to deep rip the ground to get rid of the hardpan so that the soil below the hardpan could interact with the topsoil. Deep ripping allowed oxygen to get down deeper and it allowed the roots and the water to penetrate.

Compaction and hard pans are caused by over tilling, so I started going over the ground fewer times. Instead of spraying the fields with RoundUp I started incorporating the green manure into the soil so that that I was actually feeding the soil at the same time that I was getting the ground prepared. Sometimes the ground cover would just be what had grown since the previous crop. Sometimes it was oats that I had put in specially. I bought a Howard square plough that just turned 10 cm of topsoil over and turned the crop under the soil. Since then I've actually sold that plough because now I don't think it's the right way to plough the soil.

I was still using RoundUp and herbicides. I started reducing the amount I was using by adding some sugar and molasses to the sprays so that they were less harmful to the soil and the plants. There were stages when I was using humic and fulvic acid. I was also using molasses when I added fertilizers.

I changed my fertilizers. I did trials with and without MAP and I cut down my MAP application rates and added sugar. I worked out that the acid fertilizers only lasted in the ground for a couple of months before they locked up. By adding sugar I was able to prolong the effectiveness of the chemical fertilizers by creating a buffer that stopped it locking up so quickly.

I wanted to promote biologically grown produce as a transition step because I thought changing to growing organically was too hard. I had one crop I was growing organically and by chance I ran two advertisements at the one time. One advertised biologically grown produce and the other organically grown produce. The organic market was very small but even so I got a better response for the organic produce and none at all for the biologically grown produce. As a result I basically dropped the biological system and went straight to organics, even though the market was still very small and we were geared to a big turnover.

We changed a lot of things in what I now see was a transition phase, and in hindsight I went too far and too fast with the changeover. Yields dropped right off and the cost of growing produce went through the roof. I now understand that you have to increase soil inputs markedly as a first step because the chemical farming process you've been using has stripped everything from the soil. High levels of inputs are needed to provide enough energy for the crops to use when they grow.

I purchased some biological fertilizer from Victoria. It was called Triple 6 and it contained 6% phosphorus and 6% potassium, nitrogen and other carbons and microbes. Some of the phosphorus was soft rock. We added trace elements, depending on what our soil tests showed, to bring everything into balance.

When we started this process our soil organic levels were around 2%. We've built them up to somewhere between 5% and 6% and I don't believe it needs to be any higher than that.

During the next 8 years we struggled to stay afloat. It was as if I was just pouring money down the drain. I didn't have a cost effective process for growing organically and I wasn't getting the yields or the quality I wanted either. Basically it took 8 years of losses before the penny dropped and I started to learn how to manage this system properly and efficiently and how to make money out of it. It took me that long to learn the ropes. It involved changing all our strategies for running the farm.

We were growing crops conventionally and organically at the same time so I was switching from one system to another all the time. That was difficult. The reason I was hanging onto the conventional areas was to maintain a cash flow to keep the farm running. At the same time the prices for conventionally grown vegetables were going down.

We had a 260-acre property 7 kilometres away. That was where I lived. When things got difficult we sold 100 acres of that farm. That was in 2002. In 2004 we sold the rest, including my home. That helped us to stay afloat but it didn't solve the problems. A year later I sacked all three of my full time workers.

I did go back later and ask one of the people I'd sacked to stay on and he agreed to do that, but without all the extra workers I had to go out and do the work myself. That was the best thing I could have done. By doing everything myself I actually started planting more stuff. Every job I did I found short cuts on how to do it and how to work with time saving strategies. With the organic vegetables I doubled the fertilizer rates and I started using compost. The more compost I put on the crops, the more they responded.

I realise now that in the transition phase the soil is very hungry and you need to build up the levels of organic matter very quickly. I used green manures and compost. The chemical fertilizers we had used had just ripped the carbon out of the soil, which is like robbing the bank all the time. I really needed to incorporate green manures and add compost and use soft fertilizers to build up the carbon levels.

In my second year of growing organically I imported a container load of fertilizers from New Zealand. I bought bio-phos, which was a biologically activated phosphate. I bought a fish product that was made using a cold process. I bought kelp and trace elements. It cost a small fortune but I saw some brilliant results from using the right fertilizers. That got me really excited. I started to see the potential. Fertilizers like the ones I bought from New Zealand are now available everywhere but they weren't back then.

What sort of application rates were you using for compost and fertilizers?

In the early days I was probably only putting on 5 or 10 cubic metres of compost per hectare. I increased the quantity and in some areas I was putting on 40 and 50 cubic metres per hectare. That was a bit much. I gradually learned how much to put on and I believe 15 to 30 cubic metres per crop per hectare is the right amount. Sometimes, when we've had a really strong crop of a vegetable like broccoli I mulch that into the soil and follow it with potatoes. When we do that we don't need to put much on at all.

In the beginning I was trying to save money by using less fertilizer, but in the end I realised I should have been using more, rather than less.

I'd been on several bus tour workshops in the USA, New Zealand and NSW and visited farms where they talked a lot about minimum inputs, which was where I got the idea that it was possible to reduce fertilizer inputs. From my own experience I know that you've got to get the soil working and to do that you have to increase your inputs as well as having high levels of bacteria and fungi. When you put on a lot of compost you really allow a lot of microbes to get into the soil.

Have you done anything other than adding compost to build the microbe population in the soil?

I've bought lots of microbes and mycorrhizal fungi and a few other blends of microbes. I make cocktails of different varieties. I spray them regularly on the leaves and the soil.

I went through a couple of years of putting compost teas on the leaves and the soil, and now every year I put on a biodynamic prepared 500. I throw as much of a smorgasbord of everything I can at present and sometimes I overdo it. I should just be working with biodynamic preparations. With biodynamics you use the 500 a few times and compost. Biodynamics is a really different system and it's the next area I really want to study and work with. That's why I've got the new farm registered for biodynamics certification. I can apply the biodynamics principles there and start to understand it.

What are your strategies for controlling pests?

The only spray I use is in the broccoli for the diamond black moth and the white butterfly. I use BT on the brassicas, which is an allowable input. It's a bacterial spray, which goes on the leaves. The little larvae eat it and it upsets their stomachs.

I don't have any problems with potatoes. When I used all the chemicals I had black beetle and white fringe beetle. As the health of the soil improves those bugs just don't want to be there. I did have some potato moth in the potatoes a few years ago. It was a late season crop in February or March. The potato moths came in and I was at my wits end worrying what to do. I rang up a guy who works for the Department of Agriculture in Victoria and was involved with brassicas over here. He told me to collect some of the leaves with cocoons on them and send them across so that he could analyse them. I must have sent across 20 or 30 leaves. The results of their test showed that every cocoon had a parasitic wasp in it. None of those eggs would have hatched. The Ag Department guy said it was the only time he'd ever seen all the eggs attacked by parasites. The potato moths came into the crop in such numbers that they attracted the wasps and the wasps then destroyed all the eggs. I was thinking of spraying pyrethrum, but luckily I didn't spray, because that would have knocked out all the wasps.

A lot of the time when you get an insect problem it pays to stand off a bit, because the predators won't turn up unless the food source is there. I've got lucerne in one of the pivots and I was getting the lambs out one day on my motorbike and there were aphids all over the paddock. I couldn't find anything to explain why the aphids were there except that if a crop is high in nitrates it'll attract aphids. I took the sheep out of the paddock for a week, thinking that the urine might have been too rich in nitrates. A week later I went back and the whole paddock was full of ladybirds. They'd cleaned up the aphids and the problem was gone. Nature really co-operates to eliminate problems.

Have you found the cost of growing organically much higher than the cost of growing conventionally?

It's not much higher. In the early days I tried to make it cheaper and that didn't work. I swung back to putting on much higher levels of fertilizers and organic matter. It costs me more for fertilizers and microbes than it did when we were growing conventionally, but my costs of herbicides and insecticides are down to zero, so I save money there.

How long have you been happy with what you're doing?

Since 2007, which is three years. My organic produce now looks the same as or even better than the conventional produce that's available. I've completely switched to growing organically and I know it's the only way to go.

You've had a huge learning curve. Did you ever doubt that you were doing the right thing?

I had no doubt about what I was doing. I just wasn't doing it the way I should have been doing it.

How did your family react to what you were doing?

I was the driving force behind the changes and Mum and Dad certainly questioned what I was doing. They could see the long-term benefits and they could see we were moving in the right direction, but the transition process was very expensive and took a long time. We went forward as a group and I've been extremely fortunate to have parents and family who were supportive and encouraging. I'm still doing experiments all the time and trying to improve the way we do things.

What has been your greatest challenge?

From the beginning I should have been more aware of the market and the scale I needed to operate at. I thought the market wasn't large because there was no supply and that if I could push the market by growing a bit extra all the time, we might be able to increase the market size. A lot of retailers were telling us they couldn't buy organic produce. My strategy has worked but it took a lot longer than I expected. Even now, 2 tonnes of potatoes is what we can sell each week. It's not a huge market. There are times when you can't sell what you've grown because there just aren't enough people out there who want to buy it.

I could go into Coles and Woolworths but I'm trying to stay away from them and just supply smaller retailers. Obviously I could sell more if I sold to the supermarkets, but I don't like the way they operate. When you deal with them you have to accept that your prices will drop.

In respect of my farming practice, the biggest challenge has been getting the yields up and growing produce organically that looks as good as the stuff that's grown conventionally.

Do you sell just in Western Australia?

We sell all our vegetables in Western Australia. The avocados and plums from my farm go to the East. We're thinking about exporting to Singapore, but we're not ready to do that yet.

You've obviously been through a steep learning curve and have learnt a lot. Where did the information you needed come from?

I subscribe to both the Australian and American *Acres* magazines. I joined the Biodynamic Association. I joined

Biological Farmers of Australia. I went to workshops in Western Australia and in the Eastern states. I did a tour of American farms. I built close relationships with sustainable fertilizer companies and organic agronomists. My very good mate, Neville Simcock, was a lot of help in the early days and he still is. When I have a problem I confer with him. I know quite a few people around the place and I get information from everyone.

Tell me about your American tour.

It was a biological farming tour organized by Ken Bailey. Fifteen of us from all over Australia went on that trip. We visited twenty farms in the Mississippi area. All of them were different. The networking on the bus meant there was a great sharing of information about the soil and plants and about human health and its connection to the health of the soil.

The last farm we saw was an Amish farm. They were so advanced in their farming technology that 10 years ago, when I was there, they were making compost out of crops that were being grown for the purpose of making a specific type of compost for a particular crop. They were planning and organizing 2 years in advance for the crops they were planning to grow. They were using a variety of different energies. They had a probe in the soil while they were planting and they'd operate the fertilizer shute at different rates depending on the crop that was in the soil. They made the fertilizers themselves.

We started digging in the soil in a crop of corn and commented that we couldn't find any worms. We thought that indicated a problem. They told us: "When we see worms in the soil we know we've got a problem. We believe our soil has gone past the worm stage and is now in the high energy microbe phase." Our jaws just dropped. We've been taught all our lives the worms are the key to good healthy soil and they were telling us that when their soil has worms in it, it means it's going backwards. It opened up our minds to a whole different world. Hearing that and seeing what they were doing is one thing, but being able to achieve it myself is a different matter, though I guess that's what we're moving towards.

Are you doing things differently on your new farm?

Yes. I'm using biodynamic methods. With the avocados I'm just starting to see signs of phytophthera. I'm going to put on more biodynamic preparations and more fungi to help the soil. I'll put out lucerne hay as a home for the fungi and I'll add some fish fertilizer as well. The fish should stimulate the good fungi to grow and outnumber the bad fungi.

Bad fungi is a bit like having nematodes in the soil. Most, 80%, are good guys. The rest, the other 20%, are the bad guys. Instead of putting on a poison that will kill both the good and the bad guys you just have to feed the good guys and let them to the job for you. I'm planning to feed the good fungi so that they'll outnumber the bad fungi.

Is there something you feel strongly about that you haven't yet shared with us?

I've read a huge number of books and looked at all sorts of information, but one book I've come across that really struck a chord was Percy West's book called "Cancer Causes and Cures". He only died a couple of years ago. He was 105. He did a lot of experiments with his farm. By changing fertilizers he could put his sheep into a paddock with a low pH and they'd come back into the yard with cancers all over their ears and noses. Then he'd turn them into an alkaline paddock and all the cancers would go. For me, he really brought home the message about the difference between acid and alkaline farming.

We need to get our soil with a pH level between 6 and 6.5, which is perfect. It's the same pH our bodies should have. Soil is like our stomach. It takes care of the digestive process so it has to be slightly acidic. The rest of our body is slightly alkaline.

When you grow food in acidic conditions the makeup of that food is different from what it should be. Growing using organic or biodynamic principles creates food that has great energy and high nutritional value. If anyone is hesitating about making the transition to growing organically, they should just start. It just takes one step at a time. There are a variety of different ways of doing it and there are many people out there who want to help.

Basically we all are what we eat and if anyone is interested in being healthy and living a long and productive life, they must understand that what they put in their mouths affects their health. I don't want to be a farmer who grows food that doesn't make people healthy. At least half the food we eat should be alkaline, and that includes all the vegetables, particularly raw vegetables. Raw vegetables have so much more goodness than cooked ones.

The more you learn about the health of the soil, the more you understand about the health of your body and the relationship between the two. Sometime in the future I'd like to have people come to our farm to buy our produce. I'd also like to organize yoga, detox and raw food workshops and perhaps develop farm stay accommodation.

When others read your story, they'll be more informed about making the transition to organics. Thank you.

Kenneth Keogh

Potato grower on the Evelyn
Tableland in northern Queensland

Kenneth Keogh is a fourth generation farmer on the Evelyn Tableland area in Northern Queensland. With his father and his younger brother, Clinton, Kenneth raises cattle and grows potatoes on their 800-acre property, five hundred acres of which are cleared.

After a 2-year agriculture course at Burdekin Agricultural College, Kenneth worked on the farm for 10 years. He spent some time on one of the mines in Queensland before returning. Kenneth had always expected to be a farmer and it is something he is truly passionate about.

One of the highlights of Kenneth's farming experience has been a three week tour of American farms with medical doctor and agricultural consultant, Dr Arden Andersen, whose regular visits to Australia have convinced many conventional farmers to experiment with biological farming methods. For Kenneth, the thing that stood out most on that tour was that all the farmers he visited seemed to be happy with their lives and happy with what they were doing. This was in great contrast to Kenneth's experiences in Australia where he finds conventional Australian farmers are always complaining about something: the government, their crops, the weather or taxes.

Tell me a little about the history of your property, Kenneth.

My great-grandfather came from Ireland to Melbourne and then by horse and buggy to northern Queensland. He stopped for a while in the Burdekin country to cut cane and it was here that he met his wife-to-be before proceeding through to Ravenshoe. He must have been a very brave man. He liked the tableland area but was told not to try to farm there because the Aborigines were extremely hostile. To everyone's amazement he got on well with the Aboriginal tribes and worked with them.

Why do you think he chose the tableland area?

Good climate. Good soil. There must have been a lot of timber in the early days. Much of our property is cleared but the remainder is blue gum, bloodwood and stringy bark eucalypt scrub forest. The soil is red volcanic. The Evelyn Tableland area is usually hot because this is a tropical region, but in winter temperatures have been known to fall below freezing point at night because the tableland is 3,000 metres in altitude. Daytime temperatures are usually around the 25^0 - 30^0C mark, even in winter. Summer is wet, often very, very wet.

You seem to live in an ideal place for farming with plenty of water, good soil, moderate to high temperatures. Do you have any problems with the physical environment?

Weeds, such as wild hops, wild turnips and nutgrass are probably our greatest problem, and I firmly believe we've actually created the problem with our NPK farming methods. The other problem is that we have to work around the wet season with the potatoes. We plant as soon as the rain stops, before the temperatures start to drop, because it can get as low as -10^0C on the ground in winter.

What steps are you taking to overcome your weed problem?

I'm still working on that! I'm concentrating on trying to balance the soil minerals. I've seen other farms where they've used more of a biological approach than I have and their weeds aren't nearly as much of a problem as ours are so there's obviously a solution.

What do you consider to be your greatest problem on the business side of farming?

The biggest problem is definitely distance from major markets and the cost of freight. We send our potatoes by rail and sometimes by semi-trailer. The closest rail station is Innisfail.

What's been the biggest obstacle you've had to confront in making the change to a more biologically sustainable approach?

Opposition from my family has been the big challenge. Everyone says it can't be done. We did try to make the change a few years ago, but that was a disaster, and it's probably the reason why Dad and Clinton are so adamant that a biological approach won't work.

We did a soil test, applied a prescription blend to bring the soil into mineral balance, used leaf sprays, applied compost tea sprays for 2 to 3 months before and after we planted. It seemed to be working, but I think now that we didn't give it enough time. We probably should have been using compost tea for 2 to 3 years before planting to give the soil time to recover.

When we did our first inspection the young potato plants had up to 28 tiny potatoes forming which was great, but the plants just ran out of steam. When it came to harvest time, each bush only had 3 or 4 potatoes. We lost a lot of money with that trial and we did it on too big an area. The soil just ran out of nutrients to feed the plants.

I know now that our soil has been totally reliant on using NPK fertilizers and now, instead of going cold turkey as we tried to do then, I'm going through a process of weaning my crops off NPK. We've farmed here for 60 years with NPK and there's no way you can just switch from one approach to another. I still use NPK, but I'm starting to use other fertilizers and other strategies.

Our soil isn't dead but it's so close to it so as to not make any difference. All but dead! Even dad's commenting that the soil is getting harder and harder and lumpier and lumpier. He's gone back to using muriate of potash, which is going to make it even worse. I said to dad the other day, "Do you realise muriate of potash is what they use to harden air strips?"

If we don't do anything different we've got no choice but to pour on heaps of fertilizer, pour on heaps of water and then pour on a heap of poisons to kill the insects that come in. At the moment we're farming "hydroponically" in the soil. The soil is just holding the plants up but it's not providing any nutrients. What I'm doing is making a difference. I'm sure of that.

Recently one of my workers was ploughing one of the paddocks I'm just about to plant. I've been inoculating it with kelp and some sugars. When he left the area I've been improving and moved on to dad's area, he had to shift down a gear, which is proof that the soil is improving. I can't be too hard on myself. Evidence like that shows that we must be doing something right!

How long is it since you seriously started to change from traditional farming methods to a more biologically friendly approach?

I wanted to make the switch 25 years ago but didn't because of my family. That's why I went away mining. I came back but never got it out of my system. I'm not sure what made me so determined to do this but now I've decided that it's better to try something and fail than just keep doing what others want me to do. It's taken a long time and I did make an effort some years back, as I mentioned earlier, and that wasn't successful.

For the last two years I've been giving a lot more time to going down this track. I know that sounds pretty slack because I've wanted to do this for so long. I think I've finally realised that the people I'm dealing with who are into organic, biological, biodynamic methods are very different from your typical chemical fertilizer reps who just don't understand. They understand the "hydroponics in the soil" system and they can sell you plenty of chemicals and fertilizers, because that's what pays their salaries and pays for their utilities so that they can drive around.

I'm doing it despite what my dad and brother think.

What's been your major motivation for changing?

I'm not sure why I've wanted to go down the biological track. I remember that when I first came onto the farm there was one paddock of open pollinated corn and all the rest was hybrid corn, which produces a bigger yield than the open pollinated variety. The cockatoos wouldn't even land in one of the hybrid corn paddocks. They only ate the open pollinated variety. I thought something was going on for that to happen.

I suppose I really hate spraying chemicals. One of the chemicals I use, even with overalls, gumboots, respirator and gloves, always leaves me with a headache by the time I'm finished in the afternoon. I used to think that was my body saying, "You've got to get away from that stuff!"

Anther reason why I've gone down this path is because you have to ask the questions: "Why are more and more people getting cancer?" and "Why are people getting heart disease younger and younger?" Surely the cancer and heart disease has got to be because of the food. If the body is fed the right nutrition it can get rid of these diseases.

What are you doing differently from what your family wants you to do?

You could use the term "organic" as a broad term, but I like to describe what I'm doing as biological farming.

My brother's a hydraulics engineer. If a hose breaks, you can fix it and not think anything more about it. When you ask the question, "Why did it break?" you might find something wrong with the system. That's what I'm doing. I'm asking, "Why?" I'm looking to find what's wrong with the system.

I've been asking, "Why do the insects come?" and "Why do we get this disease pressure?" I'd really like to know the answer to the question, "What's going on that's creating these problems when it wasn't like this years ago?"

The problems are getting worse and worse. We've had to use stronger and stronger chemicals, but none of them fixes the problem. And we're not the worst. We're the only farmers in the area who don't put on fungicides and poisons to kill the nematodes. Everyone else is pouring poisons into the soil. It never used to be like that, so we're doing something awfully wrong. When I talk to the reps about that their answer is that these farmers are only doing it as an insurance policy. Some insurance policy! They're totally destroying their soils as an insurance policy!

But we're almost as bad. We seem to be putting on more and more chemicals. During the growing period we side-dress our potatoes twice. We have to do this just so we can get a crop. This is something new. We didn't have to do it in the past.

So now I'm working with a couple of different companies. I'm not using any one person's ideas. I'm developing the nutrient level of my soil by putting on fish preparations, which build up the trace elements and feed the micro-organisms in the ground. It's a form of hydrolysed fish and it has all the oil still in it. It's a liquid that's been biologically broken down.

We soil test before every crop. We're deficient in calcium, boron and zinc, so we add them. I use a composted blend of calcium and put it in my pig manure. I also add liquid calcium. The product is called Calsap. The calcium / magnesium ratio of our soil is 4:1 and it should be 7:1, so I have to keep working on that. I'm adding silicon as well.

I played around with microbe inoculation but I think I was a bit too impatient. The changes didn't happen fast enough. The fish and the kelp I'm using are high in microbes but I do want to get back into compost tea brewing and spend some time getting it right. I've realised from experience that changes don't happen overnight.

I'm also going to start using some biodynamic preparations. I'm planting by the moon, and spraying by the moon. I figure that if the moon can pull the tide in and out it must have some sort of bearing on things.

I did one trial composting minerals and pig manure and I had a very good and very quick response. As a result of this I've done a deal with the piggery, which is only 800 metres away, to get manure so that I can do more mineral and manure composting. It's a minimum disease piggery and they don't use hormones. I'm also about to start working with Yeoman's rippers to aerate the soil and put food into the soil.

I'm piecing together a whole lot of ideas from a variety of places to suit what's happening here on my farm. I figure that what I'm doing here might not necessarily be good in another area. It depends also on the inputs I can get that are reasonably priced. The cost of doing something is a major factor.

Are you still using poisons?

I'm using all the softer versions. The insecticides I'm using are more like bacteria and the insects come along and ingest that and they die. The stuff I'm using doesn't take out my beneficial insects so I'm relying more on the population of beneficials to breed up and help me. I've been doing that for 2 years now and it's worked very well. I've actually been doing it longer than two years but in the beginning it was a bit hit and miss. Now I'm serious.

What's the evidence that this approach is working?

Potato moth is a big problem. They leave a black line through your potatoes, which is not something customers want. In 6 acres, I only threw away a dozen potatoes that were damaged. I did have other problems and I'm not sure what happened there, but the potato moth was controlled really well.

To use this strategy you have to be able to shut your eyes a bit. There are still potato moths in the paddock. Because

I've been brought up very conventionally, I believed that as soon as you see a potato moth or a bug in the paddock you spray it. I'm learning now that there's an alternative. You can actually just let them be.

My soil tests provide evidence that we're doing something right. Carbon levels have started to come up, even though we're working the soil. People have told me that I can't get the carbon level up unless I turn the paddock over to pasture. In only 12 months it has come up by half a percent. The level of organic matter is 6%, which is good. The CEC (cation exchange capacity) level is still very low, but it's also starting to improve.

In the past I've been very hard on myself always asking, "What am I doing that this isn't working?" and "Why aren't I getting the size of potatoes the market wants?" But there have been a lot of positives. I'm getting beautiful skins on the potatoes. They're by far the best skins on the farm. Appearance is very good. And the soil is definitely getting softer.

Have your yields gone up in the last two years?

My answer's a "yes" and a "no". All the paddocks I've taken on are the worst paddocks on the farm. They're actually the paddocks that Dad walked away from because he said they wouldn't produce any more. I'm producing potatoes in them. I figured that if I'm going to make these ideas work and I can make them work on the worst areas, I should be able to turn around the better paddocks a lot quicker. By the time we start working on them, I will have learnt a few short cuts.

Where do you think farming in Australia is heading?

I'm not seeing any change, but I'm hoping that as people continue to get sicker younger, then surely some time the penny has to drop. If the farmers don't turn around and make what they're producing healthy, how is the country's population going to be healthy? I'm just working on making my soil healthy.

Thank you for sharing your story, Kenneth.

David Slacksmith

Corn, Soy, Sorghum and Azuki bean grower from Dubbo in Central NSW

David Slacksmith is still shaking his head about the direction his farming practices are heading and much of the time is reluctant to share what he is doing with "old style" farmers in his district. David believes in the power of radionics to help solve problems, eradicate pests, and identify the correct mix of elements that his soil needs. He is also working with biodynamics principles. We are fortunate that he has chosen to explain to us some of the extraordinary and almost unbelievable events that are changing the way he farms.

The son of a doctor who bought a large farm as his version of a "sea change", David runs his father's farm. A large area of the farm is irrigated and David grows corn, azuki beans and soybeans. He is gradually moving away from dry land wheat farming, preferring to develop the land as pastures for fat lambs.

David is a strong advocate for education and training for farmers so that they can make decisions based on a big picture view of the resources available.

Tell me a bit about yourself, David.

I grew up here in Dubbo. Mum was a nurse and Dad was a specialist in radiology but all he really wanted was to have a farm and he bought one a while back. It was a horse stud. Now at the age of 68 he's retired, and he's here every day making sure everything gets done the way he likes to see it done!

I went to Hawkesbury Agricultural College and did a degree in Land Economy. I then worked as a valuer for the State Bank of New South Wales for 7 years. I got a redundancy package, which was good because I enjoyed living in Sydney. I needed to be pushed to come back home to Dubbo and work on the farm.

Dad was actually the trigger that caused me to become a different sort of farmer from most of the guys around here. One day he threw down a folder and said, "Look at this. These are the bloody spray bills! I want you to halve the amount we're spending. Do what you have to do to find out how to halve the amount of spray we're using and maybe increase yields at the same time." It was a tall order.

The timing of this conversation was fortunate. I was doing a bit of reading and just touching on Albrecht's theories as a result of reading Neal Kinsey's book, *Hands on Agronomy*. Kinsey was writing for middle-America farmers and he set out the calcium / magnesium ratios and talks about sulphur and trace elements and how they work. I got really interested in that because it seemed to imply that if you balance your cations you then look after soil structure, and this is a good way to stop some varieties of weeds coming up. Once you no longer need to have weeds with long tap-roots to aerate your ground, they stop growing. I hadn't previously thought that weeds might be a response to a particular soil condition.

Not long after the conversation with Dad, I took a 3-month job scouting sweet corn. In that job I went round visiting farms and looking at corn crops in the area to select the best ones for Simplott to buy. In my job with Simplott I got to see about 130 different crops being grown. That's a good way to sort out how you'd like to do things and what the possibilities are.

The fellow who was my boss at Simplott at the time had just come back from a course with Dr Arden Andersen in Perth, where he'd sat next to a fellow by the name of John Pannon. That meeting between my boss and John triggered a series of events, which have dramatically altered how I think and how I farm.

John had done courses with Arden prior to that particular course and had studied radionics as a result. Arden Andersen is a keen radionics practitioner. John was very accurate with the box and he also understood the Albrecht principles. He had a link with a fellow called Graham Emerson who comes from Portland in Victoria who makes fertilizers using radionics. Graham put together a calcium di-phosphate blend that wasn't acid treated and to that he added all the trace elements like cobalt, iron and molybdenum. Basically his fertilizers include all the goodies that are needed to bring your soil back into balance very quickly. You can afford to use fertilizer like that if you're growing vegetables. It's not as affordable if you're growing wheat on a much larger area. It's not affordable if your soil needs a lot of inputs to get the minerals balanced, if you need to bring up the carbon content and/or develop the soil biology. That actually describes most of the soils that are being farmed in Australia. Generally they're deficient in minerals, have low to very low organic matter levels, and farming methods have decimated the micro-organism populations. It's going to take a huge investment to bring them back to full health and productivity.

Tell me about the physical conditions on the farm.

It was a horse stud till 5 years ago. It's 1,350 hectares and it's on the Macquarie River. It has 520 hectares that we irrigate, mainly from bores and sometimes from the river. We have plenty of water but we tend to use it sparingly because it costs a lot of money to pump and our off peak electricity rate is about to be abolished, which will make it even more expensive. Rainfall here is 525 mm but it comes when it feels like it rather than in any set pattern. It's hot in summer and cold in winter and we have frosts.

We irrigate from central pivots, which spray water in a large circle. In the pivot areas we have 750 ppm phosphorous that's locked up because that's what happened when we used the simplified chemical NPK fertilizers in the past. The problem was that the NPK fertilizers actually broke down the soil organic matter faster than it was being replaced. That organic matter was food for the microorganisms so when it went, so did the microorganisms. The soil that was left was virtually dead.

We're building the organic matter levels of the soil back up to where they should be. Locked up phosphorus will then be released by micro-organisms.

We make sure we no longer put on phosphorus in a form that can convert to tri-calcium phosphate and tie up and add to the stuff that's already here. Graham Emerson's "Emfert" fertilizer does the trick there. The phosphorous in that fertilizer is less likely to lock up, probably because it's not acid treated and it's made from biologically activated soft rock phosphates.

- 214 -

We've got very fertile, fine alluvial soil near the river, which we irrigate. Soil away from the river isn't quite as good. I've finally got 100 acres down to Mitchell Grass and Dorrigo grass and some legumes on the dry area.

The soil has a calcium/magnesium ratio of 4:1 and it should be closer to 5:1. We add 500 kg lime per hectare every year and gypsum as well because we need sulphur. We're adding calcium a little at a time. I don't believe we can bring it up to the right level in one go because that would be too much for the "stomach" of the soil to accept. Molybdenum, iron, cobalt, selenium and iron are deficient. Silicon is OK, but even so we're using a form of diatomaceous earth in our broadcast blends of calcium, gypsum, and humified compost, because the silicon isn't always available. The CEC ratio is between 11 and 20.

What do you grow, David?

We've got corn under the pivots but we've not growing as much as we'd like to. We'd love to be growing a lot more but Chinese corn comes into New Zealand, gets repackaged and stamped "product of New Zealand" and competes against us. Simcott still does the harvesting. The corn is my responsibility now. All I have to do is plant it and inter-row cultivate it to take out any weeds and put some oxygen in the soil and keep the grubs out. To do that we normally use Gemstar, which is a virus. It's not a biological insecticide: it's an organic product.

We're not growing our corn organically. We use a poison to stop the African Black Beetle attacking the seedlings and wiping them out. We do that because when you invest in one of these crops you cannot afford to have a poor plant stand. We do try to get the soil healthy to reduce damage by bugs and insects.

Once the plant is up and growing I suspect that any problems we do have are the result of having only 2·3% organic carbon. I think if we had 5% organic matter we probably wouldn't have beetles eating the corn roots. They're only doing their job, which is to stop the corn reproducing. That's what insects do. They destroy the stuff that's not fit to produce seeds. The studies that Dr Phil Callahan did showed that. If the plant has high sugar levels, the heliothis grubs fall off drunk and die of alcohol poisoning. Insects and grubs can't metabolise sugar in a high concentration.

Getting a good crop is a matter of getting everything right. If you can't do that you don't get a yield or a saleable crop. You have to control your weeds and control your grubs and get a sufficiently high yield to justify the cost of harvesting. We control our weeds with inter-row cultivation and we use a lay-down chemical spray that stops the weeds for the first 30 days.

Our problems are that we don't have a perfectly balanced soil. We have to recognise that. We're trying softer options once the crop is above the ground and trying to keep beneficial insects in play because they do such a wonderful job and allow us to run a soft system that causes less damage.

This year I'm growing adzuki and soybeans, and I think I'll be growing a lot more pulses in the future.

Have you been using progressively fewer chemicals?

Yes, we have. In the corn we've cut out a whole application, which involved a 30-day herbicide. We're just relying on inter-row cultivation and radionics. We rotary hoe the residue after we've harvested and take out the grasses before they've seeded. The broadleaf weeds are becoming fewer but the grasses aren't.

What sort of soil cultivation do you do?

I tend to grow a green manure crop about 6 weeks after the corn comes off. We'll cultivate the stubble then do a second run to get everything down and level and starting to decay because we want to use the stubble in the soil to feed the micro-organisms. We spread a grazing wheat or grazing oats on the surface and run an Aerway aerator over it. The machine has four spikes to a rotation that are slightly turned out and it's designed with a little crack below the point of the knife and this mixes the seed in. We turn the pivot on if there's no rain and up comes a green manure crop that sits there with weeds and stinging nettles for 4 to 5 months feeding the little fellas. Depending on how close to planting we get we might have to use RoundUp. The better approach is to run a disc through it and turn it in, but then we've got an uneven surface to plant into which is a problem. For corn we have to have seeds coming up uniformly every 10 centimetres. We're looking for 68,000 plants established per hectare, so we really need a nice level paddock, so unfortunately we have to work it a bit and it mustn't be too dry or too wet.

How often do you use RoundUp?

Too often, to be honest! We were influenced to use a chemical no-till method on our dry land farming areas for a few years but for the past two years we've changed back to using the discs. I've had to get rid of some fairly big weeds and with chemical no-till you have to spray too often and keep the application rates too high. Chemical no-till was going on all around me while I was working on the pivot areas where we actually make all our money, and I'm finally getting to the stage where, this year, I'm converting a lot of the dry land cropping area to long-term pastures and concentrating on the irrigated cropping area.

We're minimising the use of RoundUp on our irrigated land by reducing the pH of the water that we mix the RoundUp with. When we bring the water pH down using citric acid, we can get it down to 4.2, which is lower than we get when we use spraying adjuncts. If we get it down to 4.2 there's no antagonism between the RoundUp and the water and we can use a much smaller amount of RoundUp. We get even better result when we wrap the RoundUp within a spraying oil, which protects it from associating with the water too much. We put 3 litres of the spraying oil in the bottom of our container and then pour RoundUp in at the rate of 3 litres to 17. The RoundUp folds into the oil and is wrapped in it. It doesn't affect the machinery doing this.

What are you doing to build soil micro-organisms?

I've used compost teas in the past and they worked brilliantly as a stubble reduction strategy.

I bought them ready made and had to transport two shuttles from Young to here. It was quite expensive. I've taken my time getting the equipment and I'm going to learn to do it myself. I have a microscope and I've done Elaine Ingham's basic training at Lismore. I've got the machinery ready to go. I've got to do some drilling and set up the combine to take the liquid compost down as an injection. We're going to use 30 kg of granular fertilizer and 50 litres of a brew that will be based on compost tea.

I'm not planning to make compost. I have a friend starting to do some fungal dominant compost. That's what I'm interested in. I think we've got plenty of bacteria. We need the fungus to dominate. Most of the issues we have with regard to growing crops appear to be fungal issues towards the end of the growth period because we don't have sap pressure. It's possibly caused by a lack of boron or possibly calcium or silica. I reckon if we get the critters out there they'll help, provided we've got most of the minerals right.

I've been using humic and fulvic acid to try and excite the bacteria and fungus. The biodynamic preparations are good inoculants. I've been using inoculants on the azuki bean and soybean seeds that we put out. I use a combination of specific species inoculum, biodynamic preparations and John Pannon's seed dressing. When John did that he was able to get five out of six of the germs in a wheat seed to germinate. He got five plants out of one seed by using radionics and re-mineralisation. The CSIRO thought he was genetically modifying the seed. They couldn't understand how he could make that happen.

What have been some of your concerns about switching over from conventional growing methods?

I'm trying to work in tandem with the way nature wants to work. As a foundation, the Albrecht soil test is fantastic for understanding structure and what you realistically need to grow a crop. In a mono-cropping situation, if you're looking to get a decent yield, you're hard pressed doing it in a totally natural way unless you're really committed to it and have some really good tillage methods and/or really good radionics methods to stop other plants seeding and fouling up your crop.

What strategies do you use to minimise concerns about the changes you're making?

I like to have a mentor, or several. John Pannon was my mentor until he died. I would speak to him on the phone regularly, sometimes twice a week. John had a friend called Graham Emerson, whose fertilizers we use, and the two of them developed a table so that they could work out the right amount of fertilizer with the correct mix of elements and not put out too much stuff you don't need. John could run tests from where he lived using a polaroid photograph and make changes in our cropping circumstances. If we needed additional minerals he would make up a foliar spray specifically for us and put in the radionics frequencies of the right potency. All I had to do was to spray it on.

Now I have an hour-long phone call once a week with Cheryl Kemp, who's a biodynamics expert. I met Cheryl as a result of making a phone call to the Biodynamics Association in Coffs Harbour and saying, "I'm really interested in biodynamics but I haven't got the time to sit and stir liquids." They put me onto Cheryl. Reading Rudolf Steiner's *Agriculture* isn't going to bring you close to the truth when you read it on your own. You need someone like Cheryl to help explain the significance of these things.

I went to the biodynamics people because I was looking to become less reliant on granular fertilizer. I could see real opportunities for injection of liquid fertilizer at sowing to provide nutrition and a live biological base. We'd just bought a brand new disc-opening planter, so we can put in any fertilizer and micro-organisms we want and come back in a month's time and apply a compost tea. It'll be a brewed compost tea that I'll do myself.

I probably only got into this stuff in 2004. I've read continuously and done a lot of personal spiritual development. That's important if you want to become a biodynamics farmer and use the techniques to the best advantage. Biodynamics is not as simple as applying a few preparations and hoping it all works. But it can be made simpler by putting a cosmic pipe, which consists of two poles, in your paddock. You can put your biodynamic preparations in the silica well and the calcium well. I'm not using cosmic pipes because I'm developing specific potencies and broadcasting them out through my radionics box. I already own that, so I don't need another type of device. Probably the biggest hurdle to doing this sort of thing is accepting it works, and the people who can accept it are few and far between.

I also talk a lot to Richard May. He was the agronomist that mapped the reef north of Exmouth, doing most of the work in a wet suit. He's good on microbes, microbe tea production and liquid fertilizers.

I like to take ideas from each of them and try and fit them together in a way that suits the conditions here.

I also think training and reading are important. Reading and training give you the broad picture so that you can better use any advice you get. It takes quite a lot of education to be able to appreciate the value of different things.

Radionics has obviously been important. Tell me about radionics.

The guy who took over from me at Simplott called in to show me the radionics machine he'd just bought. Of course I had to have a go. I got a "hit" within a few seconds, which is most unusual, so of course I was hooked. From that moment on I was totally excited about the prospect of learning all about it. I then trained with John Pannon in 2004. He became my mentor and we started using John as our agronomist and fertilizer provider.

John would make up foliar sprays for us and put in radionics frequencies of the right potency and I just had to put it on. He also did insect and cockatoo removal. I've done a bit of that myself. When John taught me how to do it I went out and collected grubs that had been affected by the nucleopolyhedra virus and were dying. The virus is an Australian-made remedy for killing heliothus grubs that get into corn and cotton. I placed the dying grubs in the well of my machine and broadcast the frequency of the dead and dying grubs to a photograph of my paddock that had soybeans growing in it. What happened after I did that nearly blew my mind. Never before had I seen heliothus grubs get down off a plant and crawl along the ground to get out of the paddock. When they left I was able to use a biological spray, which is organically acceptable, because I didn't have an extremely high grub pressure.

I've seen John take the cockatoos out of the sorghum paddock on the river. The gums along the river are home to thousands of cockatoos. John took a cockatoo feather and read all the sets of frequencies that made up that flock of cockatoos. A radionics box has a scanner with a pair of dials at the top that go from 1 to 100. The first dial is "condition". The second is "location". John swapped them. He did this from his home in Horsham, Victoria. Then he took a photo of the crop and sent out the frequency. The cockatoos couldn't stand it. They scattered. John turned the frequency on and off during the whole time we had the crop and the cockatoos went mad.

When we grew our first crop of corn under radionics and Emfert fertilizer it produced 24 tonnes to the hectare. It was the highest yielding super sweet corn that Edgells had ever experienced. Our previous best average was 21 tonnes to the hectare, so it was a huge improvement. Normally we'd grow about 18·5 tonnes. The brace roots of that crop were just dripping sugar at 50 days, feeding the microbes.

I can only explain radionics by the fact that everything is connected through consciousness. It's a bit like homeopathics in natural medicine. It's not the herb they use that does the work, it's the energy frequency of the herb that's used that causes the changes, and the less of the herb that is included in the homeopathic substance the greater the potency.

It's very hard to explain it to someone who hasn't understood quantum theory and the way quantum non-locality works.

There's a basic connection we can all tap into. As radionics operators we tap into the energetic field of the subject and scan the energetic levels of that "subject", which can be a soil test, a corn plant or a photograph of a farm.

Last year I did one experiment using a daytura pepper, which is sometimes called a thorn apple and is a very difficult weed to eradicate. I used the irrigation system, because I find water is a great carrier of "intent", and I used the pivot to apply my daytura pepper "essence" while I was irrigating the sweet corn. On the new moon I put a 9x potency of the daytura pepper that I'd prepared radionically through the irrigation water and then on the full moon I put a 10x potency through the irrigation water. At the end of the cropping season there were 6ft tall daytura peppers and none of them had any seedpods. This year we've not had many daytura plants at all.

These sorts of examples show me that radionics works and using it can have enormous benefits.

Where do you see farming in Australia heading?

At the local level we have a few people in town thinking of setting up a shop selling organic / biodynamic food. We need to organise some like-minded farmers to get continuity of supply and convince them that it's important to develop local outlets. If we were to do this we'd be able to supply our local town. Selling locally and doing the selling ourselves allows us to bypass agents and this means we get a much higher proportion of the selling price.

People who are farming biologically or organically haven't many ways out other than banding together and taking the "in-between" guys out of the equation. These farmers are trying to feed the people of this country and want to do it the best possible way. I believe people will have to learn that the "real" cost of producing well-grown nutritionally rich food is much higher than the prices they're accustomed to paying. "Real" food is food that will keep them away from doctors. When people realise the real costs of producing food they might be prepared to pay for the privilege of eating it.

It's too easy to rely on China to produce the food we need because it's cheaper than doing it ourselves, but that strategy has immense dangers if there's a world crisis, like a major war or something like that. Oil prices could jump dramatically overnight, because I think oil is being held at an artificially low price.

We need to convince the people on the other side of the "sandstone curtain" that if anything goes wrong, we have only 8 to 12 weeks of food in this country, and we're losing farmers fast because they can't make a decent living. Coles and Woolworths, who control 85 to 90% of food sales, and the people who import food into this country, control our ability to feed ourselves. When they import food from countries that pay workers much, much less than people in Australia earn, then our Australian farmers don't make sufficient income to stay in business.

If you were asked to give some advice to farmers who are thinking of switching from conventional agriculture to a more sustainable method, what would that advice be?

They probably don't want to try and do everything at once. Work with a 50-acre paddock and compare what happens doing something different with what's happening doing what you normally do.

You've got to wean your soil off the straight NPK inputs if you want to keep cropping, and you've also got to think about the biochemistry sequence. You have to go back 3 steps and say, "Well it really starts with boron which excites calcium and silica to play their role in the production of nitrogen, phosphorus and then potassium as your sugars develop at the very end." What I try to do is to consider the whole sequence. Unfortunately, when you use harsh chemicals such as insecticides as a rescue strategy, everything can fall over. People often don't realise that they're working with a very delicate system and the soil biology is vital. Having a diversity of soil biology is so important. Having the right minerals in the right balance is only a first step. Once you have the right minerals the soil biology can exist, so then you have to create the conditions for soil micro-organisms and fungi to thrive, and that means building the organic matter as a top priority.

That's where the bio-dynamics comes in and is the reason why I'm trying to incorporate biodynamics principles into my growing strategies.

You've just given a great account of what you're doing, David. Thank you so much.

Chapter 6
A Gourmet's Paradise

Three very different growers are featured in this chapter. The first grower, Dick Rochford grows garlic on a very small block of land which is rotated on a five year cycle. Carl Brown, can trace his farming heritage back to the middle of last century. He is descended from a family of farmers who have specialised in sheep and grain farming. In making the transition to organic growing of grapes Carl has ventured into new territory. The third grower featured in this chapter lives in the Barossa Valley in South Australia, has a very special garden which provides food for his restaurant: a gourmet's paradise, which brings together good wine, good food and the companionship of a shared table. Michael has no farming experience and is more a gardener than a farmer.

Growers featured in this chapter are:

Dick Rochford   *garlic*

Carl Brown   *wine grapes*

Michael Voumard   *a gourmet's garden*

Dick Rochford

Garlic Grower from Tenterfield, New South Wales

Dick Rochford has a small but highly successful operation. Dick grows just 1¼ acres of garlic a year and produces between 3 and 4 tonnes, which he markets through the Internet and sends through the post. He does all the planting and harvesting by hand, and uses vast quantities of mulch, made from a weed that grows prolifically in Tenterfield to control weeds.

Dick started off growing conventionally. Eight years ago he switched to growing organically. Now he is thinking of investigating biodynamics in the search for improved quality.

How did you come to be growing garlic Dick?

I've been growing it since 1990. In the beginning it was a combined venture with my next-door neighbour. We decided that garlic was an interesting proposition. It was getting $9 a kilogram, which was a pretty good price at that time. We did that for a number of years. We had a plan that we'd sell seed garlic to farmers and teach them how to grow it, and then we'd offer to buy back their garlic if they wished and we'd take care of the marketing. My partner was a retired businessman who'd worked in the corporate food industry all his life. My role was to produce the garlic.

To promote garlic sales we held seminars for interested farmers in areas where garlic will grow. That went well. We bought back the garlic and sold it at a profit through the Sydney and Brisbane markets. We did that for eight years until my partner's health declined. I continued on my own with my wife and that's how it's been for the past 8 years. When we split up the partnership I decided that I wanted to start growing organically and that's what I did.

What was your motivation for getting organic certification?

I come from Ireland. I grew up on a farm in Ireland. We were basically organic farmers back in those days without even knowing that the term existed. We never used chemicals or artificial fertilizers at all. We wouldn't have been able to afford them!

The organic industry was beginning to expand about the time I went on my own and I thought it was an opportune time to go that way. Besides, my wife and I have a really strong interest in having a healthy lifestyle, so that helped sway the decision.

Tell me about your farm, Dick.

It's 50 acres in size, mostly trees and rocks. Of the 50 acres there are probably 10 to 15 acres that I can actually farm. We're on the Tenterfield Creek, so we have an irrigation licence. The soil is very sandy. When we first tested it, the pH was far too low. It was 4·5. That was the major problem when we first stated growing garlic. It didn't do well. I didn't know the first thing about growing garlic when I started and only realised through trial and error that our pH level was way too low. We got people in to check things out and that was the major problem. We now have a pH of 6·5, which is fine.

Boron is our big deficiency. The nitrogen level is always a bit low. It seems to leave the soil and we have to boost it every year. The organic matter is very low. I think that's because the soil is so sandy. Even though the mulch is put on each year and we're adding some organic matter, it's still low but it is improving. I grow green manure crops and plough them in, so that's helping.

What have you done to correct the deficiencies and imbalances?

I do a soil test every year before I plant, so that's how I know what I need. I also do leaf tests.

I applied lime. Over the 10 years, each growing area got 2 tonnes of lime. Once I take the garlic out, I plant the area in oats for the following winter and I under-sow the oats with different varieties of clover. The clover improves the nitrogen level in the soil. I grow cowpeas as a green manure crop and plough it in about a month before I plant my garlic.

I've been working with NutriTech Solutions for a long while and I use their products. What I do to correct deficiencies depends on the soil test and the advice I receive from Nutri-Tech. It varies from year to year. I put on different applications of their products according to the programme they provide. This year I decided to do something different. I went to Ag Solutions at Gympie and bought a tonne of their Natramin. It's a mineral based product that comes as a granular fertilizer. It's certified organic. I gave them my soil test results and they recommended which of their products would be best to improve the soil.

Why do you think a dry mineral fertilizer is better?

I don't. I put on half a tonne of Natramin K-phos on last year's crop. I was experimenting because I thought the previous year's crop wasn't as good as I would have liked. As it turned out, the garlic I grew last year was the best I've ever grown from the point of view of health and colour, but it was way too small. I'm trying to rectify that this year by putting on some certified chook manure.

What are some of the different strategies you're using now compared with when you first started?

In the early days when we grew the garlic we used artificial fertilizers like ammonium nitrate. That's the stuff they made bombs out of during the War. We did use RoundUp and another chemical to control the weeds. I also used a little hand propelled scuffle for the weeds. Once I started I'd continue till it was finished, and then I'd have to start all over again. It was tough, because I was the one doing the pushing. One year I continually scuffed between the rows of 4 acres of garlic.

I'm not using the scuffle any more. There's a grass that grows here in Tenterfield called African Love Grass. We have it all over Tenterfield and it's a weed. It's a very strong grass that spreads everywhere and you can't get rid of it. People burn it each year and it grows back nice and green in spring and early summer, when it's good food for cattle and sheep. Once it dries off and when we have frosts, it's basically inedible.

I've got it on my property and I slash it every year and bale it and use it as mulch. Mulch has replaced my scuffle. I grow 1¼ acres of garlic every year and I put 500 bales of mulch on as soon as I've planted it. I've made good use of a noxious weed, which is absolutely brilliant as mulch. When the crop is finished, much of the mulch is still there, so I rake it up, bale it, and use it again the following year. I put out 500 bales and may have 350 still there to use again the following year. By the 3rd year it gets a bit fragile and chaffy. It's not something I'd want to sell outside of

Tenterfield because of the seeds, but it works really well here where we already have the problem so it can't do any harm. Most of the farmers around here see it as an absolute curse, but I've made good use of it.

Do you promote soil micro-organisms?

I applied a compost tea last year. That was the first time I'd used it.

I'm a member of the Border Landcare Organic Group, which has 120 members in the Tenterfield/Stanthorpe area. The group meets monthly, when we share ideas and do farm tours and visit sustainable backyard gardens and have regular guest speakers.

One of the members has started up a Tea for Life business making compost tea. She applied two lots of her compost tea to my garlic crop last year. While the bulbs were not as big as I would have liked, the whole garlic crop was certainly the healthiest that I've ever grown.

How often do you water?

It varies considerably. I water straight after I plant. We've got pretty good rainfall here. It's about 30 inches. That's 750 millimetres a year. When the garlic is mulched it reduces the need for watering. During the winter I seldom irrigate. Garlic grows through the winter. Frosts don't affect the garlic because the main type I grow originates from northern China. Come spring, that's when the garlic starts to take off and the growing spurt occurs. I irrigate then, when it needs moisture to really grow.

Visitors to our garlic farm tell me that the most interesting feature is our working water wheel. In 2003 I built and installed the water wheel at the base of a natural waterfall on our permanent creek. I also built a cave around it to protect it in times of flood.

The water wheel powers a small piston pump that pumps the water to three large tanks above the garlic fields. The water from the tanks is gravity fed back down to the house and gardens. The three large tanks act as a reservoir for irrigating the garlic crop. When the tanks overflow, the excess water is piped back down to the creek.

Did you have any problems changing over to growing organically?

No problems at all. When we moved to growing organically I just used the scuffle. I didn't use herbicides. The only thing I did use for a couple of years was the ammonium nitrate. Then I started using chook manure. By the time I applied for organic certification and the BFA people came to do a soil test it had been 4 or 5 years since I'd used any artificial fertilizers.

How do you grow your garlic, Dick?

I use a five-year rotation. Once I've prepared the soil I plant it in rows by hand. I have two planting machines in the shed but I never use them. It's a huge job but I do it over three weeks. I have to break up the bulbs and plant them and mulch them. I cover the soil with a 15-centimetre layer of mulch and over time, as it gets wet, it compresses to just 2 centimetres in thickness. Planting and mulching is just a matter of hanging in there until it's all finished. It's three weeks of hard work doing the mulching, but it saves lots of labour in terms of weed control through the growing period. It's an 8-month growing period, so you can imagine the problem you'd have with weeds over that period of time.

I harvest by hand as well. I plant four rows in what I call a bed. I can straddle that with my tractor. When I harvest in October and November I use the tractor with an under-cutter behind. The under-cutter is a hand made device made with grader blades. I use the tractor to drag the blades under the bed so that it cuts the roots and the garlic just sits there. I come along and lift it out of the ground. I leave it in bundles along the rows so that the stalks of one bundle cover the bulbs of the one next to it. When it's all pulled out, I collect it and put it on drying racks in the shed. I leave it to dry for at least three weeks before I start working on it and sending it out to customers. My main variety, Oriental Purple, lasts for about 8 months and I can sell it till it starts to shoot in June and July. It loses its quality by August, which is different from the Russian garlic, which lasts all year.

I keep the garlic I'm going to plant the following year on the drying racks, then I top and tail it and put it in bags.

It sounds like a lot of work. Why don't you get help?

I'm able to manage 1¼ acres on my own. I could sell twice the amount I grow but I'm happy to leave it at that.

The topping and tailing and getting it packaged to send out is the hardest part. At the beginning of the season everyone wants the garlic tomorrow. I send it as far away as Darwin and Melbourne.

How do you market your garlic?

I produce somewhere between 3 and 4 tonnes a year, which is a lot of garlic. I have a lot of enquiries though my web page. Over a period of 8 years I've built up a clientele. I have regular customers and I send out a bulletin each year. They chase me rather than me having to chase them. I send 90% of my garlic through the mail. Large quantities

I send by carrier. I send Food Connect in Brisbane 100 to 200 kilograms at a time. I've been dealing with them ever since they started. Rob Pekin turned up here one day and told me what he was doing and that got me hooked.

What variety of garlic do you grow?

I grow two varieties: Oriental Purple and Giant Russian. I sourced my main variety from Northern China many years ago. I was and still am a member of the Australian Garlic Industry Association. They established a programme where they brought in different varieties of garlic from all over the world. We paid hundreds of dollars to cover the costs involved. Everyone who'd financed the programme got at least one bulb from each variety. I ended up with 112 varieties and whittled them down to just one. It's the main variety I grow and is the one I call Oriental Purple.

My Giant Russian, which is about 15% of my whole crop, was sourced from an old German family here in Tenterfield. Their grandparents brought it from Germany over 100 years ago.

What's the biggest challenge in terms of growing garlic?

If you want to integrate garlic growing into a farming enterprise it's important to realise that there are crucial periods when you have to give garlic attention. Irrigation has to be done when it's needed, and garlic needs a lot of water if you don't mulch. You have to plant it on time. There's only a 2-week window of opportunity when you can plant. When it's growing you have to keep on top of the weeds. I walk through the garlic field once a month and pull out any weeds that are growing. Time management would be a big challenge for most garlic growers.

Yours is a really interesting story, Dick. Thank you for sharing it.

Carl Brown

Vigneron and sheep/wheat farmer
in central Victoria

Carl lives "smack bang" in the middle of central Victoria. He's a descendant of German migrants who came to Australia during the gold rush, but realised that farming was a lot more reliable way to make a living. A descendant of one of five German families to settle in the area in 1860, Carl can trace family ownership of the land around Colbinabbin back to those days.

After leaving school Carl worked for a stock and station agent for a period, but it was working as a shearer that helped earn Carl the money to buy his farm 15 years ago. Because land in this area of Victoria is highly sought after, he has had to purchase whatever land became available, so his property consists of a number of different blocks, some as much as 10 kilometres distant from one another. In total he owns 1,100 acres.

Prior to 8 or 9 years ago, Carl and his brother were doing "pretty much the same as everyone else here does: cereal cropping and sheep." His brother is still doing the same but Carl's life starting going in a different direction when he decided to grow a small area of grapes organically.

Tell me about the physical environment of the area, Carl.

We've got a temperate climate. On average we get about 18 inches of rain a year, mainly in winter, but the past 10 or so years we've averaged about 12 inches. It's been very dry.

The summer temperatures can be high. It can get up to 45⁰C but that's unusual. Most often it gets to about 35⁰C to 37⁰C. During the daytime in winter it's between 12⁰C and 15⁰C and at night it can get down to just below freezing.

Because my land is scattered over a wide area, I've got several different soil types and very different minerals in those soils. We live on the side of what was a very old volcano, so some of the area is red Cambrian volcanic soil and it runs down onto a heavy black clay soil. It's very expensive to buy here and there's just no more of it available.

We've got red soil on the home block. I can tell you most about the home block soil because that's where I've got my grapes. The pH is around 6 and the cation exchange capacity is 30. On the black soil areas the CEC is up to 50, which is very high. The major imbalance, the one that affects us most, is the calcium/magnesium ratio. In some areas, on the poorer blocks, that's down to 1:1, which makes the soil very tight, and that's what we have to fix before we do anything else. A ratio of 2:1 is not unusual. These soils tend to go very sloppy when they're wet and rock hard when they're dry. Organic matter is between 1 and 2% but in the vineyard I've got that up to between 3 and 4%.

What was your motivation for moving into organic farming?

Because we've got various soil types and different minerals in those soils, there are different plants growing in different locations, and I've always been curious as to why. I asked "why" for a long time and never got a satisfactory answer.

Also I was intrigued by how much fertilizer we were putting on compared with what my father used to use. We weren't growing any better crops than he did in spite of the fact that we were using way more fertilizer.

I was at a Field Day, going around all the tents and talking to people who were selling alternative fertilizers, and I got talking to someone who said, "You've should read Neil Kinsey's book, *Hands-on Agronomy*." I found the book and it really interested me. That's what sparked my interest. I've read lots of books since then. I think the best book I've read is Graeme Sait's *Nutrition Rules*, but you need to have some background knowledge before you read it. That's a really interesting book. He interviews farming consultants and health professionals around the world about farming. Those blokes just know so much. I actually lent it to a cousin of mine who had an accident and was laid up for a while, but I'm pretty sure he just wouldn't have believed what was in it. Garry Zimmer's book, *The Biological Farmer*, is also a good book.

When I purchased my last block I financed it through Rural Finance. They offered a small interest rebate to young farmers. I paid about half a percent less than normal, I think. When I was negotiating that loan I met a fellow called Alistair Walker, who recommended that I go to a seminar that was being held in Echuca. Now I wasn't very knowledgeable about biological farming at that point, but during that conversation with Alistair, I must have said something that caused him to tell me about this seminar. He faxed me the details and I went and did a 3-day course with Arden Andersen. He opened my eyes and it all went from there. Arden answered some of my questions. I started to understand just how important the biology in the soil is and how that should be your main focus. A lot of people don't even realise that there are things in the soil that affect what's going on. They just farm dirt.

Have you done any other training?

I did the Certificate in Sustainable Agriculture with Graeme Sait and I did Elaine Ingham's course.

From Graeme I learnt about applications and timing and how best to apply the various mixes. He was good because he transferred the information on soil health straight over to human health, making the link between the health of the soil and the health of people. Graeme vividly points out what rubbish we eat. Some of the statistics he uses are really shocking. I get the *Acres Australia* newspaper and Graeme often has interesting articles in there.

I was hoping to get some finer details of how to make compost from Elaine, but her course was about how important bacteria, and particularly fungi, are in the soil. I'd learnt a lot about all that before I did the course so I didn't get a whole lot from it. I did go back and do the small microscope course and that was very interesting. It's amazing to see just how much life there is in the soil. When you hear about so many millions of bacteria in one gram of soil, those are just numbers. When you actually see those bacteria under a microscope you realise that there's a huge amount of life in a 1/100th solution of 3 drops of soil that's from your paddock. There's just so much life in there. It's totally amazing just to see it.

Tell me about your grapes, Carl.

I decided to put them in and grow them organically. I went down the conventional organic route. You can use sulphur and copper if you want to when you grow organically. I did that for the first couple of years because I was fearful of something going wrong. We use a lot of the stuff that's out there because we're afraid of things going wrong. We're not confident that plants can look after themselves if we allow them to.

I had a bit to do with a fellow called Adrian Lawrie of Lawrieco in South Australia. He was just a farmer who started doing a few things on his farm and then he saw an opportunity to expand and make a business out of it. A lot of people who work in the organics field are like him: absolutely genuine. They never try and sell you something they don't absolutely believe in or that they don't think will work for you.

Adrian was putting out prescription blends based on Graeme Sait's recipes. In one of his base products you get brown coal dust, granite sand, soft rock phosphate and whatever minerals your soil needs and they brew up microbes and inoculate the heap with the brew. If you need heaps of calcium or potassium, they add that too. I used a lot of prescription blend, more of it in the vineyard than anywhere else. We'd already planted the vines when I did that. The changes we saw in there were substantial. The weed level decreased, the soil softened and we mulched heavily between the vine rows, so at the same time as I was doing that I was also adding organic matter. I put on that prescription blend for 4 years at a rate of about 2 tons to the acre. On other areas of the property it was applied at a lighter rate.

What I learnt from Elaine Ingham is that if you put lime out and you don't have any fungi to hold onto it, the lime will just leach away. I suppose, because our vineyard was organic, there would have been quite a lot of fungi in there to start with. The grapes didn't respond noticeably for a couple of years because with the heavy mulching using straw there would have been a lot of nitrogen draw down as the mulch rotted. I didn't apply any nitrogen to compensate for this. The vines just chugged along until there was a good enough soil life to get some nutrient cycling going on. They've only made real headway in the past 2 or 3 years. When I do leaf and petiole tests now, the results show that we have luxury levels of nitrogen and we don't put any on. Our nitrogen level is 1.21%. Rather than doing stuff to add nitrogen, I put a heap of straw on which takes nitrogen away. Four times a year I spray a fungi/microbe inoculant that contains 4 species of fungi and twenty species of bacteria.

I was doing soil tests for a while, but the organics auditor told me that the only thing they take into account is the level of organic matter. If that continues to rise, then this indicates you're doing the right thing. I've now got 3.4% organic matter in the vineyard. It took about 5 years to get to that level. It has come up about 1% over that time. I think leaf tests are more reliable than soil tests. You can put a heap of stuff in the soil, but if you don't have the micro-organisms to unlock it you're not going to get it into your plants.

Where are you selling your grapes?

We sell our grapes to a wine maker, Sergio Carlei, in Upper Beaconsfield on the outskirts of Melbourne. He bottles our wine and puts his label on it. Because ours are organic grapes and we've been certified for 6 yeas now, we do get a price premium, but the premium doesn't cover the cost of what I do to be organic. Whenever I talk to Sergio he's impressed about the quality of our wine, and last year he entered it into the Victorian Wine Show and we won the Gold Medal for Shiraz. It was good to get some positive feedback.

Because we're growing organically we're not lumped in with everyone else, and when there's an over-supply situation we've got an advantage, because we're different. I have a theory that because we don't do what everyone else does, our grapes have a distinctive flavour: a flavour that's a reflection of this environment. Because of this I can find a buyer. Others might not be able to. That's what's going to help us more than getting the price premium. It doesn't matter how well we grow grapes if we can't sell them.

In terms of the economic environment, what is your biggest problem?

The problems aren't with the economic environment, they're the result of the soil imbalance. If I could get the soil right, everything would fall into place. If I could get the soils balanced, the costs I incur wouldn't be there. I'm talking about the whole property here, not just the vineyard. The weeds I get are a response to the soil imbalance and the way we're treating our soils.

How long have you been working to get the soil into balance?

About 10 years, and I haven't met with a lot of success. I just can't see the results. I get plants with visibly bigger roots and just as many with small root systems. The same thing happens on my brother's block and he's still using conventional farming systems. Sometimes his crops have bigger roots than mine do.

Have you ever seen those promotions where they compare root systems and compare blocks? Well, I could get exactly that effect on one single paddock, even when it's all been inoculated. I don't have to go into the next paddock! I'm very sceptical that all I need to do is inoculate to get results, and it's one of the reasons I'm going into composting in a big way. It's very time consuming, making my own compost and adding my own mineral blends, but I'm doing it because then I know what I'm putting on my soil. With the knowledge I have, I can tweak things, which I can't do if I buy a product from someone else.

I'm really only learning about compost, and I'm doing things the simplest possible way. I'm using cow and chicken manure and straw and green material when I can access it. I'll make use of the grape marc from this vintage just to add a different microbial inoculant into the mix. I'm keeping it fairly basic so I can keep control of it. My first batch is just coming through now. I've probably got 300 tonnes maturing.

How much do you plan to put on your 5-acre vineyard block?

I probably won't put any on the established vineyard. Other areas need it much more. The work I've done on the 5 acres in the past 7 or 8 years is sufficient. I've just planted another 4 acres of vines in a similar area. The soil in the new vineyard area is as hard as a rock. I plan to put some of the compost there. In fact, I could put 2 to 3 tonnes to the acre on that block to see if it will loosen the soil and get it going. Those two vineyards are like chalk and cheese in terms of soil quality.

There's actually been quite a major change in the first vineyard. It's motoring along quite nicely now. It took a bit of time getting it going but there's one recurring comment people make when they see it: "It just looks so healthy!" It does. For most of the year, whether it be summer or winter, you can go to that soil and put your hand in and lift up a handful of soil and it's soft. There are lots of worms.

What about pests and diseases?

Grapes don't have a lot of insect pests attack them. They're easy that way. They do get a lot of fungal disease pressure.

Elaine Ingham talks a lot about the idea of succession. When things start out they're bacterially dominant. With each progression you get a little more fungi. In cereal crops the bacteria / fungi ratio is 1:1. Where you get fruit trees it's 5:1. I thought, "How am I going to get fungi if I keep spraying sulphur?" So I stopped doing that.

I'd been spraying it on to stop powdery mildew. Now, if I have a pressure situation with high humidity and high rainfall, I just go out and spray a fungi / bacteria inoculant called 4:20. It contains 4 species of fungi and 20 different bacteria. I brew them up in my little brewing machine. Since I've been doing this, during a period of 5 or 6 years, I've not had any problem with powdery mildew. No fungal diseases of any kind have attacked the vines. I find that very comforting. By using a fungi/microbial inoculant I get on top of most of the diseases. The theory says this is what happens and it seems to work. I've had neighbours who, even thought they're on a sulphur programme, still have problems with powdery mildew, but I don't. I actually thought that with all the straw and the fish emulsion I put out I might have gone too far in getting a high fungi population, but tests indication that it's not so.

What fertilizers are you using on your grapes?

When I put the 4:20 out I put a bit of phoslife in, a bit of fish emulsion and some molasses.

Are your grapes worth growing financially?

Yes. They're the best thing I've got. No doubt about that.

Is the cost of growing grapes the way you're doing it more or less than using conventional growing methods?

It's more expensive. The straw is expensive to put out. I cut it myself but anyone who has to buy it would find it really costly. My little patch has had 300 round bales of straw put on it: 50 bales a year. There's a risk factor with fire. If I had a fire in my vineyard it would decimate it because there's so much fuel there. The mulch is about 10 cm deep. It needs to be that deep to stop the grass coming through.

Do you think the strategies you were using before and are still using on the rest of your property are ecologically damaging?

They are. Definitely. But you're trapped when soils are run down, because they don't function as they should do. I could turn around now and say, "I'm going to switch to an organic operation on the rest of my farm", but if I were to do that, I'd go broke in 2 minutes. The soil isn't ready for that. It's like a cripple limping along. If I take away the crutches it would just fall over. That's why I'm using the compost. I'm gradually making the transition. The microbes I put out in the compost will make the difference. If I make the compost right, the soil will improve and a lot of my problems will go away. I'm still learning to do it right.

I'm also using a gradual approach to changing over. I use a stubble digester to break it down. I still sow with MAP but I also put on humate granules. I inoculate my seed and don't use seeds covered in fungicide.

Oh, man! I've put in hours trying to change over. My brother doesn't do any of the things I'm doing and it's easier for him. He just fills up with seed and away he goes. He doesn't have to mix up witch's brews, which clog up everything so that you think you're ready to start planting and find you have to clean down the machine and unblock everything. You really have to be dedicated to stick with it, because the results aren't immediately apparent. All you can do is hope that the results will be there further down the track. I'm not seeing that yet. The yields from my brother's farm are fairly similar to mine.

Even though the results don't seem to be there, I've seen some interesting things, which show that something is happening. There was one time when my brother had more feed in his paddocks than I did, and his cows broke through the fence to get to my pastures. I've got nothing specific to explain why that happened, but obviously the cows had a reason to do that. I don't know what that was.

It's going to take a lot of pushing to get people to make a change in the way they're doing things, because it takes a lot of mucking around. In our district there are perhaps only a couple of kindred spirits in over a hundred farmers. That's not a big proportion.

When Adrian Lawrie first brought out a new method of seed dressing it involved 4 different components. There were four different things you had to mix up and you needed a different quantity for each one. Then you had to apply it to the seed. It got a lot easier when they produced a single dressing. Things need to be made easier. I think we've all had trouble at some stage using new products and ideas, but as our knowledge and the products get better, it gets easier.

I think that if I hadn't had my little vineyard I'd have given it all away and gone back to doing things the way I used to. Without that little vineyard I would have lost heart. It's been like a beacon. It's shown me what you can do without any chemicals and without artificial fertilizers. It just keeps on producing grapes. This season I've been through three times and thinned the fruit. It's not that unusual to have grapes over-produce but I'm not sure how unusual it is in grapes that aren't chemically fertilised. Even more importantly, we've had a really bad season. November was awful. For such a bad season we've got an unusually high yield. The grapes have a 13.5 beaume level.

You know, even if I wasn't getting a premium price, I think I'd still grow grapes this way.

What was your motivation for making the transition from conventional farming methods?

Things didn't seem to be going in the right direction. I've never liked using chemicals. No matter how small the quantity was that I was using, I was still putting poisons out on my land. I was still blowing all this poison around myself. I really disliked having to deal with it all the time.

When I stopped to think what I was doing, I realised that I was providing food for someone else to eat and I was dousing it all with poisons. That just doesn't seem right, and the silly thing is that I still eat food that other people produce and I know it's been produced using all these poisons. That scares me sometimes.

People have become removed from what's important. A lot of people in big cities and towns don't care where their food comes from or how it's produced. Most of them don't know. If they did think about it, they probably wouldn't eat it. In a lot of cases, they'd be horrified at what's been sprayed on their food. I watched a TV programme that Jamie Oliver made. It was a great example of how people reacted when they saw how their food was produced, and he only showed snippets of what happens. He didn't show how vegetables are produced or explain that they're sprayed with poisons on a regular basis. People would be absolutely horrified if they knew the reality, but there's such disconnection between consumers and the production process that these things just don't enter people's consciousness.

What are the benefits you hope will come as a consequence of what you're doing?

If I can enhance the microbial populations in the soil, I'll be able to produce sturdier crops, ones that will withstand the shock of weeks like the one we had in November and not fall apart. I'm not there yet, apart from in the vineyard. The grapes are insulated from shock.

If I could achieve that, I'd be safer in situations that I don't expect. When you farm conventionally and you know that bad weather is coming, you can put on more water, or take some precautions. When it's not expected, you get caught.

What's your biggest challenge?

Getting the soil balanced. I could just pour lime on, but if the soil microorganisms aren't there, it's just wasted because the calcium would just leach away. Putting lime on at levels big enough to make a difference would be exorbitantly expensive on large acreage. I'm making progress. I've had four soil tests done. The magnesium level hasn't changed. It's fluctuated between 22% and 25%. The calcium level has gone from 44% to 60%. The calcium / magnesium ratio has gone from 2:1 to almost 3:1 but there's still a long way to go. For me the whole process has been a bit like using a bucket with holes in it. I keep pouring money in and it keeps falling out the other end.

Another big challenge for me has been sorting through conflicting information and being able to apply the information I do have. Elaine Ingham believes we can fix the world's soils with compost teas, but the techniques aren't foolproof and there's a lot of conflicting technology out there. She said we have to figure it out and I'm not sure that answer is good enough. You have to know how to brew compost teas correctly and how to apply them correctly, and most of us don't have the time to or knowledge to figure it out.

There's a lot of information but it's really hard to sort through what's out there. You've got to have the skills and experience to know what you're doing and you can do the wrong things awfully easily. I would have more certainty if I had a microscope and could test everything, but getting a microscope would cost a couple of thousand dollars and now I'm not even sure that I haven't forgotten what I should be looking for!

I didn't get a microscope because I realised that if I wasn't analysing my micro-organism levels every week I'd soon lose my skill in identifying which is a fungi and which is a nematode and I'd be left with an expensive microscope and nothing to show for it. I didn't think I had the time to spend doing that sort of analysis.

It would be really good if there were some sort of standardisation. For example, perhaps we could have some independent body to test brewing kits so that we know which sort is best, and then we'd have a higher level of confidence in our ability to do the right thing. It's really difficult when you can't see what you're working with and you have to trust the process. Even so, I am making progress so what I'm doing must be working even if it's not working optimally.

Where do you think agriculture in Australia is heading?

Conventional farming will continue to use higher and higher levels of chemicals and artificial fertilizers and this will lead to major deterioration in the soil. Farmers who are at least trying a more biological approach will still see their soils deteriorate but they'll deteriorate more slowly.

People who are using biological techniques like making compost will see their soils get better and better. That's the way we should be farming. We should be making sure our land is getting better and better and not just saying, "I'm not going to be here for very long so it doesn't matter if the soil fertility runs down." I don't think there are too many properties that are being passed on to the next generation that are better than they were when their current owners took them over. Not now. Not the way we're killing our soils with chemicals. Conventional agriculture isn't sustainable. It'll probably carry on fine in the short term, probably for the next 20 or so years, but it'll fall over sooner or later.

We're not getting insect attacks because of a lack of pesticides, since we're using more pesticides than ever before. We're having insect attacks for another reason: we're doing the wrong things. Insects don't attack healthy food, and the food we're growing is not healthy.

If you could pass on a word of advice to farmers who want to make the transition to a more sustainable form of agriculture, what would you tell them?

I'd advise them to talk to as many people as they can who are trying different approaches, because that will save time and effort and a lot of mucking around. Don't talk to salesmen. Talk to the people who are actually doing things differently.

The one thing I do know that I would like to pass on to others is that it's a really interesting journey and it would be a shame to miss out on it.

Thank you for telling us your story Carl.

Michael Voumard

Food gardener in Tanunda, South Australia

Michael Voumard is not your common garden-variety farmer. In fact, in his eyes he's not a farmer at all, he's the custodian of 5 acres of land. Michael and his wife are both chefs at the Rockford Winery at Tanunda in South Australia's Barossa Valley, but Michael is a chef with a difference. His restaurant doesn't have a menu. People come for a food and wine experience, sit at a large table with the other guests and leave five hours after they arrive. Michael serves what he feels like cooking on the day. The menu depends very much on what has been harvested from the garden.

As well as being a chef with a difference, Michael is also a "gardener" with a difference. His planting schedule is governed by moon cycles. He sprays preparations with specific potencies that are developed according to the energy frequencies of his garden

Michael's garden is also a garden with a difference in that it has 100 varieties of food trees. He grows all his own herbs, nectar plants, vegetables, grains including maize and sorghum, and has a variety of hens and ducks. When the restaurant has an excess of fruit and vegetables it's simply left at the cellar door of the winery for people who come in to taste the wine to buy.

Tell me what you do, Michael.

For the past 9 years my wife and I have been responsible for a 5-acre food garden. It's an old heritage garden that was part of the original subdivision of the Barossa Valley when German migrants settled here. One family has farmed it since then. When the owners got too old to maintain the property, they rented it out for nearly 20 years. When we came here there were remnants of a very old, very neglected, subsistence farm. It belongs to the Rockford Winery now.

We were asked to restore the garden, replant the orchards, make use of what was still viable and start growing fruit and vegetables. That's what we've done. The long-term plan was to use the garden to supply a restaurant at the Winery and for my wife and me to be the chefs in that restaurant.

For the past five years food that's produced in the garden goes to a "table" for an afternoon of eating around a shared table. People come in at 12 o'clock and they leave about 5 p.m. There's no menu. They eat what we've prepared and we prepare whatever is available from the garden.

We didn't come into this with a conventional point of view. I let that go as a home gardener and chef 20 years ago when I had my first plot of land and grew my own vegetables. Basically we started off in this garden growing without any chemical fertilizers or poisons. The transition we've made has been to growing using biodynamic principles.

When we started this project we agreed with the winery owners that we'd grow organically, even though we weren't exactly sure what that meant. That led us down a path towards what is now termed biological agriculture, which encompasses the management of soil biology as well as soil nourishment and balancing. At the time we started, the young people we linked up with in the wine industry were moving into biological farming and they helped us.

We started here in August when the almond blossom on the old trees was out. It looked like fairyland. My wife and I went out with shovels and string lines and decided where we wanted things to grow. We decided to start by growing a little bit of food and slowly develop more beds as we got things under control. We also wanted to nurture the existing food trees, and plant new ones.

Off we went with shovels, digging beds. We went to the seed catalogues, which for us was like going to the lolly shop. We got catalogues from all the small seed companies and seed saving clubs. We've tried a sample of everything that's suited to growing in this climate.

Our vegetable gardens are set up in dedicated rows, 50 centimetres wide. In between each growing bed we have a 60 centimetre wide walking path. The long strips between the beds have clover and grass and we mow them and put the organic matter on the garden.

When you started, did you have any knowledge that the soil was important?

No. We were having a bumper season back in 2002. The rain didn't stop. It rained all the way through to the end of December, which is unknown for South Australia.

The soils looked tired but we just tended to think, "They're not clay, they're not sand. They must be good." We've got lots more knowledge now than we had back then. We now know that we have five different soil types within the 5 acres. We also have some toxic areas because of what happened on the farm before we got here.

It took us a year to put in lots of plants. We just watched. We were using books as guides and sometimes we could pick out why some of the things were happening, and could say, for example, "That indicates a lack of boron." We began to identify some of the problems, but we needed someone to help us fix them.

Did you do soil tests?

After the first growing summer we planned to replant the orchards. We were mapping out where all the different trees and gardens would be and suddenly realised that we needed to know exactly what we were dealing with. We needed someone with a proper science background. That's when we found Lawrie & Co and asked them for help. They were distributors for NutriTech Solutions. That's when we decided to do soil tests. When we did the soil tests we discovered lots of things.

We discovered that there was no carbon in the soil. The soil was useless. We had 2 % organic matter. The pH was reasonable but we were deficient in magnesium and boron. The calcium levels weren't too bad. Some areas were excessive in potassium and some had much too much zinc. There were different imbalances in different areas, depending on what had been done in those areas before we arrived.

What did you do?

We kept talking to the people at Lawrie & Co. Some of the young people on their staff had a broad perspective and they told us what to do. We'd tell them, "The beetroot is doing this. Cabbages are doing that." Some of the solutions they suggested, we just couldn't afford. Sometimes we just didn't have the practical experience to do what they suggested.

Everyone was advising us that composting was the way to go because getting the carbon levels up was the number one priority. The problem was changing my thinking from the sort of manual composting I'd done as a home gardener to the tonnages we needed to bring the carbon levels up rapidly in a garden of this size. That was a big learning curve.

We started bringing in material from the district. There's plenty of straw available and someone gave us 40 enormous bales of straw at no cost. We brought in some green waste. We put everything together in various heaps and we used chicken manure because it's the manure that is most commonly available in the area.

We quickly learned that we couldn't make compost on that scale in summer because the amount of water that was needed for the process was huge. From then on we built massive piles of compost during autumn to keep us supplied, but it was always a problem getting enough of what we needed when we needed it. This autumn we have 16 piles of compost on the go. Some are being used. Some have only just been built this week. We do something with compost heaps every week.

We've had to make our own compost. We don't have the financial resources to purchase a really good product, even if one were available, but even so, things started to work. Once we started using the compost, the vegetables grew. We were getting more minerals into the soil and the balance of minerals was improving. Pests and weeds were still a major problem though.

By this time we were a couple of years down the track. We'd planted about two hundred trees. They're all sorts of varieties because this is a cook's garden, not a market garden. We have two of each variety. There are 10 varieties of pears.

We were starting to produce things to take to a farmers' market every week. I was an original committee member of the Barossa Valley Farmers' Market in Angaston. All of us on the committee were growing and producing a whole variety of produce because we wanted to see diversification in the productivity of the region, rather than just having grapes. Having to take produce to market took our project to a slightly higher level. We needed to have produce to sell rather than just concentrating on development. This was an interim stage for the project while the trees were growing and we weren't yet ready for the value adding stage, which was the purpose of the whole project.

People were telling us that we should go for organic certification but we weren't really sure why we needed to do this. In the end I really only had to satisfy myself. When we sold produce at the farmers' market, we stood behind the stall and people knew us. The locals who were buying our produce had faith and trust in what we told them about what we were doing. We weren't selling produce anywhere else.

What do you do about weeds?

We have a great array of tools. Just before starting this project we were working outside Canberra, where there are some amazing people who run a company called Gundaroo Tillers. They've been importing and making tools that are designed by Swiss guys or by Elliott Coleman. We have little gadgets on sticks and wheels and we have a regime that's part of the biodynamic calendar so that every part of the plant is tended according to the sign of the week. We know we have two or three days to work on root vegetables so they're weeded, seeded or harvested. By doing that and not letting the weeds get out of hand and go to seed, we manage to control them. We've just put clover and grass in all the pathways and we mow that.

What steps did you take to get rid of the pests and diseases?

While we were working on the winery garden, at the same time I was developing an interest in biodynamics and was applying biodynamics methods in my own home garden. I gradually started sneaking some of the biodynamic methodology into the winery garden because basically, how we do things here is my decision as long as it's ethical. When we started with biodynamics it was basically just a case of sprinkling stuff around under the olive trees, but we had some difficult problems that needed addressing, and the biodynamics community that I was in contact with here weren't really able to help me solve my problems. Everyone was at the same fledgling stage that I was at. I think the vineyard owners really just wanted to spray a bit of stuff on in the vineyards so they could put it on their labels that the grapes were being grown biodynamically!

We'd come as far as we were likely to come as distance members of the Biodynamics Association and we hadn't solved the complex problems that we were having at that time. That was my motivation for contacting Cheryl Kemp, who was an advisor with the Association. Cheryl became involved with what we were doing, although it was nearly a year before she was able to visit us. She talked about balance more than anything else. She told us we had to stop using chicken manure in our compost piles and start using cow manure. Using the chicken manure gave us high levels of nitrogen, which acted as a magnet for all the pests. I was reluctant to do so at first because it was really easy to source chicken manure, but she persuaded me with some very practical information. I now have a deal with a farmer who has a herd of dairy cows. We collect manure when we need it and we give him wine.

I haven't delved deeply into the philosophy behind biodynamics. I just use it. I'm aware that without belief in the interconnectedness of everything, it doesn't work. It isn't a set of chemicals. It's an expression of timings and energies.

Dr Manfred Klett spoke at the National Conference and from what he said I understand that the essence of biodynamics is that every part of the Earth, whether it is beneath the soil or above the land, is connected to every other part. There are scientific reasons why what we do affects everything else. What you do in relationship to one element, when you do it and how you do it affects everything else. I think the important thing is not to go into the "airy fairy scary" stuff because that's when you go "Hmmm".

Are you relying totally on composting?

Composting and putting out the energies on a monthly basis are the most important things we do. Those two things are all we have to do. We weed, we tend, we plant and we supply water and we just recycle everything through the system.

We layer our compost piles as we build them. We don't add any rock minerals because we don't feel we need a lot but we do add two forms of calcium, dolomite and hydrated lime. We also add seaweed powder. We have a slight deficiency in cobalt so we're adding a tablespoon of cobalt to a 3-metre heap. We're probably getting to the point where we need to run some soil tests again next spring to see whether we've got the levels back to where they should be. Once we start recycling, the trace elements that have been deficient will no longer be added.

We have a couple of young lads who have cows at home and we pay them the equivalent of half an hour's work for a 20-litre bucket of manure. If they do that for us they're also allowed to come and work on the farm during the school holidays.

Now, the only things we bring in for our compost piles are cow manure and cereal straw. We haven't sufficient land to produce our own straw, but this year we grew sorghum for the first time as a green manure crop and we're using it as a compost heap protector. Every year we try and work out how to do something that will help a problem associated with the changing climate. Sorghum stops the compost heaps from drying out in the heat. We run all our straw through our poultry yards before we add it to the compost piles. We have pens of chickens, ducks and bantams for different purposes.

Are you using biodynamic preparations?

We believe we are but we're doing it on a homeopathic level rather than on an actual level. Cheryl works on the idea that our farm has a particular frequency and she adapts the preparations to that frequency. We don't put out the actual preparations.

Cheryl presented us with the idea of radionics, but my response to that was that she was pushing me totally out of my comfort zone. After a day or two of discussion I could see that there was a degree of sense in what she was telling us, because one of the big issues in farming is having enough time to do what's needed.

At that time we were already spending 3 days a week in the kitchen and labour wasn't something our employers wanted to pay for, so we were struggling trying to keep up with the bio-dynamic processes which were necessary if we wanted to keep up with things. Radionics ended up making a lot of sense.

Every month we give the garden a spray of complete preparations radionically. Cheryl Kemp makes the preparations specially for our farm with specific potencies, depending on what she discovers when she comes to the farm each year. She determines by dowsing where we're at and what potencies we need. We brew our own teas with seaweed, using Tasmanian or Queensland dry chopped kelp. We go out on the day when the moon is opposite Saturn each month and we cover the farm with this energy and the seaweed.

I had an entomologist out last spring and she was enthralled with the place. As we get one thing under control we move on to understanding and learning about something else. Now we're learning about nectar plants to sustain the beneficial insects. Pests do come but they're controlled. To keep the beneficials we need to provide food for them. We've done that. I haven't seen the red-legged mite for three years. When we first planted, certain crops would be decimated at this time of year. This is perfect weather for them, cold and dry, and none are hatching at all. We've not sprayed. We've just worked on getting everything in balance. The fact that the red-legged mite isn't here any more is a perfect example of the fact that we're getting greater health back into the soil.

We do have a balancing spray for aphids if they start to cause problems. That spray contains boron, molasses and hydrated lime. When the sap has the right minerals it goes down into the roots. We get aphids when the sugars are all at the wrong end of the plant. There's been quite a lot of research done on that. That spray is our only form of insect control. Where we can we use the poultry and they catch things like earwigs, which are a problem. In places where the chooks can't go we trap the earwigs and try to upset their breeding cycle. The problem with hens is that they don't distinguish between what's good and what isn't.

I'd been playing with a lot of "peppering" prior to Cheryl's visit to try and reduce the pest problems. When you're first introduced to peppering you think, "Hurrah, I'm going to save the world." I'd been learning about peppering from Vicki, a lovely lady who had given me a much deeper appreciation of the esoteric processes and the spiritual connectivity that comes with this style of farming.

How have you managed in terms of labour?

In the beginning it was a full time job for my wife and me. We were lucky to come across a couple of rare young lads who were growing up in the district and were interested in what we were doing. They were both intelligent and capable lads who came to us when they were thirteen. With their energy and enthusiasm during the weekend and on school holidays we were able to develop the whole garden. The boys were committed and liked to understand and question what was going on and they also had an enormous work ethic. One is now doing a double degree at University. They loved working here, and other members of their family have come along since. It's been the school kids who've really helped us. Then over the years, people have been enthralled by the project. It really is a beautiful place. We've been doing something that people have visions of creating. People came and helped for a week or so here and there.

Now that we're in the kitchen almost full time, we have one man who works five days a week. We get lads in the school holidays, which is when we get the place back on track. It's a struggle constantly.

If people wanted to do something similar to what you've done, what would you tell them?

What we're doing is not overly sustainable because of its complexity. On a smaller scale or in a shared community situation, you could do what we're doing. If you wanted to do it on a commercial basis you'd have to specialise and then you'd need to make different decisions from the ones we've made.

Your journey over the last few years is indicative of a level of dedication that's extraordinary. What do you attribute that to?

More than anything it's the challenge of nurturing something. This is food that puts delight on people's faces. Without the winery's support the garden wouldn't be here. People wouldn't be prepared to pay the real costs of the food we produce, which is okay because we don't have any economies of scale. The fact that we produce so many different things makes us relatively inefficient. It's just the joy of doing it that's important. It reminds you how small you are in the natural scheme of things, and it rewards you and castigates you when you don't get things right. It's simply a case of "Look at those onions. Aren't they fabulous!"

Thank you Michael. One day I would love to visit your restaurant and walk through your garden.

Chapter 7
Transition Trends

As a consequence of speaking to a large number of growers who have made or are making the transition from conventional growing methods to those that are sustainable over a longer time frame, it has been possible to identify a number of trends.

These include:

1. Diversity of DIY and traditional sales strategies
2. Small scale operations
3. Marginally productive areas being farmed
4. Diversity of strategies
5. A move away from agricultural chemicals
6. Methods based on previously ignored scientific knowledge or "new" scientific findings
7. Transition accompanied by spiritual development in addition to scientific awareness.

1. Diversity of Sales Strategies

Conventional farmers rely on a centralised system of wholesalers. Over a number of years, this system has received a large amount of adverse publicity because of the perceived lack of transparency and resentment by growers who believe they are not treated fairly and honestly. Farmers have responded by establishing a diversity of sales strategies which eliminate middlemen and to retain a much higher percentage of the value of their crops. These include:
• DIY sales being made through local markets or box plans
• Internet and direct sales to a clientele that is built up over a period of years

- Personal contacts with local manufacturers
- Established wholesale distribution networks through co-operative packing and marketing systems
- Contracts with retail supermarket chains
- Direct export
- Value adding through processing.

Many of the farmers interviewed believe that their success is due to the fact that they have taken responsibility not just for the growing of crops but also for the marketing, and/or value adding of their produce. The growing number and popularity of farmers' markets provides evidence to support this trend.

DIY sales
By selling locally, competition is limited to the produce available in nearby supermarkets or being offered by other growers. People who purchase at farmers' markets and through connection to CSAs (community supported agriculture) do so because they want local, fresh, preferably organic produce. They like to be able to put a face behind the food they are buying and to be assured that the food they are buying has not had poisons sprayed on it. Ray Palmer, Heinz Gugger and Martin Brook have all personally sold their produce at farmers' markets. Dick Rochford sells his garlic through the Internet and sends to customers by mail.

Contracts with local manufacturers
Carl Brown sells his grapes to a local wine maker. Carl believes that having grapes that are of high quality assures him of being able to sell his produce, but not of getting a premium price.

David Slacksmith enters into a contract for his corn with Simplott, which harvests and transports the corn to their factory in Bathurst. Jim Velehris sells his almonds directly to manufacturers.

Conventional wholesale distribution networks
For the most part large growers continue to use the more conventional central market system, but complain that the prices they receive are low. They are concerned at the competition from imported food, which comes from countries where agriculture is subsidised or where labour costs are extremely low, compared with Australia.

Mike and Jenny Ottone watched as their banana operation was ruined by what they saw was manipulation of the wholesale market system. They believe they have survived in the pineapple industry by becoming members of a local packing and marketing co-operative which, because of the size of its turnover, is able to negotiate with wholesalers and supermarkets from a position of strength, something they could not do as relatively small, independent producers.

Tony Croft, Kevin Keogh, Ian Smith, Kym Green, Wayne Edwards and Malcolm Heather sell through the normal wholesale distribution system.

Contracts with retail supermarket chains
Ian Smith markets a great proportion of his crop directly to the large supermarkets. His move into organic production was largely motivated by his desire to have an advantage when marketing to these large distributors because generally, the Australian market is over supplied with apples.

Export
Heinz Gugger moved into horticulture after a career in export/import in the USA and immediately developed an export market for his persimmons. Geoff Bugden is developing a co-operative export initiative and is sending the pecan harvest from 30 nearby farmers to China. Kym

Green exports cherries to S.E. Asia. Ian Smith sells a proportion of his apple crop overseas. Wayne Edwards' parents used to export huge quantities of cauliflowers to S.E. Asia when there was a huge vegetable export industry based in Manjimup in Western Australia in the 1970s and 1980s. The export industry dried up because of an unfavourable exchange rate for the Australian dollar. Wayne is again thinking about exporting his organic produce.

Value Adding
Martin Brook has probably developed the most innovative and valuable marketing strategy of all the farmers interviewed. Not content just to grow macadamias, Martin has developed an award winning range of foods, which he sells in Australia and the USA. Martin has been so successful in this venture that his company has won lots of awards, both in Australia and overseas, including the Telstra "Autralian Business of the Year".

Geoff Bugden is value-adding by sizing his pecans.

Probably the most unusual example of value-adding is the Rockford Wines restaurant. Michael Voumard and his wife are both the chefs at this restaurant and the gardeners responsible for the establishment and tending of the 5-acre garden that supplies the food cooked in the restaurant.

2. Small Scale Operations

One of the surprising aspects of the research that underpins the findings in this book is that farmers do not need large areas of land to make a living. Whilst Dick Rochford does not have the smallest property, all but 5 acres is unusable for growing crops and at any one time he is using only 1¼ acres.

In Western Australia, James Fernleigh's apricot orchard is only 15 acres in size and he is raising a family from the revenue he is getting from his farm. So far he believes he has only got to 50% of the farm's earning capacity.

Carl Brown and David Slacksmith both have large farms, but have converted only small areas of those farms to more sustainable farming methods.

Three highly successful larger scale farmers are Ian Smith, Malcolm Heather and Heinz Gugger, but even so, their properties are less than 50 hectares in size.

The people who have made the transition from conventional farming have been most successful when they have done it one small area at a time. Even Ian and Andrew Smith, who have a 35-hectare apple and cherry orchard, took ten years to convert their whole property to organic, and they are still having problems with their cherries, which are the last trees to be changed over.

The one farmer who attempted to change a large area to organic farming quickly was Wayne Edwards, who found the cost of this was so large that he had to sell a farm and his home to finance the transition.

3. Marginally Productive Areas are being Farmed.

It is apparent that many horticultural farms are making use of land that is marginal in terms of soil fertility and water availability.

The major reasons why farmers are being forced to deal with physical environments that present huge challenges in terms of production are:
a) good agricultural land is scarce and expensive
b) formerly fertile land has been substantially degraded.

a) Good agricultural land is scarce and expensive
Good land is best for farming, but good land is also used for housing, industry, recreation, warehousing and large-scale commercial agriculture. Because of competing interests, good land, especially good land located near large urban areas, is very expensive. Beginner farmers cannot afford good farming land close to the city and have to make compromises.

When companies like Mulgowie Agriculture, grow about 7,000 hectares of corn on land they own in the fertile Lockyer Valley and the Darling Downs, little good land is left for small farmers, who must "make do" with what's available.

James Fernleigh has 15 acres, which consists of two separated blocks. Carl Brown's farm consists of several different blocks of land, some as much as 10 kilometres from his house block as well as being steep and with very poor quality soil.

Ray Palmer, Tony Croft and Jim Velehris do not have reliable water supply.

The fortunate people, in terms of land ownership, are those who have been born into long-term farming families and have inherited properties.

There is another group who have made sufficient money during their working lives to be in a position to purchase good agricultural land. Their challenge has been to develop the expertise to work the land effectively. It is possible that this is a trend that is growing in momentum. Disillusioned with city living, people are moving into country areas with sufficient capital to purchase small blocks of land and the desire to develop the skills and expertise needed to work that land. Often this involves a mid-life change of career. James Fernleigh, Heinz and Angela Gugger, Geoff Bugden and Martin Brook are examples of horticulture as "second career" choices, and all of them have been fortunate in that they have been able to buy farms that have good water supplies and potentially fertile soils.

It is possible that the need to use poor farming land for food production attests to the lack of importance placed on farming in Australia. If farmers wish to supply city markets, reduce food miles and provide fresh produce on a regular basis, they often have to farm marginal areas with poor soil and inadequate water supplies, because that is the only land remaining near populated areas.

Fifty years ago, much of the land along the Nepean River, in the Baulkham Hills and Windsor areas, was occupied by orchards and market gardens. This is now totally covered in houses, factories and urban infrastructure. Fruit and vegetables that were once grown close to Sydney now have to be transported from much further away, which increases food miles and the reliance on oil for transport.

b) Formerly fertile land has been degraded
On Kenneth Keogh's farm, three generations of farmers have transformed formerly fertile soil to a condition that was "as close to dead as to make little difference" before Kenneth started work to try and bring it back to life and back into production.

Martin Brook's farm was a denuded dairy farm covered in noxious weeds: lantana and camphor laurel trees.

James Fernleigh's account of the history of his farm is typical of many: "The person who owned the land before me basically ran it into the ground. As the trees failed he just pulled them out. He didn't fertilize." Similarly, when he bought it, Tony Croft's farm was "organic by neglect".

4. Diversity of Strategies

Farmers interviewed are using a variety of strategies to:
- Re-mineralise soils and get the elements back into balance
- Increase levels of organic matter in the soil
- Improve the variety and numbers of organisms in the soil
- Eliminate damage by pests and disease
- Reduce weed problems
- Restore soil cohesion.

They are doing this based on evidence provided by
- Soil testing and analysis
- Soil micro-organism testing
- Leaf testing
- Brix level monitoring
- Insect monitoring
- Radionics testing.

With few exceptions, the farmers interviewed test their soils and apply fertilizers on the basis of what is missing from an "optimally balanced" soil, as defined by Professor William Albrecht. Professor Albrecht realised that the most fertile soils in the world are all similar in terms of their mineral composition and the balance of the minerals they contain.

Most of the growers interviewed are working to enhance the number and diversity of soil organisms. Many have studied with Elaine Ingham and done courses on using microscope analysis to identify soil biology or on using and making compost teas.

Those farmers who have started investigating the role of soil micro-organisms on soils and their impact on plant health, yields and soil enhancement are totally convinced that this is the way of the future.

Some, like Ian Smith, are looking for a "formula" to follow to get the correct mix of organisms. Others, like Malcolm Heather, believe that the key is to work towards achieving the widest diversity of different organisms possible.

Many of the farmers interviewed believe that even though they are farming agriculturally marginal land, they are making it work by building up soil organic levels and soil biology.

Several of the farmers interviewed are complementing their soil improvement strategies with biodynamic preparations, and a few are basing their whole operation on biodynamic principles.

An even more surprising number of growers are using radionics as a means of enhancing production. Radionics instruments measure subtle bio-physical energies. This is made possible by the fact that each element carries an electric charge. Radionics instruments are used to analyse the fields emitted by these charges. This technology was first applied in the US in the late 1800s, survived scientific scrutiny and was further developed in the UK in the mid 1990s. Radionics practitioners believe it is a valuable tool for optimising crop nutrition and water use efficiency.

5. Movement away from Agricultural Chemicals

Without exception farmers interviewed are working to totally eliminate poisons from their farms, and many have succeeded in doing this. Some, like Ian Smith in Tasmania, are substituting "soft" alternatives. Ian Smith and Martin Brook monitor insect populations closely. Insect pests are controlled with the use of pheromones, which are hormone attractants that confuse the male moth so that it can't find a partner to mate with, which means there are no grubs to damage the apples.

David Slacksmith probably uses the most unconventional method for bird and insect pests: radionics. David firmly believes radionics works. It is undoubtedly a highly "alternative" strategy but David has witnessed its effectiveness. Heinz Gugger also believes that radionics has a lot of potential to enhance production.

This is the technology recommended by Dr Arden Andersen, High Lovel, Graeme Sait and David von Pein, all of whom are highly regarded by organic farmers around Australia.

The Rudolph Steiner soil improvement technique based on burying cow horns filled with manure has been treated with great scepticism for years. Now it is being realised that dung-filled cow horns are breeding places for billions of micro-organisms and the means for bringing in energy. When the microbe-rich material extracted from cow horns that have been buried for a long period of time is placed in compost heaps, the micro-organisms multiply and work to break down organic matter and create humus. In the process, the manure becomes charged with energy. Buried cow horns, compost and compost teas all work towards building the same result: microbe-rich soils containing high levels of organic matter. There are a number of biodynamics preparations, each of which has its own contribution to soil coherence.

6. Basis is provided by "new" science

It is very obvious from the interviews in this book that the "hick from the bush" image of Australian farmers is a long way from the truth. Many of the farmers we have spoken with are extraordinarily well-read, highly educated in their area of expertise and have a thirst for more and more knowledge. They are investing hugely in their own education for the purpose of understanding the science that underpins the technology they are using.

Hugh Lovel believes that this stems, in part, from government policies. Rather than subsiding farmers, as most governments do, the Australian policy is to provide subsidies for training. As a result of this ability of farmers to attend educational seminars and training programmes, many overseas people have visited Australia regularly, and over the past decade have had a dramatic impact on the interest in a variety of farming strategies.

Even more fascinating is the realisation that, for the most part, these growers want to share their knowledge and their experiences so that others may benefit. They want the story to be told because they believe it is important that others realise that if it is possible for one, it is possible for many to follow in their footsteps.

7. Transition is Accompanied by Spiritual Development and Scientific Awareness

One of the surprising outcomes from doing the interviews was identification of the trend towards a greatly enhanced level of awareness of the complexity of natural systems and an enhanced level of spiritual development, compared with what one would expect to find in farmers generally.

James Fernleigh is typical of where farmers started out, before they began the transition to more sustainable forms of agriculture. As James says, " I was probably as far removed as it is possible to be from the organic world. Neither Michelle nor I had ever been to a naturopath. We'd never even thought about alternatives to mainstream chemical farming practices. We used pesticides and insecticides as a matter of course."

Wayne Edwards believes that the more he has learnt about soil health, the more he has seen the connection between soil health, plant health and human health and the interrelationships between all three. Wayne's goal for the future is to develop raw food workshops, because he believes that "the more you help people, the better off the place will be."

Michael Voumard happily works with the rhythms of the calendar and tends his plants according to the biodynamic calendar, which he uses as a management tool. Michael sprays when the moon is opposite Saturn each month and does it because he thinks it works, rather than for some deep metaphysical reason.

The motivation that drives many of these farmers is also different from what you might expect. Most of them see it as a challenge to do things better so that everyone and everything benefits. Kym Green advises, " Don't do it for the money. It's not about money, it's about the challenge." He goes on to say, "We don't have blinkers on. We don't believe that just because we're doing things more naturally it's necessarily going to be better or easier. We've lifted the bar and we're still trying to clear it. We get there occasionally."

Chapter 8
Change Masters

During the interviews that have provided the information for this book, the names of a few people have come up over and over again. Speaking to farmers it is obvious that these people have been responsible for changing the face of Australian agriculture. They have done it through education, by writing, speaking, research, running workshops and training programmes and working as consultants to growers. Their influence has been dramatic and far-reaching. These people include the following:

Dr Arden Andersen

Dr Arden Andersen is an American. He was first a soil scientist and agricultural consultant, then a physician. He specialises in nutritional management and advises farmers how to build up soil biology. He has taught a variety of classes on such subjects as soil and crop management and agricultural radionics. He has been a regular visitor to Australia and has spoken to hundreds of Australian farmers.

As a world-renowned influence in biological farming, Dr Andersen is well versed in the connection between soil health, plant health and human health. He emphasises the necessity to practise healthy eating and wholesome farming practices.

He is the author of several books, including *Science in Agriculture, Real Medicine, Real Health* and *Anatomy of Life*.

Arden believes that "Good nutrition comes back to agriculture and the way our foods are grown. Western farming methods have raped the soils, depleted minerals and compromised our food resources. Real medicine must start with diet and ultimately that goes back to the nutrition of food from the farm."

In September 2004 Arden was quoted in *Acres USA* as saying that "It's pretty much common sense that you're not going to have anything in a food commodity, minerally speaking, that doesn't already exist in the soil or in the fertility programme used in growing that crop."

Elaine Ingham

Elaine Ingham is an American soil biology researcher and founder of Soil Foodweb Inc. She is recognised around the world as a leader in soil microbiology and research of the soil food web.

Elaine has a PhD from Colorado University and joined the faculties of Forest Science and Botany and Plant Pathology and remained on faculty until 2001. She is an Affiliate Professor, Graduate Research, Southern Cross University at Lismore, NSW.

By 1999, soil samples were being sent to her for analysis. Analysis of these soil samples became a large component of what she was doing and through the university she started offering a service called the Soil Microbial Biomass Service, which offered researchers and commercial clients the ability to have soil samples analysed for soil foodweb organisms. In 1995 the service was taken off-campus and Soil Foodweb Inc. became a commercial enterprise.

Since 1996 Dr Ingham and her staff have developed methods to rapidly assess soil and foliar-related organisms. She has discovered that soil and foliar biology changes with different management practices. Her work with biological products produced for farms is increasing understanding of how bio-stimulant products work to promote particular groups of organisms. She has worked with many growers to show how to make the best compost/humus material and has demonstrated conclusively that when soil foodwebs are established and fed properly, long-term benefits for plant growth occur.

Working on compost tea with many people around the world has brought greater understanding of how to properly manage thermally produced compost, vermicompost and compost tea to guarantee disease suppression, soil enhancement and nutrient retention.

Dr Elaine Ingham is author of *The Compost Tea Brewing Manual* and *The Soil Biology Primer*.

Cheryl Kemp

Cheryl's entry into biodynamics was via her interest in health issues, as she had trained as a nurse and, in her search for holistic methods of healing, also trained in homeopathy. Realising that all aspects of healing came back to food and how it was grown, Cheryl saw in biodynamics a form of "homeopathy for Earth". She travelled to New Zealand, did a Diploma in Biodynamic Agriculture, then worked for four years with Peter Proctor in the office of Biodynamics New Zealand.

When extra minerals and trace elements need to be added to the land, it can be more beneficial and cost saving to add small amounts to composted material where they become incorporated with the fungi and bacteria in a living way. When the compost is put out, the minerals and elements are taken up immediately by the soil micro-organisms and not leached. A complete compost prescription can be developed, working with soil tests, to achieve balanced soil and balanced soil life.

Since leaving the Biodynamic Association of Australia Cheryl has developed a set of homeopathic potentised remedies of the biodynamic preparations,which can be distributed through irrigation and fertigation systems.

Cheryl also works with radionics, which uses the frequencies and patterns of living of organic organisms to diagnose and/or heal by broadcasting frequencies into a given area using crystals or specific minerals.

Richard May

Richard May grew up walking the scrub and went on to obtain degrees in Agricultural Science and Ecology before spending many years in charge of planning and management of national parks in Western Australia. He now provides training, advice, programmes and systems to farmers, leading to sustainable systems. His aim is to assist farmers to produce products of high nutritional value and to value-add their products to ensure a high rate of return on investment. He does this by teaching them what is actually happening in the paddock, by allowing them to understand how plants grow in soil and atmosphere and providing information on the interrelationships between the biological, physical and metaphysical components of crop production. Richard is an authority on the process of conversion of humus to a stable form and the conversion of carbon to carbohydrate. He explains that cow horns used in biodynamic agriculture act as antennae and are the means for bringing cosmic frequencies into the soil.

Hugh Lovel

A biochemist by training, Hugh Lovel became disillusioned with biochemistry because his courses didn't include the study of anything living, so he switched to psychology. After eight years working in San Francisco as a psychologist and a chef Hugh developed the theory that people's strength of character relates to the quality of the food they eat. They have "guts" because their food has high levels of those things that provide energy and strength in people. He bemoans the fact that food today is lacking in character, taste, texture and nutritional value.

Wanting to investigate the idea of the link between food and character, Hugh decided to become a farmer. He wanted to grow "real" food, because he knew that the chemical equilibrium of plants was destroyed by the use of chemical fertilizers, particularly soluble nitrogen. He was searching for a different approach. His search led to biodynamics, which he has endeavoured to understand through the application of scientific principles, but not the scientific principles taught in agricultural schools, which favour conventional farming strategies.

Hugh moved from California to Blairsville, Georgia. His neighbour was Peter Tompkins, author of the very famous and controversial *The Secret Life of Plants*. Hugh farmed for 30 years, producing vegetables for local markets. He grew ginseng and forest herbs, milked cows and made cheese and butter and grew grains.

Hugh has taken basic radionics technology to an advanced level by developing the field broadcaster, which sends out the biodynamic patterns and sometimes the patterns of peppers for clearing specific pests or weeds from a particular area. He has also developed an atmospheric reorganizer that orders and re-organizes the atmosphere for many kilometres around it and balances weather conditions.

Hugh has become an Australian citizen and continues to lecture in biodynamics and radionics throughout Australia. He believes that conventional farmers in Australia know there is no future in using conventional methods. He speaks of one farmer who has 80,000 acres under cotton. Every time that farmer sprays his cotton it costs him $1 million. He sprays 20 times during the crop cycle and pours nitrogen into his crop. He ends up with short fibre cotton, which does not fetch a premium price.

Ray O'Grady

Ray O'Grady is based in South Lismore in New South Wales. He runs a company called Smart Bugs Downunder and sells soil bacteria and fungi mixes, the equipment to make compost teas and biochar (charcoal). Ray advocates restoring soil health by improving carbon levels in the soil. At a "Managing the Carbon Cycle" workshop at Katanning, W.A. in March 2007, Ray explained that "Soil carbon provides the energy to sustain biological activity, diversity and productivity, regulates and aids nutrient and water movement, detoxifies and degrades organic and inorganic products and acts as a sink for storing and recycling nutrients."

John Pannan

John Pannan was a biodynamics farmer from Horsham, Victoria, a radionics practitioner and trainer, and a consultant who advised and helped many growers. When he applied the principles he had learnt at an Arden Andersen workshop, John turned his farm around. That year he harvested a 3.7 t/ha crop of malting grade barley, one of the best crops he had ever grown, and grew a paddock of peas a metre high and flowering when they were hit by a -6° frost. The peas continued to grow as though nothing had happened, but his neighbours' pea crops were a blackened mass. He attributed his crops' resilience in the face of frost to high brix (sap concentration) levels. John realised that crops on most conventionally managed farms usually have brix levels in the range of 3 to 5, and that the key to successful farming was to bring the levels up to 20.

John became an expert in energy frequencies and resonances and how minerals work in the soil. He promoted the idea that that when minerals in the soil are combined in the correct balance, good things happen synergistically.

John Pannan died in 2007.

David von Pein

A retired farmer, David von Pein runs a company called "The Meter Man" through which he sells a wide range of meters, tools and instruments, including brix meters, pH meters, soil and fruit penetrometers, conductivity meters and infra-red plant stress monitors.

David strongly believes that if farmers can identify what is lacking in the soil, management techniques exist that can help restore the soil to balance. In a healthy balanced soil, it is possible to grow plants that are healthy and disease and insect resistant. David also believes that "It is imperative as a nation that we start thinking about the nutritional value of food grown and eaten in this country. If we can achieve greater nutrition in our food, more people will live healthier lives."

A strong believer that farmers and growers have to learn to think for themselves and to ask why things happen as they do, David thinks that for too long growers have looked to agronomists to tell them what to do, when to plant, what to grow and when to spray.

Robert Pekin

Ex-dairy farmer Robert Pekin is the founder of Food Connect, a not-for-profit CSA (Consumer Supported Agriculture) system. It was established in 2006. In 2009 Food Connect won the prestigious Queensland Sustainability Award. The Brisbane Food Connect operation accesses produce from more than 100 farmers whose farms are located within a 100-kilometre radius of Brisbane. Food Connect distributes boxes to more than 1,500 households in the Brisbane area and to organic restaurants. Since it started in 2006, Food Connect has grown at a rate of over 70% per annum. Its aim is to provide a distribution system for locally produced fresh fruit and vegetables to customers who wish to reduce "food miles" and to support local farmers. It operates its own accreditation system based on the inputs and methods that growers use.

Food Connect offers a highly efficient and cost effective model of food distribution that relies on "city cousins": people who are prepared to allow the use of their homes for collection of weekly food boxes by Food Connect customers who live nearby.

Food Connect now operates in Brisbane, Sydney, Melbourne and Adelaide and will shortly have distribution centres in many of Australia's larger towns.

Graeme Sait

Graeme Sait is co-founder and CEO of NutriTech Solutions. He is a sought-after keynote speaker at seminars world-wide, author of *Nutrition Rules*, a book that some of our farmers believe is an extremely valuable resource, founder of the Radiance Festival at Woodford, and an amazing educator. He runs a 5-day Certificate of Sustainable Agriculture programme throughout Australia, Norfolk Island, the Netherlands and South Africa. Graeme has written over 300 published articles on such topics as the link between nutrition and wellness.

In the early days of NutriTech Solutions, Graeme decided that his marketing strategy would be through education. For many years he has conducted workshops and seminars throughout Australia. His strength as a speaker lies in his meticulous research combined with a unique capacity to explain complex subjects in an easy-to-understand manner. His passionate presentations have often been described as life changing.

NutriTech Solutions works in conjunction with Elaine Ingham's Soil Food Web laboratory. Prescription blends, tailored specifically for farmers' needs, are available from NutriTech.

Graeme advocates building soil humus levels as a form of carbon sequestration and is in increasing demand as a speaker as the devastating implications of Peak Oil become apparent.

Neville Simcock

Neville Simcock lives in Mt Gambier, South Australia, and manufactures fertilizers specifically to meet farmers' needs. Neville has spent most of his life farming in Western Australia as a member of a very successful partnership. He experienced all the problems associated with farming, including lice and footrot in his sheep. Fascinated by what he learned from people like Arden Andersen, Neville has been committed for many years to finding ways to farm better.

It has taken Neville many years of study and investigation to be able to do what he is now doing: manufacturing fertilizers for specific needs and to solve particular problems. Neville likens what he does to making a cake. As he describes it, a cake is the sum total of all the ingredients, each added in a particular way in and in a specific sequence. The cake then needs to be cooked. This is process that adds heat and changes the structure of the ingredients.

Many fertilizer salesmen sell the equivalent of agricultural "eggs" and "flour", but this isn't the cake that farmers need: they're just selling the ingredients for making the cake.

Just like a cake, effective soil fertilizer needs a variety of ingredients, which vary depending on what is already in the soil. Each ingredient is added in a particular way and in a specific sequence and then subjected to a process to "cook" the mix. Ingredients in a cake include milk, flour and eggs. Ingredients in a fertilizer include mineral elements in various forms, organic matter and a variety of micro-organisms. This process produces a fertilizer that is fully laden with micro-organisms, a food source for the organisms, and the mineral elements such as gypsum, phosphate and/or lime that provide a home for the micro-organisms.

Neville explains that you address the shortfalls in soils by providing an input that is composed of the elements that will bring the soil into balance. He identifies shortfalls using Reams tests, which provide him with a different interpretation of what is going on from the more normal Albrecht method of testing.

It has taken 15 years of intensive study for Neville to develop the process he is now using, and he is excited by the changes he is seeing on farms where his products are being used.

Resources

Contact details for companies and services referred to by growers.

Acres Australia
PO Box 1822
Noosaville,
Queensland 4566
(07) 5471 0877
www.acresaustralia.com.au

The National Newspaper of sustainable agriculture. Editor: Lindsay Bock.

AgSolutions P/L
8 Wadell Road
Gympie
Queensland 4570
(07) 5482 8044
www. infor@agsolutions.com.au

Manufacturers of BFA registered mineral fertilizers and soil conditioners including NatraMin.

Ausmin Australia P/L
66 Chum Street
Dinmore
Queensland, 4303
(07) 3282 1200

Suppliers of fertilizers.Backed by EAL Laboratories. Sell organically certified, activated minerals, Platinum P and Vital Liquids that combine Biobrew biological inoculants

Cheryl Kemp
627 Tyringham Road
North Dorrigo
NSW 2453
Tel: (02) 6657 5396

Biodynamics consultant, tailoring methods to farmer's own needs or developing biodynamic programme for certification. Provides advice by phone. Conducts radionics and biodynamic workshops.

EAL Laboratories
PO Box 157
Lismore
NSW 2480
Tel: (02) 6620 3678
Fax: (02) 6620 3957

Provide in-depth fertility analysis of soil test data used to formulate prescription blends to provide precision nutrition for crops. Plant therapy leaf analysis provides the means to identify precise nutritional requirements of plants.

Food Connect
3/8 Textile Crescent
Salisbury,
Brisbane, 4107
Queensland
Tel: (07) 3216 7777

A not-for-profit community supported food distribution programme, which sources susainably grown food from areas adjacent to cities and towns for distribution through customer networks.

Hydrosmart
259 Fullarton Road
Parkside
South Australia 5063
Tel: (08) 8357 3334
www: infor@hydrosmart.com.au

Water treatment technology that offers solutions to problems caused by minerals and chemicals in water supplies. Prevents algae, fungal growth and crystals combining to form scale that blocks irrigation pies. Breaks down crystals into particle form.

Jack Waterman
1 Crawford Road
East Lismore
NSW 2480
Tel:0409431424
Jackwaterman@live.com.au

Manufacturer of premium compost, compost teas, brewers and accessories, protozoa inoculum.

NutriTech Solutions
7 Harvest Road
Yandina
Queensland 4561
Tel: (07) 5472 9990
www.nutri-tech.com.au

Suppliers of a wide range of organically approved and general purpose fertilizers, microbes, human health products. Provide prescription blends. Recognised for 4-day Sustainable Agriculture workshop.

Omnia Specialities Australia Pty Ltd
PO Box 3418
Morwell,
Victori, 3840a
Tel: (03) 5133 9118
Email: www.omnia.com.au

Manufacturers of specialised fertilizers including humates, and chelated plant nutrients. Produce foliar sprays, trace elements and MAP.

Optima Agriculture
Osborne Park
Western Australia, 6017
Tel: (08) 9445 1819
Email: optimaagriculture.com.au

Supplier of wide range of lime products including Calsap, a liquid calcium source, Bio-Lime and Hi-Cal, a concentrated lime.

Smart Bugs Downunder
O'Grady Rural Services
46 Woodburn Road
North Lismore
Tel: (02) 6621 6088
Email:
rogrady@bigpond.net.au

Manufacturer and importer of Bio-Char, microbe tea brewers and microbial inoculants.

The Meter Man
PO Box 7964
Toowoomba South
Queensland 4350
Tel: (07) 4635 7065
Email:the.meterman.com.au

Provides a range of tools, books and instruments including brix meters, plant stress monitors, penetrometers and conductivity meters.

TNN Industries
273 Johnson Road
Stanhope
Victoria 3623
Tel: (03) 5857 7065
Email: tnn.com.au

Plant and soil analysis services, brix meters, measurement of chemical residues and soil programmes. Sell chelated minerals, trace elements and Triple 10 nitrogen.

Vital Resource Management P/L
22 Reward Crescent
Bohl,
Queensland 4814
Tel; (07) 4774 6337
Email: vrm.com.au

Range of formulations to promote balanced microbial reactions in soils. Manufacture composts from fruit and organic extracts. Provide microbes, and manufacture products for microbial development.

Western Minerals Fertilizers Pty Ltd
PO Box 2,
Tenterden
Western Australia 6322
Email: wmf@bionet.com.au

Specialise in granulated mineral fertilizers. Developers of a biologically active silicate mineral fertilizer that mineralises soil for health and biology. Sell soil microbe blends.

Appendix

Chapter 1

[1]   http://www.dailynews.co.uk Jan 21, 2010

[2]   Jeffrey Smith "Seeds of Deception" and "Genetic Roulette"

Chapter 2

[1]   Asia Newspaper, 4th May 2005.

[2]   "The Transition Handbook" by Rob Hopkins.

[3]   Christine Jones, "Potential for High Returns from more Soil Carbon", Australian Farming Journal, February, 2006

[4]   Lester R Brown "Plan B 4.0 Mobilizing to Save Civilization".

[5]   Address by Peter Cullen, to the Brisbane Institute "Facing up to the Water Crisis in the Murray Darling Basin" given on 13th March, 2007

[6]   "WA Soil Erosion under investigation" Journal of Agriculture, 2006

[7]   www.ofa.org. au/ myth pesticides

[8]   www.ofa.org. au/ myth pesticides

[9]   www.truehealth.org

[10]   P. 9 "Bringing the Food Economy Home" by Helena Norberg-Hodge, Todd Merrifield and Stephen Gorelick

[11]   Organic is the term given to farming practices that use natural inputs, a range of "accredited" pest and disease sprays made from natural ingredients and encourage the recycling of all on-farm outputs with the ultimate aim of making the organic farm a closed system operation. Strict certification rules apply and are monitored by accreditation agents. In Australia there are several organization, which offer organic certification.

[12]   Biodynamic farming has its origins in the teachings of Rudolf Steiner. It is a form of farming that uses a variety of preparations that are made according to methods set down by Rudolf Steiner. Biodynamic farming relies on inputs of composted cow manure and advocates planting, maintenance and harvesting in accordance with moon and planetary influences.

[13]   Nutrition Farming is a form of farming that uses mineral inputs designed to bring the soil into optimum balance as defined by Professor William Albrecht who, in the early 20th Century studied the world's most fertile soils and came to the conclusion that they all contained the same balance of major and minor elements. Nutrition farming relies on introducing

micro-organisms and fungi to break down organic material and minerals into a form that is plant accessible.

Chapter 3

1   Fertigation: A method of fertilizing through the irrigation system using a variety of soluble minerals, fish emulsion, fulvic and humic acids.

2   Prescription Blend: A fertilizer blend, which is prepared so that the minerals being added to the soil will balance those already present to create the "optimum" ratio of major and minor elements according to the formula established by Professor William Albrecht.

3   Inoculant: A method of adding a variety of micro-organisms and/or fungus spores to a basic food source, so that the microorganisms will multiply quickly. The resulting "brew" is called a microbe tea or compost tea and it is spread onto the farm through the irrigation system.

4   Chelation describes the process in which a ring shaped chemical structure, based on 6 carbon atoms, holds onto free floating metal ions. Lichens chelate rock to extract minerals and are important in the formation of soil. Humus chelates mineral ions in soil, allowing them to be made soluble and available for plant uptake.

5   Cation Exchange Capacity describes the quantity of positively charged ions a clay mineral can accommodate on its negatively charged surfaces. It is used as a measure of soil fertility, and nutrient retention capacity.